THE SHERIFF
OF BIGFOOT COUNTRY

BRIAN KING-SHARP

HANGAR 1 PUBLISHING

Based on a True Story…Well..Sorta

PART I

THE HOLLOW

1

____

THE ROAD TO NOWHERE

The truck rattled down the dirt road like it was trying to shake itself apart, and I pressed my face against the window watching the trees close in around us. Georgia pines, mostly. Tall and straight as telephone poles, their branches starting way up high like they couldn't be bothered with the ground. Between them, the hardwoods were just starting to turn, splashes of orange and red mixed with all that green. It was September of 1984, a week after my twelfth birthday, and everything I'd ever known was disappearing in the side mirror.

Daddy's hands gripped the steering wheel like he was strangling it. He hadn't said more than ten words since we'd left the old place in Summerville, and that suited me fine. When Jerry Patterson got quiet, it usually meant the storm was building. Better to let it build than to be the one who set it off.

Mama sat between us, her hip pressed against mine every time Daddy took a curve too fast. She smelled like the Jergens lotion she rubbed on her hands every night and the faint sweetness of the Dr Pepper she'd been nursing since we stopped for gas an hour back. Jean Patterson was a small woman, barely five foot two, but she had a way of taking up space when she wanted. Right now, she was trying to make herself invisible, same as me.

"How much further?" I asked, not really expecting an answer.

"When we get there, we get there." Daddy's voice was gravel and cigarette smoke. He reached for the pack of Winstons on the dashboard without taking his eyes off the road.

Mama put her hand on my knee and squeezed. That was her way. She couldn't fix things, couldn't make Daddy any different than he was, but she could let me know I wasn't alone in the silence.

The road narrowed. What had been two lanes of cracked asphalt became one lane of packed red clay, and the trees pressed in even closer. Spanish moss hung from oak branches like old gray ghosts reaching down to stroke the truck as we passed. I'd seen plenty of woods in my twelve years, but nothing like this. This felt old. This felt like the kind of place that had been here long before people came and would be here long after we were gone.

Then the trees opened up, and there it was.

The house sat at the end of the road like something that had crawled there to die. It was white once, I think, but years of Georgia weather had turned it the color of old bones. The porch sagged in the middle, and one of the upstairs windows was covered with a piece of plywood that had started to warp. A rusted propane tank squatted in the side yard like a beached submarine.

"Home sweet home," Daddy said, and laughed. It wasn't a nice laugh.

I climbed out of the truck and stood there in the dirt driveway, trying to make sense of what I was seeing. Behind the house, the land rose up in a gentle slope before disappearing into woods so thick and dark they looked like a wall. Eighty acres, the landlord had said. Eighty acres of woods and hollers and creek bottoms, and all of it was ours to use as long as we paid the rent on time.

Daddy was already carrying boxes inside, his boots heavy on the porch steps. Mama stood beside me, her arms crossed over her chest like she was cold even though the September heat was thick enough to chew.

"It'll be alright," she said. I couldn't tell if she was talking to me or herself.

"Yes, ma'am."

She turned and looked at me then, really looked, the way she did when she wanted me to hear something important. "Brian, I know this isn't what you wanted. I know you had friends back in Summerville, had your school, had your life. But sometimes we gotta play the hand we're dealt. You understand?"

I nodded, even though I didn't understand. Not really. I didn't understand why Daddy couldn't hold down a job for more than a few months at a time. Didn't understand why we had to keep moving, keep running from landlords and creditors and all the messes he made. Didn't understand why Mama stayed with him, why she kept believing things would get better when everything I'd seen in my twelve years told me they never would.

But I was twelve. Understanding wasn't my job yet. My job was to keep my head down, stay out of Daddy's way, and wait for the next storm to pass.

"Go on and pick out your room," Mama said. "Top of the stairs, take your pick. Just leave the big one at the end of the hall for me and your daddy."

I grabbed my duffle bag from the truck bed and headed inside.

* * *

The house smelled like dust, old newspapers, and something else underneath. Something sour and wrong. I tried not to think about what might have happened here before we came, what kind of people might have lived and died within these walls. As I climbed the stairs, the floorboards creaked under my feet, and I swear I could feel the house shifting around me, settling into its bones like an old man easing into a chair.

There were three bedrooms upstairs. The big one at the end of the hall had two windows that looked out over the backyard and the woods beyond. The one next to it was barely bigger than a closet, with a single window that faced the driveway. But the third room, the one at the front of the house, that one called to me.

It wasn't much to look at. Water stains on the ceiling, wallpaper peeling at the corners, a closet door that hung crooked on its hinges. But the window—the window was something special. It looked out over the front porch roof, and beyond that, I could see the dirt road stretching back through the trees toward the highway. Toward civilization. Toward the world I'd left behind.

I dropped my duffle bag on the floorboards and sat on the bare mattress someone had left behind. Springs poked through the fabric, and it smelled like mildew, but I didn't care. This was mine now. This little room at the top of this dying house at the end of this dirt road in the middle of nowhere. Mine.

From downstairs, I could hear Daddy cursing at something. A box he'd dropped, probably. Or maybe he'd found the bottle he'd hidden in the truck and was just getting started on his evening. Either way, I knew better than to go back down. Better to stay up here where it was quiet. Better to wait until Mama called me for dinner.

I laid back on the mattress and stared at the water stains on the ceiling. If I squinted just right, they almost looked like a map. Rivers and mountains and vast empty spaces where anything could be hiding. Anything at all.

Outside, the sun was sinking behind the trees, and the shadows were getting long. Somewhere in the distance, a whippoorwill started calling. Whip-poor-will. Whip-poor-will. Over and over, like it was trying to tell me something.

I closed my eyes and listened.

This was home now. For better or worse. This sagging house, these endless woods, this family that was coming apart at the seams. This was all I had.

I just didn't know yet how much it would cost me.

2

THE WOODS HAVE EYES

The first few weeks in Lyerly passed in a blur of unpacking boxes and learning the rhythms of a new place. School started, and I found myself sitting in the back of classrooms surrounded by kids who'd known each other since birth, kids whose families went back generations in this little town that didn't even have a stoplight. I was the outsider. The new kid. The boy from somewhere else who didn't know the history, didn't know the stories, didn't know which families had been feuding since before the Civil War.

I kept my head down and my mouth shut. Answered questions when teachers called on me. Ate my lunch alone at a table in the corner of the cafeteria. And every day, when the bus dropped me off at the end of that long dirt road, I walked home through the trees and felt something in my chest loosen. Something that had been wound tight all day finally letting go.

The woods were my salvation.

I started exploring them that first weekend, when Daddy was off somewhere doing God knows what and Mama was too tired from unpacking to notice I was gone. I took my BB gun, a Red Ryder that Daddy had given me for my tenth birthday back when he still did things like that, and I headed into the trees behind the house.

It didn't take long to realize that eighty acres was more land than I'd ever imagined. The woods went on forever, or at least it seemed that way to a twelve-year-old boy. Hardwoods gave way to pine thickets. Pine thickets gave way to swampy bottoms where the creek ran slow and dark. And everywhere, everywhere, there was life. Squirrels chattered at me from the branches. Birds I'd never seen before flashed through the underbrush. Once, I came around a bend in a deer trail and found myself face to face with a doe and her fawn, all of us frozen in surprise before they bounded off into the trees.

I started making maps. Crude things, drawn on notebook paper with a pencil I kept sharpening with my pocketknife. I marked the big features—the lightning-struck oak that had split down the middle but kept on living, the boulder field where granite pushed up through the red clay like bones breaking free of skin, the swimming hole where the creek widened into a pool deep enough to dive into. I gave them names. The Sentinel. The Graveyard. The Baptism.

And I built forts. Lord, did I build forts.

The first was simple—just some fallen branches leaned against a big oak to make a lean-to. But it grew more complicated as the weeks unfolded. I found an old tarp behind the house, half-rotted but still mostly waterproof, and stretched it over a frame I built from saplings cut with my pocketknife. I dragged logs over for seats. I dug a fire pit, even though inside I never lit a fire because Mama would've killed me. I stashed supplies out there—a rusty coffee can full of matches, a canteen I'd found at a yard sale, some beef jerky I'd stolen from the kitchen.

That fort became my home. My real home. The place I went when Daddy was drinking and the tension in the house grew so thick you could cut it with a knife. The place I went when I needed to think, or when I didn't want to think at all. The place I went to be Brian, just Brian, not the quiet kid in the back of the classroom or the boy who flinched when his father raised his voice.

Mama knew I was spending time in the woods. She didn't say much about it, just made sure I was home before dark and that I had something in my belly before I went out. I think she understood, in her way. She knew what it was like to need a place to escape. She just didn't have one of her own.

* * *

By October, I thought I knew those woods pretty well. I'd mapped maybe forty or fifty acres, crisscrossing back and forth until the trails were worn into the dirt from my footsteps alone. I knew where the deer bedded down. I knew where the squirrels nested. I knew which trees were good for climbing and which would snap under your weight.

But there was one section I hadn't explored. One corner of the property, way back at the far edge where our land butted against the national forest, that I'd been avoiding without really knowing why.

It started with a feeling. The first time I got close to that area, maybe two hundred yards from the property line, I felt this wrongness wash over me. Like walking into a cold spot in a warm room. Like the moment before a thunderstorm breaks, when the air thickens with electric and every hair on your body stands up. I stopped dead in my tracks, my heart pounding for no reason I could name, and turned around to walk back the way I'd come.

I told myself it was nothing. Told myself I was being stupid, being a baby. There was nothing in those woods that could hurt me. Bears, maybe, but I'd never seen sign of any. Snakes, sure, but I knew to watch where I stepped. There was nothing to be afraid of.

But I stayed away regardless.

Weeks passed. The leaves changed and fell. Daddy came and went, sometimes gone for days at a time, and when he was home, he was either drunk or getting there. I learned the signs—the way his eyes flattened two drinks in, the way his hands shook when he needed another. I learned to make myself scarce. I learned to be invisible.

Mama tried. She really did. She cooked dinner every night, even when Daddy didn't come home to eat it. She helped me with my homework, asked about my day, did all the things a mother is supposed to do. But there was something fading in her, something going dim behind her eyes. The light that had always been there, the spark that made her Jean instead of just Daddy's wife, it was getting harder to see.

I escaped to the woods whenever I could.

And that section I'd been avoiding? It started calling to me. I don't know how else to describe it. It was like an itch I couldn't scratch, a song I couldn't get out of my head. Every time I was out in the woods, I'd find myself drifting in that direction, getting a little closer before that wrongness pushed me back. It was like the world's worst game of chicken, me against whatever was back there in the dark.

Finally, on a Saturday in late October, I decided I'd had enough. I was twelve years old, almost thirteen. Too old to be scared of the dark, too old to let my imagination run wild. I was going to go back there and prove to myself there was nothing to be afraid of. Just trees. Just woods. Just another part of the property I hadn't mapped yet.

After breakfast, I grabbed my BB gun and headed out, telling Mama I'd be back before lunch. She barely looked up from the dishes. Daddy was still asleep, sleeping off whatever he'd been doing the night before. The house was quiet in that heavy way it always was on weekend mornings, and I was glad to get out.

The walk took about half an hour. I followed my usual trails, past the Sentinel and around the edge of the Graveyard, until I hit the deer path that led back toward that forbidden corner. My heart was already beating faster, and I made myself slow down. Take a breath. There's nothing out here. Just trees.

The wrongness hit me when I was about a hundred yards out. That cold-spot feeling, that electric tingle. Every instinct I had was screaming at me to turn around, to go home, to stay away from this place. But I gritted my teeth and kept walking.

Fifty yards. The trees were thicker here, older. Less underbrush, but more shadows. The ground sloped upward toward a ridge I couldn't quite see.

Twenty-five yards. The hair on the back of my neck was standing straight up. My hands were sweating on the stock of my BB gun. I could hear my own breathing, ragged and fast, and underneath it, the woods were silent. No birds. No squirrels. Nothing moving, nothing making a sound.

That should have been my warning. That silence should have sent me running. But I was twelve and stubborn and I had something to prove, so I kept going.

I pushed through a thick patch of briars that tore at my jeans and scratched my arms. On the other side was a small clearing, maybe thirty feet across, carpeted with dead leaves and ringed by trees so tall I couldn't see their tops. In the center of the clearing, there was a depression in the ground, like something big had been bedding down there. And the smell—God, the smell. Like a wet dog mixed with a dumpster behind a butcher shop. Thick and organic and wrong.

I stood at the edge of the clearing, frozen in place, trying to make sense of what I was seeing. What I was smelling. What I was feeling.

And then I heard it.

Footsteps. Heavy footsteps. Not the delicate step of a deer or the scrabble of a squirrel. These were big. These were bipedal. These were something walking on two legs, something that weighed as much as a man and then some.

They were coming from somewhere behind me. From the thick stand of trees and briars I'd just pushed through.

I spun around, my BB gun raised like it could do anything against whatever was making that sound. But I couldn't see anything. The underbrush was too thick, the shadows too deep. I could only hear it. Hear it getting closer. Hear those footsteps, those impossibly heavy footsteps, crunching through the dead leaves.

Then it stopped.

For a long moment, there was nothing. No sound. No movement. Just me and the silence and the pounding of my own heart.

And then it huffed.

I don't know how to describe that sound except to say it was the most primal thing I'd ever heard. Like a horse snorting, but deeper. Like a bear growling, but not quite. It was a challenge. A warning. A Get out of my territory that needed no translation.

Another huff. Closer now. Maybe forty feet away, hidden somewhere in that wall of green and shadow. And then a growl that started low and built until I could feel it vibrating in my chest, vibrating in my teeth, vibrating in my bones.

I wanted to run. Every cell in my body was screaming at me to run. But my legs wouldn't move. They felt like they'd been planted in the ground, like four-by-four fence posts driven deep into the red Georgia clay. I couldn't run. I couldn't even breathe.

More sounds now. Snorting. Heavy breathing. Something that sounded almost like words but wasn't—grunts and clicks that rose and fell in patterns that seemed to mean something, even if I couldn't understand what. And underneath it all, those footsteps again. Circling. Moving around the edge of the clearing. Getting closer.

I couldn't see it. That was almost worse than if I could. I strained my eyes against the shadows, tried to catch a glimpse of whatever was out there, but the underbrush was too thick. All I had were sounds. Sounds and that god-awful smell and the absolute certainty that something was watching me. Something big. Something that could end me if it wanted.

Then it charged.

I heard the explosion of movement through the underbrush—branches snapping, leaves scattering, something massive coming straight at me through the trees. The sound was like nothing I'd ever heard. Like a freight train. Like a landslide. Like the end of the world.

It stopped maybe twenty feet away. I still couldn't see it—the briars and the shadows hid it from view—but I could hear it breathing. Heavy, ragged breaths. I could smell it stronger than ever now, that rank animal stink filling my nostrils until I thought I might gag.

We stood there like that for what felt like forever. Me frozen in the clearing, clutching my useless BB gun. It hid in the trees, breathing and watching and waiting. I don't know what it was deciding. I don't know why it didn't finish what it started.

All I know is that after a long, terrible moment, I heard those footsteps again. But this time they were moving away. Fading into the distance. Getting quieter and quieter until they were gone.

For another long moment, I couldn't move. My legs were still fence posts, my lungs were still locked, my heart was still trying to beat its way out of my chest. And then, all at once, something broke loose inside me.

I ran.

I don't remember much about that run. It's all a blur of trees and briars and my own panicked breathing. I fell once, twice, maybe more. My jeans ripped. My arms bled from the thorns. But I didn't stop. Couldn't stop. I ran like something was chasing me, even though I knew in some deep part of my brain that it wasn't. It had let me go. Whatever was out there had looked at me—or smelled me, or sensed me somehow—and decided I wasn't worth the trouble, and it had let me go.

I ran until I saw the house through the trees. Ran until I hit the barbed wire fence at the edge of the backyard. I didn't stop to find the place where the wires were loose enough to slip through. I just jumped, catching my leg on one of the barbs and leaving a piece of my jeans and a streak of blood on the rusty wire.

And then I was in the yard, falling to my knees on the patchy grass, gasping for breath and shaking so hard I thought I might fly apart.

Mama was inside. I could see her through the kitchen window, standing at the sink, washing dishes or peeling potatoes or doing one of the thousand things she did every day to keep our broken little family running. I could have gone to her. Could have told her what I'd heard, what had happened, what was out there in those woods.

But I didn't.

I couldn't.

How do you tell someone that you've heard a monster? How do you explain that everything you thought you knew about the world is wrong, that there are things out there that aren't supposed to exist but do? How do you put that into words without sounding crazy?

So I didn't say anything. I sat there in the grass until my breathing slowed, until my heart stopped racing, until my hands stopped shaking. Then I got up, brushed myself off, and went inside.

Mama looked up from the sink. "You're back early. Everything okay?"

"Yes, ma'am," I said. "Just got tired."

She nodded, accepting this. Why wouldn't she? It was just another Saturday. Just another day. She didn't know that everything had changed. She didn't know that her son had heard something impossible, something that would live in his nightmares for years to come.

I shambled upstairs to my room and closed the door. Sat on my bed and stared at the wall. Tried to make sense of what had happened.

I couldn't.

So I did what I'd learned to do with all the things I couldn't make sense of. I buried it. Pushed it down deep, locked it away in a box in my mind, and told myself it didn't happen. Told myself it was just a bear. Just my imagination. Just the wind playing tricks on me.

But I knew. Deep down, in the place where the truth lives even when you don't want to look at it, I knew what I'd heard.

And I knew I'd never forget it.

3

____

WHAT DARKNESS KNOWS

After that day in the woods, something shifted. Not just in me, though that was part of it. The whole world seemed different, like I was looking at it through a lens that had been slightly out of focus my whole life and had suddenly snapped into clarity. Everything I thought I knew was wrong. Everything I'd been taught about what was real and what wasn't—wrong. And I couldn't tell anyone about it.

So I did what kids do when they can't talk about something. I read about it.

The Chattooga County Library was a small brick building in the middle of Summerville, about fifteen miles from Lyerly. Mama took me there on Saturdays when she went shopping, and while she was at the Piggly Wiggly loading up on groceries we could barely afford, I was in the stacks, hunting for answers.

At first, I didn't even know what to look for. I wandered through the sections, running my fingers along the spines, waiting for something to jump out at me. And then I found it. A book with a dark cover and yellow letters. The title was simple: BIGFOOT.

With shaking hands, I pulled it off the shelf.

The first chapter talked about sightings going back hundreds of years. Native American tribes had stories about these creatures, calling them different names—Sasquatch, Ts'emekwes, Oh-Mah—but the descriptions were always the same. Tall. Hairy. Walking on two legs. Incredibly strong. Incredibly fast. And incredibly good at staying hidden.

I read until Mama came to pick me up, and then I checked out the book and read it again at home. Then I went back for more. Books about the Loch Ness Monster. Books about the Yeti. Books about creatures that science said didn't exist but that people kept seeing, kept reporting, kept swearing were real.

I devoured them all.

The librarian, a gray-haired woman named Mrs. Hendricks, started noticing my interests. She'd save books for me, set them aside behind the counter with a little sticky note that said "Brian" on it. She never asked why I was so interested in monsters. Maybe she thought it was just a phase. Maybe she understood more than she let on.

But here's the thing about reading those books: they didn't make me feel better. If anything, they made me feel worse. Because now I knew I wasn't the only one. Now I knew that people had been encountering these things for centuries, had been reporting them, had been laughed at and dismissed and called crazy. And nothing had changed. The creatures were still out there. And the world still refused to believe.

* * *

Meanwhile, life at home was getting worse.

Daddy's drinking had always been bad, but that fall it got dangerous. He'd switched from beer to the hard stuff—bourbon mostly, though he'd drink anything with alcohol in it if bourbon wasn't available. And he'd started taking pills. Downers, I learned later. Quaaludes. Pain pills. Anything that would slow down the world, make it soft and fuzzy around the edges.

When he was on that stuff, he was unpredictable. Sometimes he'd go quiet, sitting in his recliner for hours, staring at the TV with glassy eyes. Those were the good times. Then he'd get mean. He'd pick fights with Mama over nothing—the way she'd cooked the potatoes, the fact I'd left a light on, the noise the floorboards made when we walked across them.

He never hit her. Not while I was around, anyway. But he came close. I saw him get right up in her face, screaming so loud that spit flew from his lips. I saw him punch holes in walls. I saw him throw a plate of food across the kitchen because it wasn't hot enough.

Mama took it. That's what kills me, looking back. She just took it. She'd clean up the broken dishes, patch the holes in the walls with spackle she bought from the hardware store, and go on like nothing had happened. Like this was just the price you paid for having a family.

I hated him for it. I hated him so much it scared me sometimes. I'd lie in bed at night and imagine all the ways I could make him pay. Make him hurt the way he hurt us. But I was twelve years old and he was a grown man, and there wasn't anything I could do. Not yet.

So I escaped to the woods. Not to that corner of the property—I never went back there—but to my forts, my trails, my secret places. I'd spend hours out there, alone with my thoughts and my BB gun and the animals that didn't judge me, didn't expect anything from me. It was the only place I could breathe.

And sometimes, late at night when I couldn't sleep, I'd sit by my window and look out at the tree line and wonder if that thing was out there. Listening. Waiting. If it knew I'd stumbled into its territory. If it remembered me the way I remembered it.

I never heard it again. But I never stopped believing.

* * *

November came, and with it, the cold. Not cold like up north, where the snow piles up and the temperature drops below zero. Georgia cold is different. It's wet and raw, the kind of cold that sinks into your bones and stays there. The old house had no insulation to speak of, and the heating system was an ancient oil furnace that rattled and coughed and barely put out enough heat to keep the pipes from freezing.

We wore layers inside. Mama knitted me a sweater from yarn she'd bought at a yard sale, and I wore it over my regular clothes every day after school. At night, I piled every blanket I could find on my bed and still woke up shivering.

But the cold wasn't the worst thing about that November.

One night, I woke up to voices.

Not Daddy's voice, not Mama's. These were different. Whispery and indistinct, like someone talking in another room. But my room was at the end of the hall, and there was no one else up here.

I lay in bed, perfectly still, and listened.

The voices seemed to be coming from the walls. From inside the walls. I could hear them murmuring, chattering, having conversations in a language I couldn't understand. Sometimes they laughed. Sometimes they cried. Sometimes they screamed.

I pulled the covers up over my head and told myself it was just the house settling. Old houses made noises. That's what Mama always said. Old houses had stories to tell, and sometimes they told them at night.

But this didn't feel like a house settling. This felt like something else. Something alive. Something that was aware of me, that knew I was listening, that wanted me to hear.

The voices stopped around dawn. I got out of bed with dark circles under my eyes and headed downstairs to find Mama already up, making coffee in the kitchen.

"You look tired," she said.

"Couldn't sleep."

She nodded, understanding. She'd been having trouble sleeping too. I could see it in her face, in the way she moved. The house was wearing her down, same as it was wearing me.

I didn't tell her about the voices. What was the point? She had enough to worry about without adding her son's nightmares to the list.

* * *

Next night, the voices came back. And the night after that. And the night after that.

But that wasn't the worst of it. No. The worst was what started happening around the end of November.

I woke up one night to the feeling that I wasn't alone.

You know that feeling. Everyone does. That prickle on the back of your neck, that certainty someone is watching you. I felt it, and my eyes snapped open, and there it was.

A figure. Standing at the foot of my bed.

It was tall and dark, darker than the darkness around it. I couldn't see its face, couldn't see any features at all. It was just a shape, a void, a place where the light refused to go. And it was staring at me. I knew it was staring at me even though I couldn't see its eyes.

I tried to scream. Nothing came out.

I tried to move. I couldn't. My body was locked in place, frozen like it had been in the woods that day. Like those fence posts I'd become when I heard the thing charging me. I couldn't move, couldn't speak, couldn't do anything but lie there and stare at this impossible figure at the foot of my bed.

It stood there for what felt like hours. Just watching. Just waiting. And then, without any sound or movement, it was gone. One moment it was there, and the next moment I was alone in my room, gasping for breath, my heart hammering so hard I thought it might crack my ribs.

I didn't sleep the rest of that night. Or the next.

The figure came back. Not every night, but often enough. Sometimes it stood at the foot of my bed. Other times it stood in the corner. Once, I woke to find it looming over me, so close I should have felt its breath on my face. But there was no breath. No heat. Nothing but that impossible darkness, that void where a person should have been.

And I could never move. Never speak. Never do anything but lie there and wait for it to go away.

I know now that there's a name for what I was experiencing. Sleep paralysis. Night terrors. The medical explanations are very tidy, very scientific. Your brain wakes up before your body, and you hallucinate, and it's all perfectly normal.

But here's the thing. Those explanations assume that what you're seeing isn't real. They assume that the figure at the foot of your bed is just a trick of your mind, a remnant of a dream, a misfire in your neurons.

They don't account for what happened next.

* * *

It was a week before Christmas when I heard the scratching.

I was lying in bed, trying to fall asleep despite the cold and the fear and the weight of everything that was happening in that house. Mama had been tired lately, more tired than usual. She'd been having headaches, been feeling weak. Daddy was gone, off somewhere for three days now, and part of me hoped he'd never come back.

The scratching started in the wall next to my bed.

At first, I thought it was mice. We had mice—every old house in Georgia had mice. I'd heard them scurrying in the walls before, their tiny claws clicking against the wood. But this wasn't the sound of tiny claws. This was bigger. Heavier. Something was in that wall, something that was scratching at the plaster like it wanted to get out.

I lay perfectly still, holding my breath, listening.

The scratching moved. From beside my bed to the corner of the room. From the corner of the room to the closet. From the closet to the other wall. It was circling me, moving through the house like it owned the place, like I was the intruder and it was just trying to scare me off.

And then it stopped.

I waited. One minute. Two. Five. Nothing.

I had just started to relax when three loud knocks shook my bedroom door.

I shot up in bed, my heart in my throat. Mama wouldn't knock like that. Mama barely knocked at all—she'd just tap lightly and call my name. These knocks were heavy, deliberate. Demanding.

"Mama?" My voice came out as a whisper.

No answer.

I got out of bed and crossed to the door on legs that didn't want to cooperate. My hand was shaking as I reached for the doorknob. I turned it. Pulled the door open.

The hallway was empty.

But not dark. There was a light coming from downstairs, a flickering orange glow that threw shadows against the walls. I could smell smoke. Something was burning.

I ran down the stairs to find Mama standing in the living room, staring at the fireplace. We never used the fireplace—Daddy had said the chimney was blocked, that it wasn't safe—but now there was a fire burning in it. A big fire, flames licking up toward the flue, casting dancing shadows across the ceiling.

"Mama?"

She turned to look at me, and her face was pale. Paler than I'd ever seen it.

"I didn't light it," she said. "Brian, I didn't light it."

We stood there together, mother and son, watching that impossible fire burn in our blocked chimney. And I knew then, with a certainty that went beyond reason, that there was something in this house. Something that had been here before us. Something that didn't want us here.

Something that was just getting started.

4

THE SLOW FADE

Christmas came and went without much fanfare. Mama did her best—she always did her best—putting up a small tree in the corner of the living room, wrapping a few presents in newspaper because we couldn't afford real wrapping paper. I got a new pocketknife and a pair of jeans that actually fit. Daddy showed up on Christmas Eve, sober for once, and for a few hours it almost felt like we were a normal family. Almost.

But January brought something we weren't prepared for.

Mama had been scratching at her arms for weeks. I'd noticed it— the way she'd dig at her skin when she thought no one was looking, the red marks that appeared on her forearms and stayed there. She said it was dry skin, the winter air, nothing to worry about. But it kept getting worse. The scratching became constant. The red marks became welts. And then the welts became something else entirely.

I came home from school one afternoon to find her sitting at the kitchen table, staring at her arms. The skin was raised in patches, red and angry, like something was trying to push its way out from underneath.

"Mama?"

She looked up at me, and I saw fear in her eyes. Real fear. The kind of fear I'd only seen in my own reflection after nights when the dark figure visited.

"I need to see a doctor," she said.

* * *

The doctor in Lyerly took one look at her arms and sent us to a specialist in Rome. The specialist took one look and sent us to Atlanta. And the doctors in Atlanta—a whole team of them, it seemed like—ran test after test after test.

I remember sitting in the waiting room of Emory University Hospital, watching Mama disappear through door after door, coming back looking more tired and more scared each time. Daddy was there for the first visit, but after that he started finding excuses not to come. Work, he said. Bills to pay. Couldn't take time off.

We both knew it was lies.

Finally, after two weeks of tests, a doctor sat us down in a small room with no windows and told us what they'd found.

Mycosis fungoides.

I didn't know what that meant. The words sounded foreign, clinical, like something out of one of those medical shows Mama liked to watch. The doctor explained it in terms I could understand, but even then, it took a while to sink in.

Skin cancer. Mama had skin cancer. A rare kind that started in the white blood cells and showed up in the skin. It had been growing for a while, he said. Maybe years. By the time it showed itself on the surface, it was already everywhere underneath.

"How long?" Mama asked. Her voice was steady, but I could see her hands shaking in her lap.

The doctor didn't want to answer. I could see it in his face, the way he looked away, the way he shuffled his papers.

"How long?" Mama asked again.

"Six months," he said. "Maybe a year, with treatment."

The world stopped. I know that sounds dramatic, but it's true. In that moment, everything I thought I knew about my life, about my future, about what would happen next—all of it just stopped. Like someone had hit pause on a tape player and forgotten to hit play again.

Six months.

My mama had six months to live.

* * *

They admitted her to the hospital that day. Started treatment immediately—chemotherapy, they called it. Poison to kill the cancer, but the poison killed everything else too. Her hair. Her appetite. Her strength. Day by day, I watched my mama fade away, watched her become someone I barely recognized.

I was fourteen years old. My birthday had come and gone in December without much celebration. Fourteen years old, and I was losing the only person in the world who'd ever really loved me.

Daddy disappeared.

Oh, he came by the hospital a few times in the beginning. Stood in the corner of Mama's room with his hands in his pockets, not knowing what to say or do. But as the weeks passed, his visits became shorter and less frequent. And then they stopped altogether.

I found out later that he'd shacked up with some woman over in Trion. Found out he was spending his days drinking and popping pills and doing whatever else people do when they're too much of a coward to face reality. But at the time, all I knew was that he was gone. Just gone. Like I didn't matter. Like Mama didn't matter. Like we were just problems he could walk away from.

I hated him for it. I hated him more than I'd ever hated anything in my life.

But I didn't have time for hate. I had to survive.

* * *

The Hendersons saved my life.

Brad Henderson was my best friend—my only friend, really. We'd met at school a few months after we moved to Lyerly, bonding over a shared love of comic books and hatred for the bullies who made our lives miserable. He was a skinny kid with red hair and freckles, quiet like me, the kind of kid who faded into the background and liked it that way.

His parents, Bill and Angie, were good people. The kind of people who went to church on Sundays and actually meant it. The kind of people who saw a kid in trouble and stepped up without being asked.

When they found out about Mama, when they found out that Daddy had vanished and I was living alone in that house at the end of the dirt road, they didn't hesitate. Angie showed up at our door one evening with a casserole in her hands and a look on her face that said she wasn't taking no for an answer.

"You're coming to stay with us," she said. "Just until your mama gets better."

I wanted to argue. Wanted to say I could take care of myself, that I didn't need charity, that I'd be fine. But the truth was, I wasn't fine. I was fourteen years old and terrified and alone, and the house I was living in had something wrong with it, something that came alive at night and whispered in the walls and stood at the foot of my bed with no face and no mercy.

So I went.

* * *

The Henderson house was small but warm. Two bedrooms, one bathroom, a kitchen that always smelled like something baking. Brad gave up his room for me and slept on the couch, even though I told him he didn't have to.

"You need it more than me," he said, and that was that.

I went to school. I did my homework. I ate dinner with the Hendersons every night and pretended that everything was normal. And on weekends, Bill drove me to Atlanta to visit Mama.

Those visits were hard.

The chemotherapy was brutal. Mama lost all her hair within the first month, and she was so weak she could barely lift her head off the pillow. The cancer was everywhere now—the doctors talked about it in hushed voices, using words I didn't understand. Spreading. Aggressive. Resistant to treatment.

But Mama fought. God, did she fight.

"I'm not going anywhere," she told me one Sunday afternoon, her voice barely more than a whisper. "You hear me, Brian? I'm not leaving you."

I held her hand—so thin now, the bones standing out like sticks under paper—and I believed her. I had to believe her. Because if I didn't, if I let myself think for even one second that she might really die, I would fall apart completely.

"Yes, ma'am," I said.

She squeezed my hand. "That's my boy."

* * *

The months crawled by.

Spring came, and with it, the first signs that maybe the doctors had been wrong. Mama's numbers started improving. The cancer wasn't growing anymore—it wasn't shrinking either, but it wasn't growing. The doctors called it a plateau. A holding pattern. They said it was rare but not unheard of. They said we shouldn't get our hopes up.

We got our hopes up anyway.

Summer came. I turned fifteen in a hospital room, eating cake that Angie had baked and watching Mama smile for the first time in months. She was still weak, still bald, still a shadow of the woman she'd been. But she was alive. She was fighting. And she was winning.

Fall came. The leaves changed outside Mama's hospital window, and she watched them with something like wonder in her eyes.

"I didn't think I'd see another fall," she said.

"You'll see a lot more," I told her.

She smiled. "Promise?"

I couldn't promise. I couldn't promise anything. But I nodded anyway, because that's what she needed. That's what we both needed.

* * *

December came. My birthday came and went. And then, three days before Christmas, almost a year to the day after she was diagnosed, the doctors called a meeting.

I sat in that same windowless room where they'd first told us about the cancer. Bill and Angie sat on either side of me, their hands on my shoulders like anchors keeping me from floating away. The doctor who entered wasn't the same one who'd given us six months a year ago. This was someone new, someone younger, someone with a smile on her face that I didn't dare interpret.

"Jean's cancer is in remission," she said.

I didn't understand. The words didn't compute. I just sat there, staring at her, waiting for the other shoe to drop.

"The tumors have shrunk significantly," the doctor continued. "Her blood work is improving. She's not out of the woods yet—she'll need monitoring, follow-up treatments, regular checkups. But for now, the cancer is retreating."

"She's going to be okay?" My voice came out cracked and strange.

The doctor's smile widened. "She's going home, Brian. Your mama's coming home for Christmas."

I cried. I'm not ashamed to admit it. I sat in that windowless room and I cried like a baby, and Bill and Angie held me, and for the first time in almost a year, I let myself believe that everything might actually be okay.

* * *

Mama came home on December 22nd.

She weighed maybe eighty pounds. Her head was bald and smooth, covered with a scarf that Angie had knitted for her. She was so weak she could barely walk, and Bill had to carry her from the car to the house while I held the door open and tried not to cry again.

But she was home. She was alive. She'd beaten the odds, beaten the doctors' predictions, beaten death itself.

And the first thing she did, once she was settled on the couch with a blanket over her legs and a cup of tea in her hands, was look at Daddy's empty chair and make a decision.

"We're leaving," she said.

I thought I'd misheard her. "What?"

"We're leaving, Brian. This house. This marriage. All of it." She turned to look at me, and despite everything she'd been through, despite how weak and frail she was, there was steel in her eyes. The steel I remembered from before she got sick. The steel that had always been there, hiding under the surface, waiting for its moment.

"Your daddy isn't coming back," she said. "And even if he did, I wouldn't take him. I spent a year fighting to stay alive, and I'll be damned if I'm going to spend whatever time I have left living like this." She reached out and took my hand. "It's just you and me now, baby. You and me against the world. You ready for that?"

I looked at my mama—this small, fierce woman who'd stared down death and won—and I nodded.

"Yes, ma'am," I said. "I'm ready."

But I wasn't ready for what happened next.

Nobody could have been ready for what happened next.

5

FIRE IN THE NIGHT

The hospital had sent Mama home with pain medication. Strong stuff—oxycodone, morphine, things I didn't know the names of back then. She was supposed to take them for the lingering pain from the cancer and treatment, to help her sleep, to make the transition back to normal life a little easier.

She never took them.

Not because she didn't hurt—Lord knows she hurt. I could see it in the way she moved, the way she held herself, the way she sometimes stopped in the middle of doing something and just stood there with her eyes closed, waiting for a wave of pain to pass. But she'd seen what pills did to Daddy. She'd watched him disappear into bottles and baggies, watched him choose chemicals over his family. She wasn't about to follow him down that road.

"I'd rather hurt than not be here," she told me once, when I asked why she didn't take her medicine. "Pain means I'm alive. I can live with pain."

So the pills sat in the medicine cabinet. A whole pharmacy's worth of narcotics, just waiting.

Daddy found them within a week.

I don't know how he knew we were back—maybe someone in

town told him, maybe he'd been watching the house, maybe he just got lucky. But two days after Christmas, he showed up at the front door like nothing had happened. Like he hadn't abandoned us for almost a year. Like he hadn't left his wife to die and his son to fend for himself.

He looked bad. Worse than I'd ever seen him. His face was gaunt, his eyes were bloodshot, and his hands shook so bad he could barely hold his cigarette. Whatever he'd been doing for the past year, it hadn't been good to him.

"Jean," he said, when Mama opened the door. "Baby, I'm so sorry. I'm so—"

"Don't." Mama's voice was ice. "Don't you dare."

"I know I messed up. I know I shouldn't have—"

"You left." Mama stepped forward, and even as small and frail as she was, Daddy took a step back. "I was dying, Jerry. I was dying, and you left. You left me alone. You left Brian alone. And now you show up at my door with sorry on your lips like that's supposed to fix anything?"

"I was scared," Daddy said. "I didn't know how to handle it. I—"

"You were a coward," Mama said. "You've always been a coward. And I'm done. You hear me? I'm done."

She tried to close the door. Daddy stuck his foot in it.

"Just let me get my stuff," he said. "I'll be out of your hair. I just need my stuff."

Mama stared at him for a long moment. Then she stepped back and let him in.

I watched from the hallway as he moved through the house, gathering things. Clothes. Tools. A few bottles of booze he'd hidden in places Mama hadn't found. And then he entered the bathroom, and I heard him rummaging around in the medicine cabinet, and when he came out his pockets were bulging.

He'd taken Mama's pills. All of them.

"Jerry—" Mama started.

"I need them more than you do," he said. And then he was out the door, climbing inside his truck, disappearing down that long dirt road.

We never saw him again.

Well. That's not entirely true. We saw what he did with those pills. In a town as small as Lyerly, word travels fast.

* * *

Lyerly was the kind of place where everybody knew everybody's business. Population maybe a thousand, no stoplight, one gas station, one grocery store, two churches. The kind of place where you couldn't sneeze without three people asking if you were coming down with something.

Word got around quick about what Daddy was doing. He wasn't just taking the pills—he was selling them. Trading them. Using them to buy more of the downers he really wanted. He'd become a small-time dealer, operating out of whatever hole he was living in, feeding his habit by feeding other people's.

And word got around about us too. About Mama's cancer. About how the church had taken up a collection to help with medical bills. About how the community had rallied around us while Daddy was nowhere to be found.

People were angry. Not at us—at him. At this man who'd taken their charity and their goodwill and thrown it away for pills and booze. At this husband who'd abandoned his dying wife. At this father who'd left his child to fend for himself.

I didn't know how angry until that night in January.

* * *

I was asleep when the noise started.

At first, I thought I was dreaming. The sounds were muffled, distant—voices, vehicles, the crunch of tires on gravel. But then Mama was shaking me awake, her hand on my shoulder, her face pale in the darkness.

"Brian. Brian, wake up."

"What's wrong?"

"Something's happening outside."

I got out of bed and followed her to the window. What I saw there is burned into my memory like a brand.

The front yard was full of people. Twenty, maybe more. All of them dressed in white robes. All of them wearing masks or hoods that covered their faces. And in the center of the yard, right in the middle of the dead winter grass, was a wooden cross. Twenty feet tall, at least. And it was burning.

The Ku Klux Klan had come to our house.

I'd heard of the Klan, of course. Everyone in Georgia had. They were supposed to be a relic of the past, something from the bad old days that didn't exist anymore. But here they were, standing in our front yard, their robes glowing orange in the firelight, their faces hidden behind white cloth.

"Get away from the window," Mama said. Her voice was steady, but I could see her hands shaking. "Get down."

We crouched beneath the windowsill, listening to the crackle of the flames and the murmur of voices outside. I couldn't make out what they were saying—it was just a low rumble, a crowd noise, punctuated by the occasional shout or cheer.

"Why?" I asked. "Why are they here?"

Mama didn't answer for a long moment. When she did, her voice was barely a whisper. "Your daddy," she said. "This is because of your daddy."

I learned later what had happened. The Klan in that part of Georgia, what was left of it anyway, had gotten wind of Daddy's activities. They'd heard about the collection the church had taken up for us. They'd heard about Daddy abandoning his family, about him stealing the pain medication meant for his dying wife, about him selling drugs in a community that had shown us nothing but kindness.

They didn't approve.

Now, I want to be clear about something. The Klan is evil. Always has been, always will be. What they did that night wasn't justice—it was terrorism. Burning a cross in someone's yard isn't a warning, it's a threat. A promise of violence if you don't fall in line.

But I also understood, even then, that this wasn't really about us.

Mama hadn't done anything wrong. I hadn't done anything wrong. This was about Daddy, about his choices, about the shame he'd brought on his family in a community that took such things seriously.

We stayed huddled under that window for what felt like hours, listening to the fire burn and the crowd murmur. And then, just as suddenly as they'd appeared, they were gone. The headlights of their trucks receded down the dirt road, the murmur of voices faded into the night, and we were alone with the smoldering remains of a twenty-foot cross in our front yard.

Mama called the sheriff. He came out, took some notes, shook his head a lot. Said he'd look into it, but we all knew nothing would come of it. The Klan protected their own, and the law in that part of Georgia wasn't exactly eager to go poking around in their business.

"Y'all might want to think about moving," the sheriff said before he left. "Might be healthier."

Mama looked at the burned cross, then at me, then back at the sheriff.

"We're already planning on it," she said.

* * *

We left Lyerly two weeks later.

Mama had already filed for divorce—turns out it's not hard to get a divorce when your husband has abandoned you for a year and has multiple witnesses to his drug dealing. The paperwork went through quick, quicker than I'd expected. And just like that, we weren't the Pattersons anymore. Well, I was still a Patterson—I kept Daddy's name because it was the only name I'd ever had—but Mama went back to her maiden name. Jean Turner. Like she was reclaiming something that had been taken from her.

We couldn't afford much. What little money we had went to first and last month's rent on a tiny apartment in the low-income housing complex over in Summerville. Two bedrooms, one bathroom, a kitchen the size of a closet. The walls were thin enough to hear our neighbors' TVs, and the carpet was stained in ways I didn't want to think about.

But it was ours. And it was safe. And most importantly, it was far away from that house in Lyerly, far away from the woods and the things that lived in them, far away from the darkness that had followed us for too long.

Or so I thought.

* * *

The thing about trauma is that it doesn't care where you live. You can move across town or country, but you can't outrun the things that live inside your head. I know that now. I didn't know it then.

The nightmares followed me to Summerville. The dark figure that had stood at the foot of my bed in Lyerly—he came with us, appearing in my new room at random intervals, standing in the corner or looming over me while I lay frozen and unable to scream. The voices in the walls were gone, and the scratching was gone, but the dreams remained. Vivid, terrible dreams of something chasing me through endless woods, something that huffed and growled and never quite let me see its face.

I didn't tell Mama. She had enough to worry about.

After we got settled, she started looking for work. It wasn't easy— she was still weak from the cancer treatment, still bald under the scarves she wore, still dealing with follow-up appointments and medications and all the aftermath of almost dying. But Jean Turner wasn't the kind of woman to sit around feeling sorry for herself.

She got a job at the grocery store first. Part-time, minimum wage, standing on her feet for six hours a day bagging other people's groceries. It wasn't much, but it was something. And then she got a second job, cleaning offices at night. And then, because apparently two jobs weren't enough, she enrolled in classes at the community college.

"I'm going to get my degree," she told me one night, her textbooks spread out across the kitchen table while she drank coffee to stay awake. "I'm going to make something of myself. For you. For us."

I wanted to tell her to slow down. I wanted to tell her that she didn't have to do this, that we'd be fine, that her health was more important than any degree. But I saw the determination in her eyes, the same steel that had helped her beat cancer, and I knew better than to argue.

"Yes ma'am," I said instead.

And because I was my mother's son, I got a job too.

* * *

I was fifteen years old and working at the Dairy Queen after school, flipping burgers, making Blizzards, and mopping floors at the end of the night. The pay was terrible, but I didn't complain. Every dollar I earned was a dollar that Mama didn't have to worry about. School clothes. Lunch money. The electric bill when it got too high. These were the things I bought with my minimum-wage paycheck, and every one of them felt like a victory.

I didn't have time for the woods anymore. Didn't have time for forts or maps or reading about cryptids in the library. My life had narrowed down to three things: school, work, and taking care of Mama. Everything else was a luxury I couldn't afford.

But I never forgot what I'd heard in those woods back in Lyerly. Never forgot the huffing and the growling and the footsteps that sounded too big to be real. Never forgot the thing that had charged at me and stopped just twenty feet away, hidden in the underbrush, breathing and watching and deciding whether I was worth killing.

I knew it was real. I knew it was out there. And someday, when I had the time and the resources and the freedom to look for answers, I was going to find it again.

But first, I had to grow up.

First, I had to survive.

PART II

FINDING MYSELF

6

———————

THE YEARS BETWEEN

The next several years passed in a blur of work, school, and the slow, steady process of healing.

Mama got her degree. It took her four years of night classes and weekend study sessions, four years of working multiple jobs while her body slowly recovered from the cancer that had nearly killed her. But she did it. I remember sitting in the audience at her graduation ceremony, watching her walk across that stage in her cap and gown, and feeling something I hadn't felt in a long time. Pride. Real, honest pride in someone I loved.

She cried when she got her diploma. I did too.

I graduated high school without much fanfare. My grades were decent—not great, but decent. Good enough for a place at the local state college if I wanted. But college cost money we didn't have, and besides, I'd spent the last few years working. I knew how to hold down a job, how to show up on time, how to do what needed doing without being told twice. That seemed more valuable than any degree.

So I kept working.

The Dairy Queen gave way to a convenience store, which gave way to another convenience store, which eventually led to a management position at a gas station on the edge of town. I was good at it—good at dealing with people, good at handling problems, good at keeping my cool when things were hectic. By the time I was twenty, I was running the place. By the time I was twenty-two, I was managing multiple locations for a restaurant chain.

I was making money. I was building a life. I was doing everything society said I was supposed to do.

And I was absolutely miserable.

* * *

I need to talk about something now that I didn't talk about then. Not to anyone. Not for years.

I knew I was different from other boys pretty early on. Even before I knew the words for it, I knew something about me didn't fit the mold. While my classmates were chasing girls and bragging about their conquests, I felt... nothing. No interest. No desire. The whole performance of teenage masculinity felt like a foreign language I was supposed to speak but had never learned.

I told myself it would change. Told myself I was just a late bloomer, that the right girl would come along and everything would click into place. But the right girl never came. The right person did, eventually, but it wasn't a girl.

His name was Marcus, and he worked at the restaurant with me. We started as coworkers, became friends, and then one night after closing, became something more. It was terrifying and exhilarating and absolutely right in a way that nothing in my life had ever been before.

I was gay.

There. I said it. Three words that seem so simple now but felt like a death sentence back then. This was rural Georgia in the early nineties. People didn't talk about things like that. And if they did, it wasn't with kindness.

Marcus and I kept our relationship secret for as long as we could. We were careful—always meeting in private, never showing affection in public, maintaining the fiction that we were just good friends. But secrets have a way of getting out, especially in small towns.

Someone saw us. Someone talked. And within a week, everyone knew.

I lost friends. People I'd known for years suddenly couldn't look me in the eye. Coworkers who'd laughed at my jokes and shared their lunch started avoiding me in the break room. Even some of my family —aunts, uncles, and cousins I'd grown up with—stopped calling, stopped visiting, stopped acknowledging that I existed.

It hurt. Lord, did it hurt. But it also clarified something for me. The people who left weren't people worth keeping. The ones who stayed— Mama, Brad, a handful of others—those were the real ones. Those were the ones who loved me for who I was, not for who they wanted me to be.

Marcus and I didn't last. He moved to Atlanta, I stayed in Summerville, and the distance proved too much. But I don't regret any of it. He helped me figure out who I was. That's worth more than I can say.

* * *

By my mid-twenties, I'd settled into something resembling a stable life. I had a decent apartment, a reliable car, a job that paid well enough. Mama was doing better than ever—the cancer had stayed in remission, she'd earned a promotion at her company, and for the first time in my memory, she wasn't struggling just to survive.

But I wasn't happy. I was comfortable, sure. I was getting by. But there was a restlessness in me that wouldn't go away, a feeling that I was meant for something more than counting inventory and scheduling shifts and dealing with customer complaints.

I'd always wanted to be a cop.

I know that sounds strange, given everything I'd been through. Given my experiences with the sheriff back in Lyerly, with the system that had failed us again and again. But that was exactly why I wanted it. I'd seen what happened when the people in charge didn't care, when they let problems fester because solving them was too hard or too dangerous or too politically inconvenient. I wanted to be different. I wanted to be the kind of cop who actually helped people.

The problem was, I didn't know how to make that happen. I was twenty-six years old with no college degree and no law enforcement experience. The idea of starting over, of going through academy training and working my way up from the bottom, seemed impossible.

And then I saw an ad in the paper.

"Corrections Officer Wanted," it said. "Georgia Department of Juvenile Justice."

It wasn't exactly what I'd imagined. But it was a start.

* * *

The youth detention facility was a maximum-security lockup about an hour from Summerville. The kids inside—and they were kids, some as young as thirteen—had done terrible things. Murder. Rape. Armed robbery. Gang violence. The worst of the worst, locked away from society until the courts decided what to do with them.

My first day on the job, I watched a sixteen-year-old try to stab another kid with a sharpened toothbrush. My second day, I broke up a fight that left two teenagers bleeding on the floor. By the end of my first week, I'd been threatened, spat on, and called names I won't repeat here.

I loved it.

Not the violence—I never loved that. But I loved the work. I loved trying to reach these kids, trying to find the human beings underneath all that anger and pain. Some of them were beyond reaching, too far gone into whatever darkness had claimed them. But some of them weren't. Some of them just needed someone to see them, to listen to them, to treat them like people instead of problems to be managed.

I worked at that facility for seven years. Started as a corrections officer, worked my way up to supervisor, then assistant director, and finally director. By the time I left, I'd overseen a complete transformation of how the place operated. Less punishment, more rehabilitation. Less isolation, more counseling. The recidivism rates dropped. The violence decreased. Kids who came in as monsters started leaving as something closer to human.

I was proud of what I'd accomplished. But I still wasn't satisfied.

Because the whole time I was working at that facility, I was thinking about the streets. About the real work. About being a cop the way I'd always imagined—out there in the world, making a difference where it counted.

I was in my early thirties when I finally made the leap.

It was time.

7

BADGE AND BLUE

The police academy was harder than I expected.

Not the physical stuff—seven years in juvenile corrections had kept me in pretty good shape. It was the mental stuff that got to me. The laws and procedures and protocols, the endless acronyms and forms and codes. I'd spent my career learning how to handle kids who'd already been caught. Now I had to learn how to catch them in the first place.

But I made it through. Graduated in the middle of my class, which wasn't bad for a guy who'd never been to college. And then I got my first assignment.

Suches, Georgia.

Population: maybe a few hundred, depending on who was counting. Elevation: three thousand feet, up in the Blue Ridge Mountains where the air was thin and the winters were cold and the nearest backup was forty-five minutes away. It was the kind of place that time had forgotten, the kind of place where people came to get away from everything—or to hide.

The police department consisted of me, the chief, and one other officer. We covered an area the size of some counties, all of it mountains and hollers and dirt roads that turned to mud every time it rained. Most of our calls were domestic disputes and drunk drivers, with the occasional drug bust or burglary thrown in to keep things interesting.

I loved it.

After years in the youth facility, dealing with the concentrated misery of incarcerated teenagers, Suches felt like freedom. I spent my days driving through the mountains, checking on residents, getting to know the community. The people were suspicious at first—mountain folk always are with outsiders—but I worked to earn their trust. Showed up to church suppers and community meetings. Learned who was related to who, which families had been feuding for generations, which houses to approach carefully and which to avoid altogether.

And I met Daniel.

* * *

Daniel was a deputy with the Union County Sheriff's Office, which overlapped our jurisdiction in places. We met at a multi-agency training exercise, spent the whole day partnered up for scenario work, and by the end of it, I knew there was something there. Something I hadn't felt since Marcus, all those years ago.

He was tall, dark-haired, with a smile that could light up a room and a laugh that made you want to join in even if you didn't know what was funny. He was from the area—his family had lived in these mountains for generations—but he'd spent a few years in Atlanta before returning home. Like me, he'd found his way into law enforcement almost by accident. Like me, he'd discovered it was what he was meant to do.

We started slow. Coffee after shift. Dinner on our days off. Long conversations about everything and nothing, the kind of talking you do when you're getting to know someone you hope to know for a long time.

And then one night, parked on an overlook with the whole Blue Ridge spread out below us like a crumpled blanket, he kissed me.

"I've been wanting to do that for weeks," he said.

"What took you so long?" I asked.

He laughed. And that was it. That was the beginning of us.

* * *

We moved in together after six months. Got a little cabin outside of town, nothing fancy, just a place where we could be ourselves without the whole world watching. Being gay in rural Georgia was easier than it used to be, but it still wasn't easy. We weren't hiding, exactly, but we weren't advertising either. The people who needed to know knew. The people who didn't could mind their own business.

Work was good. Life was good. For the first time in as long as I could remember, I was genuinely happy.

But there was still that itch. That restlessness that had never quite gone away. And it had a name now, a shape, a direction.

Bigfoot.

I'd never stopped thinking about what had happened in those woods back in Lyerly. Never stopped wondering what I'd heard that day, what had charged at me and stopped just short of—what? Killing me? Scaring me off? I didn't know. And that not-knowing had haunted me for almost two decades.

I started researching again. Reading everything I could find about Sasquatch, about encounters, about the long history of sightings throughout the Appalachians. The mountains of North Georgia, it turned out, were a hotspot. Reports going back centuries. Native American legends. Modern encounters from hikers and hunters and forest rangers who'd seen or heard things they couldn't explain.

I started keeping files. Newspaper clippings. Interview transcripts. Maps marked with sighting locations. At first, Daniel thought I was crazy, but he humored me. "Your Bigfoot stuff," he called it, with a smile that said he didn't quite believe but didn't quite disbelieve either.

And then, a few years into our relationship, we started talking about the future.

* * *

"I want to own land," I told him one night. We were sitting on the porch of our cabin, watching the sun go down behind the mountains. "Real land. Somewhere we can build something that's ours."

"I've always wanted that too," Daniel said. "Somewhere quiet. Somewhere away from everything."

"North Carolina," I said. "I've been looking at properties up there. Land's cheaper, and there's—" I hesitated.

"There's what?"

"There's a lot of forest. A lot of wilderness. The kind of place where things might still be hiding."

Daniel looked at me for a long moment. Then he smiled.

"Let's do it," he said.

* * *

It took two years to make it happen. Two years of saving every penny, of me cashing out my retirement account, of Daniel picking up extra shifts whenever he could. We looked at dozens of properties, drove thousands of miles on our days off, rejected one piece of land after another because it wasn't quite right.

And then we found it.

Forty acres in Caldwell County, North Carolina. Rolling hills covered in hardwood forest, a creek running through the middle, no neighbors for a mile in any direction. The property backed up to thousands of acres of national forest—the Pisgah, one of the largest wilderness areas on the East Coast.

It was perfect.

We closed on a cold day in November. Drove up that afternoon and walked the property line, breathing in the clean mountain air, listening to the silence that was somehow fuller and richer than any silence I'd heard before.

"We did it," Daniel said.

"We did it," I agreed.

That night, we pitched a tent near the creek and slept under the stars. And I dreamed—for the first time in years—of something moving through the trees. Something big. Something watching.

But this time, I wasn't afraid.

This time, I felt like I was home.

8

______

WHISPERS IN THE WILDERNESS

We lived off-grid while the tiny house was being built.

That first winter was brutal. We'd set up a temporary camp with a heavy-duty tent and a propane heater, but there were nights when the temperature dropped into the single digits and we huddled together under every blanket we owned, wondering if we'd made a terrible mistake.

Daniel had left the sheriff's office. He'd tried to transfer to a department closer to our new property, but nothing was available, and the commute from Caldwell County back to Union County would have been three hours each way. So he'd turned in his badge—temporarily, he said—and taken a job at a pizza place in Lenoir, the nearest town of any size.

"It gets me out of the house," he said, when I asked if he was okay with it. "And I don't want you to worry about me out here alone while you're still figuring out what you're going to do."

What I was going to do. That was the question, wasn't it? I'd left law enforcement too, at least for the moment. My plan was to take some time off, help build the house, settle into our new life. Maybe eventually I'd look for work with a local department, or maybe I'd try something completely different. For the first time in my adult life, I didn't have a job waiting for me. It was terrifying and liberating in equal measure.

But I wasn't idle. Not by a long shot.

* * *

The first strange thing happened about three weeks after we arrived.

I was alone at the camp—Daniel was at work, wouldn't be home until after midnight. I'd spent the day clearing brush and marking trees for the construction crew that would arrive in the spring. Exhausting work, but satisfying. By the time the sun went down, I was ready for a hot meal and an early night.

I was heating up some soup on the camp stove when I heard it.

A howl.

It came from somewhere behind the property, deep in the national forest. It started low and rose in pitch, hanging in the air for what felt like forever before trailing off into the darkness. It wasn't a coyote—I knew what coyotes sounded like, had heard them plenty of times in Georgia. It wasn't a wolf—there were no wolves in these mountains, hadn't been for a hundred years. It wasn't anything I could identify.

But I'd heard it before.

Years ago, back when I first started researching Sasquatch, I'd come across an audio recording from Ohio. The Ohio Howl, people called it. A sound captured in the woods in the early nineties, never explained, never identified. It had sent chills down my spine when I first heard it.

This sound was the same.

Not similar. The same.

I stood there in the darkness, my soup forgotten, my heart pounding. And then I did something that probably wasn't smart. I howled back.

Not a perfect imitation—I couldn't have matched that sound if my life depended on it. But close. Close enough to be understood as a response, maybe. Close enough to say I'm here, I hear you, what are you?

For a long moment, nothing. Just the wind in the trees and the distant sound of the creek.

And then, from a different direction—closer this time, maybe half a mile away—the howl came again.

* * *

I didn't tell Daniel about the howl. Not right away. I wasn't sure what to say, how to explain it. "Hey, honey, I think there might be a Sasquatch living behind our property," isn't exactly normal dinner conversation, even in a relationship as unconventional as ours.

But over the next few weeks, more things happened.

Rocks appeared in places they shouldn't be. Not thrown—I never saw or heard anything throwing them—but placed. Stacked, sometimes, in little towers near the edge of our camp. Other times scattered in patterns that seemed almost deliberate.

I found footprints along the creek. Big ones. Much bigger than any human foot, much wider than any bear track. They were partially obscured by dead leaves, like whatever made them had been trying to hide its trail, but they were there.

And then there were the lights.

The first time it happened, I thought I was dreaming. I woke up in the middle of the night to a brightness that shouldn't have been there. Not moonlight—this was something else, something that lit up the inside of our tent like someone was shining a spotlight directly at us.

I scrambled out of the tent, expecting to see—what? A car? A helicopter? I didn't know. But there was nothing. Just the trees, and the stars, and a darkness that seemed somehow deeper than it should have been.

The second time, Daniel was with me. He woke up too, saw the same light, stumbled outside to find the same nothing.

"What the hell was that?" he asked.

"I don't know," I said. And I didn't. But I was starting to have suspicions.

* * *

The tiny house was finished in late spring.

It wasn't much—five hundred square feet, barely enough room for the two of us and our stuff. But it had running water and electricity from a solar setup, and after months of living in a tent, it felt like a palace.

We celebrated our first night in the new house the way you'd expect—a nice dinner, a bottle of wine, and then a long soak in the hot tub we'd splurged on as a housewarming gift to ourselves. It sat on the back deck, facing the forest, and as we relaxed in the warm water and watched the stars come out, I felt a peace I hadn't known I was missing.

"This was worth it," Daniel said. "All of it. The saving, the planning, the freezing our asses off all winter. This was worth it."

"Yeah," I agreed. "It was."

And then, from somewhere in the darkness behind our property, that howl rose again.

Daniel froze. "What was that?"

"Listen," I said.

The howl held, rose, fell, and faded. And then, from another direction, another howl answered. And then another. And another. A chorus of voices, rising and falling in the night, surrounding us with sound.

"Brian." Daniel's voice was barely a whisper. "What is that?"

I didn't answer. I just listened, my heart full of something that wasn't quite fear and wasn't quite joy. Something more like recognition. Like coming home.

After all these years, I'd found them again.

Or maybe they'd found me.

9

THE MAN IN THE BADGE

Word travels fast in small towns, and Caldwell County wasn't that big.

I'm not sure how it started—maybe someone at the hardware store mentioned my background, maybe one of the construction workers looked me up, maybe it was just the kind of rumor that takes on a life of its own. But within a few months of settling in, people started approaching me. At the grocery store. At the gas station. At the little diner in Lenoir where Daniel and I had Sunday breakfast.

"Heard you used to be a cop."

"Heard you ran a juvenile facility."

"We could use someone like you around here."

At first, I brushed it off. I was retired, I said. Taking time off. Enjoying life. I'd done my time in law enforcement, paid my dues, earned my rest. The last thing I wanted was to get back into the game.

But the more I learned about Caldwell County, the more I understood why people were asking.

The current sheriff was a man named Vernon Oates, who'd held the position for sixteen years, running unopposed in the last three elections. And in those sixteen years, the department had become—well, let's just say it wasn't what it should have been. Response times were slow. Cases went unsolved. There were rumors of corruption, of deputies on the take, of evidence disappearing when it inconvenienced the right people.

People were frustrated. People were scared. And they were looking for someone to do something about it.

* * *

The first time someone explicitly asked me to run for sheriff, I laughed.

I was in the feed store, picking up supplies for some landscaping work, when an older man approached me. His name was Harold Whitmore, and he owned about a hundred acres adjacent to the national forest. He'd introduced himself a few weeks earlier, told me about a problem he was having with trespassers on his property, asked if I had any advice.

"You should run against Oates," he said, without preamble.

"What?"

"The election's next year. He's going to run again, but nobody wants to go up against him. Nobody except you."

"I'm not—I don't even know if I want to be in law enforcement anymore."

Harold fixed me with a look that made me feel like I was twelve years old again, caught doing something I shouldn't have been.

"Son," he said, "I've lived in these mountains my whole life. I know what's happening up in that forest. People going missing. Strange things happening. And I know the sheriff's office isn't doing a damn thing about it because they don't want to look too close." He leaned in. "You're the kind of man who looks close. I can tell. We need someone like that."

I wanted to ask what he meant about strange things happening, about people going missing. I wanted to ask a lot of things. But he just patted me on the shoulder and walked away, leaving me standing there with a bag of mulch in my hands and a head full of questions.

* * *

I went home and told Daniel about the conversation.

"You should do it," he said, without hesitation.

"I don't know the first thing about running for office."

"You know how to be a good cop. You know how to lead people. You know how to get things done." He shrugged. "The rest is just logistics."

"The rest is politics. Fundraising. Debates. Shaking hands and kissing babies."

Daniel smiled. "You're good at shaking hands. And I've never seen you kiss a baby, but I bet you'd be okay at that too."

"I'm serious."

"So am I." He crossed the room and took my hands in his. "Brian, you've been restless ever since we got here. I can see it in you, even when you're pretending everything's fine. You need something to do. Something that matters. And this—" He gestured vaguely at the walls around us, at the forest beyond them. "This place needs you. Those people need you. Maybe it's time to stop hiding and start doing something."

I didn't have an answer for that. So I didn't answer. I just held his hands and thought about what he'd said.

That night, I dreamed about the woods again. About something moving through the trees, something that watched and waited and knew things it shouldn't know. And in the dream, I wasn't running away from it.

I was running toward it.

* * *

I announced my candidacy for sheriff of Caldwell County in March.

The response was—well, mixed would be an understatement. Vernon Oates wasn't happy. He'd gotten used to running unopposed, gotten used to the power and prestige and all the little benefits that came with being the only game in town. Having someone actually challenge him was an insult he wasn't prepared to handle gracefully.

He started spreading rumors. Digging into my past. The fact that I'd never lived in the county before—I was an outsider, a carpetbagger, someone who didn't understand how things worked around here. The fact that I was gay—which he never said directly, of course, but he made sure everyone knew. The fact that I'd spent seven years working with juvenile offenders—clearly, I was soft on crime, a bleeding heart liberal, probably wanted to hug criminals instead of arrest them.

I won't lie. It got ugly. There were times I wanted to quit, when I wanted to tell everyone to go to hell and retreat back to my forty acres and tiny house and the peace I'd worked so hard to find.

But I kept thinking about what Harold Whitmore had said. People going missing. Strange things happening. A sheriff's office that didn't want to look too close.

I needed to know what he meant. And the only way to find out was to win.

* * *

The election was closer than anyone expected.

Oates had been in power for sixteen years. He had name recognition, he had funding, he had the backing of pretty much everyone who benefited from the status quo. I had—well, I had me. And Daniel. And a handful of people who believed that things could be better.

We knocked on doors. We attended every community event we could find. We talked to anyone who would listen about what kind of county we could have if we just tried a little harder, looked a little closer, cared a little more.

And on election night, by a margin of less than two hundred votes, I won.

Brian Patterson. Sheriff of Caldwell County, North Carolina.

I called Mama that night to tell her. She cried, of course. Told me how proud she was, how far I'd come from that scared little boy in Lyerly. How proud Daddy would have been—and then she caught herself, remembering who Daddy really was, and we both laughed at the absurdity of it.

"You did good, baby," she said. "You did real good."

"Thanks, Mama. I couldn't have done any of it without you."

"Yes, you could have. You just might not have wanted to."

She was right. As usual.

* * *

My first day as sheriff, I met Zach.

He was a ranger with the U.S. Forest Service, assigned to the Pisgah National Forest. We crossed paths at a jurisdictional meeting—the kind of boring administrative thing that happens when multiple agencies operate in the same area. I was expecting a stuffy bureaucrat, someone who'd want to talk about forms and procedures and staying in our respective lanes.

What I got was a young guy in his early thirties with an intensity in his eyes that I recognized immediately. The intensity of someone who'd seen something he couldn't explain.

We were making small talk after the meeting when he said, almost casually, "So you're the new sheriff. Heard you're interested in weird stuff."

I kept my face neutral. "Weird stuff?"

"You know. Unexplained phenomena. Things that go bump in the night." He smiled, but it wasn't a joking smile. "Things in the woods that aren't supposed to be there."

I looked at him for a long moment. Made a decision.

"Let me buy you a cup of coffee," I said.

It was the beginning of a partnership that would change everything.

10

THE MISSING

Zach's office was a cramped room in the ranger station near Blowing Rock, walls covered with maps and photographs and charts tracking everything from wildlife populations to trail maintenance schedules. But behind his desk, hidden from casual visitors, was another set of documents. A filing cabinet that he unlocked with a key he kept on a chain around his neck.

"This is off the record," he said, as he pulled out the first folder. "Way off the record. If anyone asks, we never had this conversation."

I nodded. I knew how to keep secrets.

What he showed me that afternoon changed everything I thought I knew about the Pisgah National Forest.

People were going missing. A lot of people. More than the official statistics showed, more than the news reports mentioned, more than anyone outside a very small circle was willing to acknowledge.

Over the past twenty years, according to Zach's files, at least forty-seven people had vanished in or around the Pisgah without explanation. Not all of them were in Caldwell County—the forest spanned twelve counties in western North Carolina—but a disproportionate number were. Hikers who left for a day trip and never returned. Hunters who disappeared during deer season. Campers whose tents were found empty, their gear undisturbed, no sign of struggle or animal attack or anything that would explain where they'd gone.

"Jesus," I said, flipping through the files. "How is this not national news?"

"Because the Park Service doesn't want it to be." Zach's voice was bitter. "Every time someone goes missing, there's pressure to keep it quiet. Don't scare the tourists. Don't hurt the local economy. Just file it as a missing person case, assume they got lost or fell off a cliff or decided to start a new life somewhere, and move on."

"But you don't think that's what happened," I said, matter-of-fact.

"I know it's not." He pulled out another folder, thicker than the first. "Look at this."

It was a collection of photographs. Crime scene photos, mostly, showing abandoned campsites and empty trails and all the places where people had last been seen. But there were other photos too. Photos of footprints—huge footprints, much bigger than any human. Photos of trees with strange markings, like something had clawed at the bark. Photos of hair samples, reddish-brown and coarse, collected from branches and bushes throughout the forest.

"I've sent those samples to three different labs," Zach said. "They all came back the same. Unknown primate. Not human. Not any known ape. Something else."

I stared at the photos for a long time. "You're saying what I think you're saying."

"I'm saying there's something out there. Something that's been out there for a long time. And I'm saying that the Park Service knows about it, and they're covering it up."

* * *

Over the next few weeks, Zach and I spent every spare moment going through his files. He'd been building this case for years, ever since his own encounter in the forest—an encounter he was reluctant to talk about in detail, but which had clearly shaken him to his core.

The pattern was unmistakable. The disappearances clustered in certain areas of the forest, areas that were remote and hard to access. They happened most often in spring and fall, during the transitional seasons when the forest was changing. And in almost every case, there were reports of strange sounds in the days before the disappearance—howls, screams, wood-knocking, things that didn't match any known wildlife.

"They're territorial," Zach said one evening, spreading a map across his desk. "See how the disappearances cluster? These aren't random points. They follow a pattern, a boundary. This is their territory, and anyone who enters it—"

He didn't finish the sentence. He didn't need to.

"So what do we do?" I asked. "We can't exactly go public with this."

"Not yet. Not without more evidence." He looked at me, his eyes intense. "But we can investigate. We can document. And when the time is right, we can blow this whole thing wide open."

I thought about my encounter back in Lyerly, all those years ago. The huffing, the growling, the bluff charge. The creature that had let me go when it could have killed me.

"They're not all aggressive," I said. "The one I encountered—it could have hurt me. It didn't."

"Maybe some of them aren't. Maybe some of them are." Zach shrugged. "All I know is, people are going missing. And someone needs to find out why."

* * *

The call came in on a Thursday morning in October.

A twenty-year-old student from Appalachian State University had failed to return from a solo hiking trip in the Pisgah. His name was Austin Mercer, and according to his roommate, he'd been planning to spend a week camping in a remote area of the forest. Something about researching local legends. Something about looking for proof of Bigfoot.

"Sounds like one of yours," the dispatcher said.

I didn't respond to that. I just grabbed my jacket and headed for the door.

Zach met me at the trailhead two hours later. We hiked in together, following the route Austin had logged with the ranger station before he left. It took us most of the day to reach the area where he'd planned to set up camp.

What we found there stopped us both in our tracks.

The tent was shredded. Not collapsed, not blown over by wind. Shredded, like something had ripped through the fabric with claws or teeth. Austin's gear was scattered around the campsite—his backpack, his sleeping bag, his cooking supplies. But there was no sign of Austin himself.

"Over here," Zach called.

I joined him at the edge of the clearing. He was pointing at the ground.

Footprints. Huge footprints, easily nineteen inches long and eight inches wide. They led from the tree line to the tent and back again, a clear trail that any tracker could follow.

"Jesus Christ," I whispered.

But that wasn't the worst of it.

We found the trail cameras next—three of them, positioned in a triangle around the campsite. Austin had been smart, setting up surveillance to catch anything that approached. Zach pulled the memory cards and we reviewed them on his laptop right there in the field.

The first camera showed nothing unusual. Just woods, trees, the occasional deer or raccoon wandering past.

The second camera showed the same.

But the third camera...

The timestamp said 2:47 AM. The image was grainy, shot in infrared, but clear enough to see what was moving through the trees.

It was big. Eight feet tall, maybe more, with broad shoulders and arms that hung past its knees. It was covered in dark hair—brown or black, hard to tell in the infrared. And it was walking upright, on two legs, moving with a fluid grace that seemed impossible for something that size.

It was a Sasquatch.

And it was walking directly toward Austin's tent.

* * *

We found his phone near the fire ring, half-buried in leaves.

The screen was cracked, but it still worked. I picked it up with gloved hands, careful not to disturb any potential evidence, and navigated to the video folder.

There was one video, recorded the same night as the trail camera footage. I pressed play.

Austin's face filled the screen. He was young, early twenties, with the kind of eager energy that reminded me of myself at that age. But there was something else in his expression. Something that made my stomach clench.

Fear.

"I don't know if anyone will ever see this," he whispered, his voice barely audible over the background noise. "But something's out there. I've been hearing it all night. Howls, screams, something big walking around in the trees. I thought I was prepared for this, I thought I was ready, but—"

He stopped. Turned toward the wall of the tent. In the background, I could hear it too—those vocalizations I knew so well, the huffing and the growling and the strange almost-speech that had haunted my dreams for thirty years.

"Oh, God," Austin said. "It's coming closer. It's—"

And then the tent ripped open.

The phone spun, capturing glimpses of movement—dark shapes, thrashing fabric, Austin's screaming face. And then he was dragged out of frame, still screaming, his voice getting fainter and fainter as he was pulled into the darkness.

The phone landed face-up, pointing at the ceiling of the ruined tent. For the next forty-three minutes, it recorded nothing but silence.

Until the battery died.

* * *

Zach and I stood in that clearing for a long time after the video ended. Neither of us spoke. There wasn't anything to say.

We had our proof. After all these years, we had undeniable evidence that these creatures existed. Evidence they were dangerous. Evidence they had taken a young man who might still be alive somewhere, or might already be dead.

But what were we supposed to do with it?

If we went public, we'd be laughed out of the room. Sasquatch doesn't exist, everyone knew that. We'd be mocked, discredited, probably fired. All our work, all our evidence, dismissed as hoax or hallucination.

But if we stayed silent, more people would die. More families would never know what happened to their loved ones. The cover-up would continue, and the creatures would keep claiming victims in the deep woods where nobody was watching.

"We have to do something," I said finally.

"I know." Zach's voice was hollow. "But what?"

I thought about it. Thought about everything I'd learned since becoming sheriff, everything Zach had shown me, everything I'd experienced myself going back to that day in the woods behind our house in Lyerly.

"We go public," I said. "Not with everything. Not yet. But we start asking questions. We hold a press conference, talk about the disappearance, mention that there are some unusual circumstances. We plant seeds. See what grows."

"That's dangerous," Zach said. "If the wrong people find out what we know—"

"I know. But I'm the sheriff of this county. It's my job to protect people. I can't do that if I'm keeping secrets that might get them killed."

He looked at me for a long moment. Then he nodded. "Okay," he said. "Let's do it."

We started packing up the evidence. Neither of us knew it then, but we'd just set in motion something that couldn't be stopped.

And something was watching us from the trees, even then.

Waiting to see what we'd do next.

11

VISITORS IN THE DARK

The press conference was a calculated risk.

I didn't mention Bigfoot. Didn't mention the trail camera footage or the footprints or the video of Austin being dragged from his tent. I just stood in front of a handful of local reporters and said that we were investigating unusual circumstances surrounding the disappearance, that we were pursuing all leads, that we were asking anyone with information to come forward.

It was enough.

The story was picked up by a few regional outlets. Then some national ones. "Small-Town Sheriff Hints at Strange Circumstances in Hiker Disappearance." The headlines wrote themselves. And in the comments sections, in the forums, on the social media pages that sprang up overnight, people started talking.

About Bigfoot. About the Pisgah. About all the other disappearances that had never been explained.

I watched it all unfold from my home office, feeling like I'd lit a match next to a powder keg. This was bigger than me now. Bigger than Caldwell County. Bigger than anything I'd anticipated.

And then, exactly one week after the press conference, they came.

* * *

It was after midnight. Daniel was asleep beside me. I was half-asleep myself, drifting in that liminal space between consciousness and dreams.

The driveway alarm woke me.

We'd installed a simple system—just a sensor that triggered a chime inside the house whenever anything larger than a deer crossed the property line. It had gone off a few times since moving in, usually for black bears or the occasional lost hiker. Nothing to worry about.

But this time, something felt different.

I slipped out of bed and moved to the security monitor we'd set up in the corner of the bedroom. The camera showed the driveway clearly, lit by infrared.

Two men were walking toward the house.

They were dressed identically—black suits, black ties, white shirts. Their faces were hard to make out in the infrared, but something about their movements was wrong. Too smooth. Too coordinated. Like they were moving according to a choreography they'd practiced a thousand times.

I felt a chill run down my spine.

"Daniel." I shook him awake. "We've got company."

* * *

By the time I got to the front door, the men were already on the porch. I'd grabbed my rifle—a Henry 45/70, heavy enough to stop a bear or anything else that might come at me—and I held it ready as I stepped outside.

"That's far enough," I said.

They stopped. Two men in their forties, maybe fifties. Clean-shaven. Expressionless. They looked like government agents, or what you'd imagine government agents to look like if you'd only seen them in movies.

"Sheriff Patterson," one of them said. It wasn't a question.

"That's right. You want to tell me what you're doing on my property in the middle of the night?"

"We're here to have a conversation."

"At one in the morning?"

"The timing was necessary."

I kept the rifle pointed at them. "Start talking."

The man who'd been speaking—the one on the left—reached inside his jacket. I tensed, my finger tightening on the trigger. But all he pulled out was a folder.

"Your press conference last week created some... complications," he said. "People are asking questions that shouldn't be asked. Looking into things that shouldn't be looked into."

"Things like what?"

"You know what."

I didn't respond. Just waited.

"The creatures in the forest," the man continued. "The ones you've been investigating with Ranger Holloway. The ones you seem to think are responsible for the Mercer boy's disappearance."

"You know about that."

"We know about a lot of things, Sheriff. We've known about them for a very long time."

"Who's 'we'?"

The man smiled. It didn't reach his eyes. "That's not information you need, Sheriff. What you need is to understand that this investigation is over. You will not hold any more press conferences. You will not discuss the Mercer case with the media. You will close the file and move on to other matters."

I stared at him. "And if I don't?"

"Then your career as sheriff will come to an abrupt end. And your partner—Daniel, isn't it?—may find himself facing some legal difficulties that would be... inconvenient."

"Is that a threat?"

"It's information, Sheriff. What you do with it is up to you."

He extended the folder toward me. I didn't take it.

"The evidence you've collected," he said. "The trail camera

footage. The hair samples. The footprint casts. You're going to destroy all of it. And you're going to forget this conversation ever happened."

"What about Austin Mercer? What happened to him?"

"The Mercer boy got lost in the woods. It happens. His body will be found eventually, or it won't. Either way, it's no longer your concern."

"His family deserves to know—"

"His family will know what we tell them to know." The man's voice hardened. "You're out of your depth, Sheriff. You've stumbled into something that's bigger than you, bigger than this county, bigger than you can possibly imagine. And if you have any sense of self-preservation, you'll step back and let the people who understand these things handle them."

He set the folder on the porch railing and stepped back.

"You have forty-eight hours to make your decision. Choose wisely."

And then they turned and walked away, disappearing down the driveway into the darkness. I stood there long after they were gone, the rifle still in my hands, my heart pounding in my chest.

Behind me, the door opened. Daniel stepped out, his face pale in the moonlight.

"Brian? Who were those men?"

I looked at him—this man I loved, this life we'd built together—and I didn't know how to answer.

Because I didn't know if I could protect him anymore.

I didn't know if I could protect anyone.

* * *

I didn't sleep the rest of that night. Just sat on the porch with my rifle across my lap, watching the tree line, thinking about everything that had happened and everything that might happen next.

The folder the men had left contained photographs. Surveillance photographs. Of me, of Daniel, of Zach. Of our movements over the past several weeks, every meeting we'd had, every piece of evidence we'd collected. They'd been watching us the whole time. Watching and waiting for us to become a problem.

And now we were.

I thought about backing off. Thought about doing what they said—destroying the evidence, closing the case, pretending none of this had ever happened. It would be easy. Safe. The smart play.

But then I thought about Austin Mercer. Twenty years old. His whole life ahead of him. Dragged screaming into the darkness by something that wasn't supposed to exist.

I thought about all the others. The forty-seven names in Zach's files. The families who never got closure. The people who would keep disappearing, year after year, while the government covered it up and the creatures in the forest kept hunting.

I thought about that twelve-year-old boy in Lyerly, frozen with fear as something charged at him through the trees. The boy who'd spent his whole life wondering what was out there, what he'd escaped from, what he was supposed to do about it.

Maybe this was what I was supposed to do.

Maybe this was why everything had led me here—the childhood encounter, the dysfunctional family, the years in law enforcement, the move to North Carolina, the run for sheriff. Maybe it was all building to this moment, this choice, this chance to finally do something about the secrets that had been hidden for far too long.

As the sun came up over the mountains, I made my decision.

I wasn't backing down.

Whatever came next, whatever they threw at me, I was going to see this through.

For Austin.

For all of them.

For that scared little boy I used to be.

I picked up my phone and called Zach.

"We need to talk," I said. "They've made their move. Now it's time to make ours."

PART III

INTO THE DARK

12

LINES IN THE SAND

Zach arrived at the house just after sunrise. He looked like he hadn't slept either—dark circles under his eyes, coffee in a thermos that he kept refilling, that same intensity burning in his gaze that I'd come to recognize as obsession. The good kind. The kind that keeps you going when everything else tells you to stop.

Daniel made breakfast while I filled Zach in on what had happened. The men in black. The threats. The photographs proving they'd been watching us for weeks. By the time I finished, Daniel had stopped cooking and was just standing at the stove, spatula in hand, staring at me.

"They threatened you," he said. His voice was flat, controlled, but I could hear the anger underneath. "They came to our home and threatened you."

"They threatened both of us. You specifically."

"What are we going to do?"

I looked at Zach. He looked at me. We'd already had this conversation in the driveway, in low voices while Daniel was still getting dressed. We knew what we had to do. The question was whether we could bring Daniel along for the ride.

"We're not backing down," I said.

Daniel set down the spatula. "Brian—"

"I know it's dangerous. I know what's at stake. But if we let them scare us into silence, nothing changes. People keep disappearing. The cover-up continues. And they win." I reached across the counter and took his hand. "I didn't become a cop to look the other way when bad things happen. I can't start now."

"Even if it gets you killed?"

"It won't come to that."

"You don't know that."

"No," I admitted. "I don't. But I know that I can't live with myself if I walk away from this. Can you?"

Daniel was quiet for a long moment. Then he squeezed my hand and let out a breath.

"What do you need me to do?"

* * *

The first thing we did was make copies of everything.

All the evidence we'd collected—the trail camera footage, the footprint casts, the hair samples, Austin's phone, Zach's files going back twenty years—we duplicated it all. Multiple times. Physical copies, digital copies, copies stored in locations that only we knew about. If they came for the originals, we'd still have backups. If they came for the backups, we'd have backups of the backups.

Then we started reaching out.

Zach had contacts in the cryptozoology community—researchers, investigators, people who'd been studying these creatures for decades. They operated on the fringes of mainstream science, dismissed as crackpots and true believers, but they had resources and connections that we didn't. More importantly, they had experience dealing with government suppression.

"There's a network," Zach explained, as we sat around the kitchen table with laptops open and phones charging. "People who've been gathering evidence for years. Most of them have had run-ins with the same kind of men you met last night. They know how to operate under the radar, how to protect their sources, how to get information out without getting caught."

"Can we trust them?"

"As much as we can trust anyone. They want the truth out as badly as we do."

I thought about it. Thought about the risks, the potential for infiltration, the possibility that reaching out would just paint a bigger target on our backs.

"Do it," I said. "Make the calls."

* * *

While Zach worked his contacts, I focused on the official investigation.

The men in black had told me to close the Mercer case. They'd told me to destroy the evidence and move on. But they hadn't actually done anything—yet. They'd made threats, but threats weren't action. And until they took action, I was still the sheriff of Caldwell County. I still had a job to do.

Austin Mercer was still missing. His family was still waiting for answers. And regardless of what was really responsible for his disappearance, I owed it to them to conduct a thorough investigation.

So that's what I did.

I assembled a search team—deputies, volunteers, anyone willing to hike into the backcountry and look for signs of the missing student. We spent three days combing the area around his campsite, expanding our search radius until we'd covered nearly ten square miles of forest.

We found traces. A torn piece of fabric caught on a branch. A shoe —just one, the left one—lying in a creek bed half a mile from the camp. More footprints, the same impossible size as those we'd found before, leading deeper and deeper into the wilderness.

But we didn't find Austin.

On the third day, I called off the official search. We'd done everything we could with the resources we had. The case would remain open, classified as an active missing person investigation, but without a body or more evidence, there wasn't much else to do.

At least, not officially.

Unofficially, the real investigation was just beginning.

* * *

The forty-eight-hour deadline the men had given me came and went. I half expected them to show up again, to follow through on their threats, to make good on all the dark promises they'd implied. But nothing happened. No midnight visitors. No mysterious phone calls. No sudden career-ending scandals.

It made me nervous.

"They're watching," Zach said, when I mentioned it to him. "Waiting to see what we do. They won't move until they have to."

"And when will that be?"

"When we become a real threat. When we start making enough noise that they can't ignore us anymore."

"So what do we do? Keep our heads down?"

Zach smiled. It wasn't a nice smile.

"No," he said. "We make noise."

* * *

The documentary was Zach's idea.

He'd been contacted by a filmmaker—a woman named Amanda Jones who'd made several well-regarded documentaries about unexplained phenomena. She'd seen the news coverage of the Mercer disappearance, heard the rumors about strange circumstances, and wanted to know more.

"She's legitimate," Zach assured me. "I've seen her work. She's not one of those sensationalist hacks who makes everything about aliens and conspiracy theories. She takes this stuff seriously. She does real investigative journalism."

"And you think we should talk to her?"

"I think we should do more than talk. I think we should give her everything."

I stared at him. "Everything?"

"The footage. The files. The whole twenty years of cover-up. All of it, on the record, on camera." He leaned forward. "Think about it, Brian. If we try to go public ourselves, we get dismissed as crackpots. Two guys in the woods chasing Bigfoot. But if a respected documentary filmmaker tells the story—if she brings in experts, corroborating witnesses, all the evidence we've collected—suddenly it's not just us anymore. Suddenly it's a real story that people have to take seriously."

"And suddenly we're in the crosshairs of whoever those men work for."

"We're already in the crosshairs. At least this way, we're not alone."

I thought about it for a long time. Thought about Daniel, about the life we'd built here, about everything we stood to lose. Thought about Austin Mercer's parents, about the families of all those missing people, about the truth that had been hidden for so long.

"Set up a meeting," I said finally. "Let's hear what she has to say."

* * *

Amanda arrived in Caldwell County two weeks later.

She was younger than I expected—mid-thirties, maybe, with sharp eyes and a no-nonsense demeanor that I recognized from my years in law enforcement. The kind of person who asked hard questions and didn't accept easy answers.

We met at a coffee shop in Lenoir, neutral ground where we could talk without being overheard. She listened while Zach and I laid out the basics—the disappearances, the evidence, the cover-up, the visit from the men in black. She didn't interrupt. Didn't react. Just listened and took notes and occasionally asked a clarifying question.

When we finished, she sat back and looked at us for a long moment.

"Do you have proof of any of this?" she asked.

"Some of it," I said. "The trail camera footage, the footprints, the video from Austin's phone. The rest—the cover-up, the government involvement—that's harder to document."

"But you believe it's real."

"I know it's real. I've experienced it firsthand. When I was twelve years old, I had an encounter with one of these creatures. I didn't see it, but I heard it. Smelled it. Felt it. It's been with me ever since."

Amanda studied me. I could see her assessing, weighing, trying to decide if I was credible or just another true believer with a story to tell.

"And you're willing to go on camera with this? Knowing what it could do to your career, your reputation?"

"I'm the sheriff of this county. A young man is missing, probably dead, and I know what happened to him even if I can't prove it. I'm not going to stay silent because it's easier."

"Even if it puts you in danger?"

"Especially if it puts me in danger. That's when it matters most."

Amanda nodded slowly. Then she reached into her bag and pulled out a contract.

"Let's talk terms," she said.

13

THE GATHERING STORM

The documentary crew arrived in early November.

There were five of them—Amanda, two camera operators, a sound guy, and a researcher who spent most of her time buried in documents and databases. They set up shop in a rental house outside Lenoir, and for the next several weeks, they were a constant presence in our lives.

Amanda interviewed everyone. Me. Zach. Daniel, though he was reluctant at first. Harold Whitmore, the old man who'd first encouraged me to run for sheriff. Park rangers who'd had their own experiences. Families of the missing. Researchers who'd been studying the Pisgah for years.

She was thorough, I'll give her that. Every claim we made, she verified. Every piece of evidence we showed her, she had analyzed by independent experts. Every witness we produced, she cross-examined until she was satisfied they weren't lying or crazy.

And what she found confirmed everything we'd suspected.

"The cover-up goes back decades," she told us one evening, spreading documents across the kitchen table. "I've found references to suppressed reports going back to the 1940s. The Forest Service, the

Park Service, the Army Corps of Engineers—they all have files on these creatures. And they've all been systematically buried."

"Who's behind it?"

"That's harder to pin down. It's not one agency—it's a network. People in different departments who coordinate to keep this quiet. Some of them are true believers who think they're protecting the public. Others are just following orders. And at the top—" She shook her head. "I haven't been able to identify who's running the show. Whoever they are, they're very good at staying hidden."

"Like the creatures themselves," Zach said.

"Exactly like the creatures themselves."

* * *

The filming took place over several weeks. They followed me on patrol, documented the ongoing search for Austin Mercer, interviewed witnesses and experts. Amanda pushed for access to the original campsite, and after some hesitation, I agreed to take her team out there.

It was different in daylight, with cameras rolling and people talking. Less ominous. More like any other crime scene I'd worked over the years. But I could still feel it—that sense of being watched, of something lurking just beyond the edge of perception.

"You feel it too," Amanda said, coming up beside me while the camera crew filmed the clearing.

"Feel what?"

"That presence. Like something's out there, just out of sight."

I didn't answer. I didn't need to.

"I've been doing this work for ten years," she continued. "Investigating unexplained phenomena, talking to witnesses, trying to separate fact from fiction. And in all that time, I've never felt anything like this." She turned to look at me. "They're real, aren't they? The creatures. They're actually real."

"I've known they were real since I was twelve years old."

"And the government knows too. They've known for decades."

"At least that long. Maybe longer."

Amanda was quiet for a moment. Then she shook her head.

"This is going to change everything," she said. "When this documentary comes out, when people see the evidence—everything's going to change."

I wanted to believe her. I wanted to believe that the truth would come out, that the cover-up would end, that all those families would finally get answers about what happened to their loved ones.

But I'd been around long enough to know that the truth doesn't always win. Sometimes the people in power are too strong, too connected, too willing to do whatever it takes to keep their secrets.

Sometimes the darkness wins.

I just hoped this wasn't one of those times.

* * *

The first sign of trouble came two weeks into filming.

Amanda's researcher—a young woman named Jessica—was working late at the rental house when someone broke in. They didn't take anything valuable. Didn't touch her laptop or phone or the cash she had in her purse. All they took was a box of documents. Physical copies of some of the files Zach had shared with us. Records of disappearances, internal memos, evidence of the cover-up.

"They knew exactly what they were looking for," Amanda said, when she called to tell me what had happened. "They went straight for that box and left everything else untouched."

"Is Jessica okay?"

"Shaken up, but fine. She was in the other room when it happened. Didn't hear anything until it was over."

"Did she see who did it?"

"No. Whoever it was, they were professionals. In and out in less than five minutes, no witnesses, no evidence."

I felt a chill run down my spine. "The men in black."

"That's what I'm thinking. They're sending a message. Letting us know they can get to us whenever they want."

"What do you want to do?"

Amanda's voice hardened. "I want to keep going. I didn't get into this business to be scared off by thugs in suits. Did you?"

"No, ma'am, I did not."

"Then let's give them something to really worry about."

* * *

We doubled down on security after that. Changed locations. Varied our routines. Made sure someone was always with the crew, always watching for signs of surveillance.

It wasn't enough.

A week later, one of the camera operators—a guy named Marcus—found a tracking device on his car. Small, sophisticated, the kind of thing law enforcement uses for surveillance. He found it by accident, only because he dropped his keys and had to get down on the ground to retrieve them.

"They've been following us," he said, turning the device over in his hands. "Probably since we got here."

"At least since the break-in," Amanda agreed. "They want to know who we're talking to, what we're finding, how much we know."

"Should we get rid of it?"

Amanda thought for a moment. Then she smiled.

"No," she said. "Let's use it. Let them think they know where we are and what we're doing. And meanwhile, we'll do our real work somewhere they're not watching."

It was risky. Everything about this was risky. But we were past the point of playing it safe.

We were committed now.

* * *

The interviews continued. Amanda sat down with Zach for a full day, going through his files piece by piece, documenting every disappearance, every suppressed report, every piece of evidence that pointed to a systematic cover-up. She interviewed former Park Service employees who'd been forced out for asking too many questions. She talked to scientists who'd analyzed hair samples and footprint casts and couldn't explain what they'd found.

And she interviewed me.

I told her everything. The move to Lyerly when I was twelve. The feeling of wrongness in that corner of the woods. The encounter—the huffing, the growling, the bluff charge that stopped just twenty feet away. The creature I never saw but knew was there, knew was watching, knew could have ended me if it had wanted.

I told her about Mama's cancer, about Daddy's abandonment, about the Klan burning a cross in our front yard. I told her about growing up poor, about working my way through life, about becoming a cop because I wanted to help people and discovering that the people who were supposed to help were often the ones making things worse.

I told her about Daniel. About loving him, about building a life with him, about the fear that all of this would destroy everything we'd worked so hard for.

"Why are you doing this?" Amanda asked, near the end of the interview. "You could walk away. Close the case, forget what you've seen, go back to your quiet life. Why risk everything?"

I thought about the question for a long time before answering.

"Because I spent thirty years pretending it didn't happen," I said finally. "Thirty years telling myself that what I heard in those woods was just a bear, just my imagination, just a trick of the light. And in all those years, I never stopped wondering. Never stopped questioning. Never stopped feeling like there was something wrong with the world, something hidden, something that I was supposed to understand but couldn't."

I looked directly into the camera.

"I'm not pretending anymore. I know what's out there. I know what happened to Austin Mercer. I know what happened to all those people who disappeared over the years. And I'm not going to be quiet about it. Not anymore. Not ever again."

Amanda held my gaze for a moment. Then she nodded and signaled for the camera operator to cut.

"That was good," she said. "That was really good."

I didn't feel good. I felt exposed, vulnerable, like I'd stripped away all my armor and left myself open to attack.

But I also felt free. For the first time in thirty years, I felt truly free.

Whatever came next, at least I'd told the truth.

At least I'd finally told the truth.

14

THINGS THAT LURK

Thanksgiving came and went without much celebration. Daniel and I had a quiet dinner at home—just the two of us, a turkey breast instead of a whole bird, all the fixings Mama used to make when I was growing up. We didn't talk about the investigation or the documentary or the men who were watching our every move. We just ate and talked about nothing important and tried to remember what normal felt like.

It wasn't easy. Normal felt very far away.

After dinner, we sat on the back deck with glasses of wine, watching the stars come out over the mountains. The air was cold enough to see our breath, and we huddled together under a blanket, drawing warmth from each other.

"Do you ever regret it?" Daniel asked.

"Regret what?"

"All of this. Running for sheriff. Starting this investigation. Stirring up things that maybe should have stayed buried."

I thought about it. Really thought about it.

"No," I said finally. "I regret that it's put you in danger. I regret that our lives aren't what we thought they'd be when we moved up here. But do I regret trying to find the truth? No. I can't regret that."

"Even if the truth destroys everything?"

"The truth is the only thing worth destroying everything for."

Daniel was quiet for a long moment. Then he reached over and took my hand.

"I love you," he said. "Whatever happens. Whatever comes next. I love you."

"I love you too."

We sat there in the darkness, holding hands, watching the stars. And somewhere out there, in the vast wilderness surrounding our little patch of land, something watched us back.

I could feel it. That familiar sensation of being observed, of something large and intelligent taking note of our presence. It wasn't threatening—not exactly. More like a reminder. A reminder that we weren't alone out here. A reminder that the forest had eyes.

"They're out there tonight," I said quietly.

Daniel tensed beside me. "How do you know?"

"I can feel it. The same way I could feel it back in Lyerly, all those years ago."

"Should we go inside?"

I shook my head. "They're not going to hurt us. If they wanted to hurt us, they would have done it already."

"Then what do they want?"

"I don't know. Maybe they're just curious. Maybe they're watching to see what we do next." I squeezed his hand. "Maybe they know we're trying to help."

"That's a lot of maybes."

"Yeah," I agreed. "It is."

We stayed on the deck for another hour, watching and waiting. Nothing happened. No vocalizations. No movement in the trees. Just that presence, that weight, that feeling of being observed by something we couldn't see.

When we finally went inside, I locked the door behind us and checked all the windows. Not because I was afraid of the creatures—I wasn't. But because there were other things out there to be afraid of.

Human things. Things in black suits who made threats in the middle of the night.

Those things scared me a lot more than anything in the forest.

* * *

December brought snow.

Not a lot—just a few inches, enough to turn the mountains white and make the roads treacherous. The documentary crew had finished their initial filming and headed back to California to start editing. Amanda called every few days with updates, said the footage was amazing, said this was going to be bigger than anything she'd ever done.

"We're looking at a spring release," she told me. "Maybe earlier if we can get everything cut in time. The network's excited. They think this could be huge."

"What about the people watching us? Have they made any moves?"

"Nothing overt. A few attempts to access our servers, some suspicious activity around the editing facility. But we've got good security. They're not going to get to the footage."

I wanted to believe her. I wanted to believe that we'd outmaneuvered them, that the truth was going to come out no matter what they did to stop it.

But I'd been in law enforcement long enough to know that powerful people have ways of making problems disappear.

"Be careful," I said. "They're not going to give up just because we've made it hard for them."

"I know. We're being careful. You be careful too."

"Always."

* * *

The call came on a Tuesday afternoon, two weeks before Christmas.

I was at the office, working through a stack of paperwork that had piled up during the investigation, when my personal cell phone rang. Unknown number. I almost didn't answer.

"Sheriff Patterson," I said.

"Sheriff." The voice was familiar. Smooth, controlled, with an undertone of menace that I recognized immediately. It was one of the men from that night. The one who'd done most of the talking.

"What do you want?"

"To give you one final warning. The documentary you're helping produce—it needs to stop. The footage needs to be destroyed. The investigation needs to end."

"Or what?"

"Or there will be consequences. Consequences for you, for your partner, for everyone involved in this project."

"You've already threatened me once. It didn't work then, it's not going to work now."

"This isn't a threat, Sheriff. It's a promise." The voice hardened. "We've been patient. We've given you multiple opportunities to walk away. But our patience has limits, and you've reached them."

"Then do what you have to do. I'm not backing down."

A long pause. Then: "You have no idea what you're dealing with. The creatures in that forest—they're not the only things you should be afraid of. There are forces at work here that you can't begin to understand. Forces that have been managing this situation for longer than you've been alive."

"Managing it how? By covering up disappearances? By threatening anyone who gets too close to the truth?"

"By keeping the public safe. By maintaining order. By ensuring that certain... complications... don't destabilize society."

"Complications. You mean Bigfoot."

"I mean things that are better left unknown. Things that would change the way people see the world. Things that certain interests have decided should remain hidden."

"And you're the ones who decide what people get to know? You're the ones who get to play God?"

"Someone has to. The alternative is chaos."

I laughed. I couldn't help it. "Chaos. A few big hairy creatures in the woods, and you think that's going to cause chaos? People have been reporting these things for centuries. The world hasn't ended."

"It's not just about the creatures, Sheriff. It never has been. The creatures are just one piece of a much larger puzzle. A puzzle that you're not equipped to understand."

"Then explain it to me."

Another pause. When the voice came back, it was softer. Almost sad.

"I can't. Even if I wanted to, I couldn't. You'd never believe me. And even if you did—" The voice stopped. Started again. "Walk away, Sheriff. For your own sake. For your partner's sake. Walk away while you still can."

"I can't do that."

"Then I'm sorry for what's going to happen. I truly am."

The line went dead.

I sat there for a long time, staring at my phone. Trying to process what I'd just heard. Trying to understand what he meant about larger puzzles and things I couldn't understand.

What wasn't he telling me? What was so big, so dangerous, that the existence of Sasquatch was just a small piece of it?

I didn't know. But I had a feeling I was about to find out.

* * *

That night, I told Daniel about the call.

He listened without interrupting, his face growing more concerned with every word. When I finished, he was quiet for a long moment.

"Maybe we should listen to them," he said finally.

"What?"

"I'm serious, Brian. Whatever this is, whatever they're protecting —it's bigger than us. Bigger than this investigation. Maybe they're right. Maybe some secrets are better left buried."

"You don't believe that."

"I don't know what I believe anymore. All I know is that I don't want to lose you. I don't want to wake up one morning and find out that you've disappeared like all those other people."

"That's not going to happen."

"You don't know that. You can't know that." He reached for my hand. "Brian, I love you. I love our life together. And I'm terrified that this investigation is going to destroy everything we've built."

I pulled him close. Held him. Felt his heart beating against mine.

"I know," I said. "I'm scared too. But I can't walk away from this. I've spent my whole life running from the truth, pretending things didn't happen, burying my head in the sand. I can't do it anymore. I won't."

"Even if it kills you?"

"Even if it kills me."

Daniel pulled back and looked at me. His eyes were wet.

"Then I guess we're in this together," he said. "Whatever happens. Whatever comes next. We're in it together."

"Always," I said. "Always."

We held each other for a long time after that. And outside, in the darkness, something howled.

15

THE PIECES FALL

Christmas was quiet. We spent it alone, just Daniel and me, trying to pretend that everything was normal even though nothing was normal anymore. Mama called from Georgia—she was doing well, still in remission, living her best life with the new husband she'd met a few years back. A good man, finally. Someone who treated her the way she deserved to be treated.

"You sound tired," she said, her voice crackling through the phone line. "You working too hard?"

"Just busy," I said. "Sheriff stuff."

"Uh huh." She wasn't fooled. She never was. "You know you can tell me anything, right? Whatever's going on, I'm here."

I wanted to tell her. Wanted to unload all of it—the investigation, the threats, the creatures in the forest, the men who watched our every move. But I couldn't bring myself to do it. She'd been through enough. She'd spent her whole life worrying about me, taking care of me, putting my needs ahead of her own. She deserved peace now. She deserved to enjoy her retirement without her son's problems weighing her down.

"I know, Mama," I said. "Everything's fine. Just the usual craziness."

"If you say so." She said. "I love you, baby. You know that, right?"

"I know. I love you too."

After we hung up, I sat by the window for a long time, watching the snow fall while thinking about everything that had led me to this moment. The move to Lyerly. The encounter in the woods. Mama's cancer. Daddy's abandonment. Coming out. Becoming a cop. Meeting Daniel. Moving to North Carolina. Running for sheriff.

Every step of the journey had brought me here. To this house, on this mountain, in the middle of an investigation that might get me killed.

Was it fate? Was it coincidence? Or was it something else—something larger, something I couldn't understand?

I didn't know. But I had a feeling I was about to find out.

* * *

New Year's came and went. The documentary editing continued. And then, in the second week of January, everything changed.

It started with a phone call from Zach.

"You need to come see this," he said. "I found something. Something big."

"What is it?"

"I can't explain over the phone. Just get here as soon as you can."

I grabbed my jacket and headed for the door. Daniel was at work—he'd taken an extra shift at the pizza place to cover for someone who was out sick. I texted him to let him know where I was going, then climbed into my truck and headed for the ranger station.

Zach was waiting for me in his office, pacing back and forth like a caged animal. When I walked in, he closed the door behind me and locked it.

"This can't leave this room," he said. "Not yet. Not until we figure out what it means."

"What did you find?"

He sat down at his computer and pulled up a document. A PDF, heavily redacted but still partially readable. The header said "DEPARTMENT OF DEFENSE - CLASSIFIED."

"How did you get this?"

"One of my contacts. She's been digging through old archives, looking for anything related to the cover-up. She found this buried in a file that was supposed to have been destroyed in the 1970s."

I leaned in to read. Most of the text was blacked out, but a few passages remained visible.

"...ongoing surveillance of subject populations in designated wilderness areas..."

"...evidence suggests intelligence levels significantly higher than previously estimated..."

"...recommendation to maintain current containment protocols until further study can be completed..."

"...potential implications for national security cannot be overstated..."

I looked up at Zach. "What is this?"

"It's from 1962. A report on a military operation called Project Threshold. And from what I can piece together, it was all about them. The creatures."

"The Department of Defense was studying Bigfoot?"

"Not just studying. Managing. Controlling." Zach pulled up another document. "I found references to similar programs going back to the 1940s. After World War II, when the government started getting serious about national security, they became aware of these creatures. And they decided to keep them secret."

"Why?"

"That's the part I'm still trying to figure out. But based on what I've read, it wasn't just about public safety. It was about something else. Something bigger."

He scrolled to another passage, this one even more heavily redacted than the first.

"...connection to [REDACTED] confirmed through [REDACTED] analysis..."

"...implications for understanding of [REDACTED] and [REDACTED] remain under investigation..."

"...recommend continuation of suppression protocols until [REDACTED] can be contained..."

"What is that?" I asked. "What are they talking about?"

"I don't know. But whatever it is, it scared them enough to spend sixty years covering it up." Zach leaned back in his chair. "Brian, I think we've stumbled into something much bigger than Bigfoot. Something the government has been hiding since before we were born. And whatever it is, they're willing to do anything to keep it secret."

I stared at the screen, trying to make sense of what I was seeing. A sixty-year cover-up. Military involvement. National security implications.

What the hell had we gotten ourselves into?

* * *

I took copies of everything. Zach had already made backups—he wasn't stupid—but I wanted my own set. If something happened to him, if something happened to his files, I wanted to make sure the information survived.

On the drive home, I kept turning it over in my mind. The creatures were real—we knew that. The government was covering them up—we knew that too. But there was something else. Something they were even more afraid of than the creatures themselves.

What could be scarier than Bigfoot?

The answer came to me as I was pulling into my driveway, and it stopped me cold.

What if Bigfoot wasn't the only thing out there? What if the creatures we knew about were just the tip of the iceberg?

I thought about all the strange things that had happened since we'd moved to North Carolina. The vocalizations. The lights in the night. The sense of being watched by something we couldn't see.

What if it wasn't just Sasquatch watching us?

What if there was something else?

* * *

I didn't tell Daniel about the documents that night. He came home exhausted from his shift, and I didn't want to pile more worry on top of his fatigue. Instead, I made dinner, we watched TV, and I tried to act like everything was fine.

But I couldn't sleep.

I lay in bed, staring at the ceiling, listening to Daniel's steady breathing beside me. My mind was racing, jumping from thought to thought, trying to connect dots that didn't want to be connected.

The creatures. The cover-up. The men in black. The redacted documents. The references to things the government considered national security threats.

What wasn't I seeing? What piece of the puzzle was I missing?

Around two in the morning, I gave up on sleep. I got out of bed quietly, trying not to wake Daniel, and went to the living room. Pulled up my laptop. Started searching.

I searched for Project Threshold. For government programs related to unexplained phenomena. For military involvement in cryptid research. For anything that might explain what I'd seen in those documents.

What I found shook me to my core.

There were others. Not just Zach and me, not just Amanda and her documentary crew. There were researchers all over the country who'd been piecing together the same puzzle. Some of them had been doing it for decades. And they'd all come to the same conclusion.

The cover-up wasn't just about Bigfoot.

It was about everything.

UFOs. Cryptids. Paranormal phenomena. Everything that mainstream science said was impossible, everything that the government officially denied—it was all connected. All part of the same vast system of suppression that had been operating for more than half a century.

And at the center of it all was something that nobody understood.

Something that the people in charge were desperately trying to keep hidden.

Something they were afraid of.

I sat in the dark, staring at my laptop screen, feeling the weight of it all pressing down on me. This was bigger than I'd ever imagined. Bigger than Austin Mercer. Bigger than the missing people. Bigger than everything I thought I knew.

And I had no idea what to do about it.

* * *

The knock on the door came just before dawn.

I was still in the living room, still staring at my laptop, when I heard it. Three sharp raps, deliberate and precise. The same knock I'd heard before.

I closed the laptop and stood. Grabbed my rifle from where it rested against the wall. Moved to the door.

"Who's there?"

No answer.

I opened the door, the rifle raised and ready.

Nobody was there. The porch was empty. The driveway was empty. The morning was gray and cold, the mountains still shrouded in pre-dawn darkness.

But there was something on the doormat. A thick manila envelope, no markings, no indication of where it had come from. Just a single word written on the front in block letters:

TRUTH

I scanned the tree line, looking for movement, looking for whoever had left this package. Nothing. No sound except the wind in the pines, no motion except the gentle swaying of branches.

I picked up the envelope and carried it inside. Set it on the kitchen table. Stared at it for a long moment, wondering if this was some kind of trap—a bomb, maybe, or anthrax, or some other threat designed to take me out before the documentary could air.

But my instincts said otherwise. Whoever had left this wanted me to see what was inside. Wanted me to know something that someone had gone to great lengths to keep hidden.

I grabbed a knife from the drawer and carefully slit the envelope open, taking care not to touch the contents directly in case there were fingerprints worth preserving.

What I found inside would haunt me for years.

* * *

The envelope contained a stack of documents—maybe fifty pages, some original, some photocopies, all of them bearing the stamps and classification markings of official government records.

The first page was a cover sheet. The header read: "PROJECT VULCAN - CLASSIFIED - EYES ONLY."

Below that, a date: May 18, 1980.

I felt the hair on my arms stand up. May 18, 1980. The day Mount St. Helens erupted. The day that fifty-seven people died in the largest volcanic event in United States history. The day that changed the landscape of the Pacific Northwest forever.

But according to these documents, something else had happened that day. Something that had been hidden from the world for over forty years.

Daniel came into the kitchen, rubbing sleep from his eyes. "What's going on? I heard you up."

"Someone left this on the porch." I held up the envelope. "You need to see this."

He sat down beside me, and together we began to read.

The document was a field report from something called the "Biological Containment Unit"—a team I'd never heard of, operating under the authority of agencies I didn't recognize. The report described a deployment to the Mount St. Helens disaster zone in the immediate aftermath of the eruption.

But they weren't there for the human casualties.

"Following confirmation of multiple Type-B biological entities within the primary blast zone," the report read, "BCU teams were deployed via helicopter to conduct recovery and containment operations. Initial surveys identified seventeen (17) deceased specimens and three (3) specimens exhibiting signs of life but severe trauma consistent with exposure to pyroclastic flows and associated volcanic phenomena."

I read the sentence again. And again. And again.

Seventeen deceased specimens. Three severely injured.

The report continued with clinical precision: "Living specimens were extracted to Field Hospital Delta for emergency medical treatment. Standard containment protocols were implemented. Two specimens expired during transport due to severity of thermal injuries and respiratory damage. One specimen survived initial triage and remains under observation at the field facility. All deceased specimens were transported to [REDACTED] for analysis and long-term storage."

"Jesus Christ," Daniel whispered.

I kept reading.

The document described, in clinical detail, the physical characteristics of the "specimens." Height: seven to nine feet. Weight: estimated 600 to 900 pounds. Covered in "dense hair-like follicles, coloration ranging from dark brown to reddish-auburn." Bipedal locomotion. Opposable thumbs. Cranial capacity "significantly exceeding Homo sapiens parameters."

There were photographs. Grainy, washed-out images that looked like they'd been taken in field conditions—helicopters in the background, men in military uniforms standing beside shapes covered in tarps. The quality was poor, but the scale was unmistakable. Whatever was under those tarps was massive.

But one photograph was different. Clear. Unmistakable.

A creature on a stretcher, being carried by four men in hazmat suits. Its eyes were closed. Its massive chest was wrapped in bandages soaked through with something dark. One arm hung limply over the side of the stretcher, the hand—five-fingered, with thick black nails— nearly touching the ground. The face was visible in profile: heavy brow ridge, flat nose, lips pulled back to reveal large teeth. Hair covered most of the visible skin, matted and singed in places from the volcanic heat.

It was real. It was documented. It was undeniable.

And the United States government had covered it up for over forty years.

"This changes everything," Daniel said, his voice barely above a whisper.

"This changes everything," I agreed.

I turned to the next page, and the next, and the next. Each one added another piece to the puzzle, another layer to the cover-up, another reason why the men in black had been so determined to keep us silent.

They weren't just hiding the existence of these creatures.

They'd been studying them. For decades.

And according to these documents, they'd learned things that would shake the foundations of everything we thought we knew about the natural world.

16

THE MOUNTAIN'S SECRET

I spent the next three days going through the documents, page by page, making notes, cross-referencing dates and locations, building a picture of what had happened in the aftermath of Mount St. Helens.

The story that emerged was staggering in its scope and implications.

In the immediate aftermath of the eruption, military and government teams had conducted a massive, secret operation to recover the bodies of creatures killed by the blast. The operation had been code-named Project Vulcan—named, I assumed, for the Roman god of fire and volcanoes. Helicopters had flown in and out of the disaster zone under the cover of legitimate rescue operations, extracting remains before civilian responders could discover them.

The timing had been crucial. The eruption had created chaos—thousands of people displaced, entire communities destroyed, emergency services stretched to the breaking point. In the confusion, it had been relatively easy to slip in additional teams with additional objectives. No one was paying attention to what was being loaded onto military helicopters. Everyone assumed it was bodies—human bodies, victims of the disaster.

No one suspected the truth.

The dead creatures had been transported to a facility in Nevada—the documents referred to it only by a code designation, but the state was mentioned in passing. I thought of Area 51, of all the conspiracy theories that had circulated for decades about secret government facilities in the desert. Suddenly, those theories seemed less like paranoid fantasies and more like the tip of a very large iceberg.

But the most disturbing documents were the medical reports.

Three creatures had survived the initial blast, though all were severely injured. Two had died during transport or shortly after—their autopsies were included in the file, and the details were both fascinating and horrifying. Internal organs that didn't quite match any known primate. Brain structures that suggested cognitive capabilities far beyond what anyone had expected. Vocal apparatus capable of producing complex sounds, including frequencies outside the normal human hearing range.

The pathologist who'd conducted the autopsies had written extensive notes. "Subject displays anatomical features consistent with prolonged bipedal locomotion," one entry read. "Pelvic structure, spinal curvature, and lower limb proportions suggest this species has been walking upright for millions of years—far longer than previously theorized for any great ape."

Another entry was more provocative: "Cranial capacity exceeds 1800cc, significantly larger than modern Homo sapiens. Brain structure shows enlarged prefrontal cortex and highly developed language centers. This species is almost certainly capable of complex communication and abstract reasoning."

The third survivor was different.

According to the medical reports, this creature—designated "Specimen 47-C—had survived for nearly three weeks after the eruption. It had been treated by a team of military doctors who'd been sworn to secrecy, and during that time, it had displayed remarkable behaviors.

"Subject displays clear signs of intelligence and problem-solving abilities," one report noted. "Responds to vocal stimuli with apparent recognition. Has demonstrated understanding of basic commands and can identify individual human handlers. Appears to distinguish between medical personnel and security staff, showing increased agitation when approached by armed guards."

The report continued: "Vocalizations appear to follow patterns consistent with intentional communication, though decoding efforts have proven unsuccessful. Subject has produced over forty distinct vocalizations, many repeated in consistent contexts suggesting semantic content. Recommend expanded linguistic analysis if subject survives."

But Subject 47-C had not survived.

The creature had died on June 8, 1980. The cause of death was listed as "multiple organ failure secondary to blast trauma and thermal injury." But a handwritten note in the margin, scrawled in different ink than the typed report, suggested something else:

"Subject appeared to give up. Stopped eating on June 3. Stopped responding to stimuli on June 5. Made continuous low vocalizations for approximately eighteen hours, then fell silent. Expired at 0347 on June 8. Almost like it knew there was no point in trying anymore."

I set down the documents and stared at the wall.

For forty years, this had been hidden. For forty years, the government had known that these creatures were real—intelligent, capable of recognizing individual humans, responding to communication attempts, displaying what looked very much like grief or despair—and they had said nothing. Done nothing. Let the world believe it was all a myth, a hoax, the delusions of crazy people in the woods.

Why?

What were they so afraid of?

* * *

"What do we do with this?" Daniel asked, after he'd finished reading through the documents himself.

"I don't know." I rubbed my eyes. "This changes everything. The documentary, the investigation—this is the proof we've been looking for. Not just evidence of the creatures, but evidence of the cover-up. Documented. Photographed. Undeniable."

"But who sent it? And why?"

That was the question. The envelope had appeared from nowhere, delivered by someone who didn't want to be seen. Someone who had access to classified government documents. Someone who wanted me to have this information.

A whistleblower? A sympathetic insider? Or a trap—bait to draw me into something dangerous?

"We need to verify this," I said. "Make sure it's authentic before we do anything with it."

"How?"

"I know some people. Researchers who specialize in this kind of thing. They can analyze the documents, check the paper, the ink, the formatting. If this is real, they'll be able to confirm it."

"And if it is real?"

I looked at Daniel. At this man who'd stood beside me through everything, who'd never wavered even when the cost kept climbing.

"Then we release it. We give it to Amanda, let her include it in the documentary. We show the world what the government has been hiding."

"They'll come after us. The men in black, the agencies—they'll do everything they can to stop us."

"They're already coming after us. At least this way, we'll have something worth fighting for."

Daniel was quiet for a long moment. Then he nodded.

"Okay," he said. "Let's do it."

* * *

Over the next few weeks, I had the documents analyzed by three independent experts. Two were researchers I'd connected with through the investigation—scientists who'd been studying cryptid phenomena for years and knew how to evaluate evidence. The third was a former government archivist who specialized in classified materials.

All three reached the same conclusion: the documents were authentic.

The paper was consistent with government stock from the early 1980s. The classification markings matched protocols used during that era. The formatting, the language, the bureaucratic structure—all of it checked out. The typewriter fonts were period-appropriate, the stamps showed the right kind of wear, even the staples were the correct vintage.

Someone had leaked genuine classified documents about a government operation to recover Sasquatch remains from Mount St. Helens.

The question was: why now? And why to me?

I got my answer on a Friday afternoon, when I found another envelope on my porch.

This one was smaller, containing just a single sheet of paper. A handwritten note:

"There are more of us than you know. We've been waiting for someone brave enough to tell the truth. Keep going. Don't let them stop you.

You're closer to the truth than you realize. The missing people in your forest—they're not the first. And they won't be the last unless someone exposes what's really happening.

The creatures are not what you think. They are not gentle giants hiding in the woods. Some of them are dangerous. Very dangerous. The government knows this. That's why they've been hiding it.

A friend."

I read the note three times. Then I burned it, just as I'd burned the first envelope after photographing all its contents.

Whoever was helping me, they were taking enormous risks. The least I could do was protect their identity.

But their words stayed with me, especially the warning about the creatures being dangerous. I thought about Austin Mercer, about the footage we'd recovered, about the thing that had chased him through the forest until his screams cut off and there was only silence.

Not all of them were harmless. Not all of them meant well.

Some of them were predators.

And the government had known this all along.

* * *

The Mount St. Helens documents opened floodgates I hadn't known existed.

Once Amanda began making inquiries—carefully, through back channels, reaching out to people who'd been involved in the 1980 disaster response—stories started surfacing. Stories that had been buried for four decades, told only in whispers, dismissed as trauma-induced fantasies.

"You're not going to believe this," Amanda called to tell me one evening. "I found a witness. A first responder who was actually there."

"There where?"

"In the blast zone. The day after the eruption. He saw them loading the bodies onto helicopters."

"He's willing to talk?"

"He's eighty-two years old and dying of lung cancer. He says he's been carrying this secret for too long. He wants someone to know before it's too late."

* * *

His name was Harold Jennings. He'd been a county sheriff in Washington state in 1980—the same job I held now, three thousand miles away and four decades later. When Mount St. Helens erupted, he'd been part of the emergency response effort, one of thousands of first responders who'd rushed to help in the aftermath of the disaster.

"We were out there the next day," Harold told me, his voice thin and raspy through the phone connection. The cancer had spread to his lungs, Amanda had warned me, and he tired easily. But his mind was sharp, and his memory was clear. "Search and rescue. Looking for survivors, though we knew there wouldn't be many. The blast had leveled everything for miles. Trees down like matchsticks. Ash everywhere. It looked like the surface of the moon."

"What did you see?"

"At first, nothing unusual. Just devastation. Trees down everywhere, ash covering everything like gray snow, the landscape unrecognizable. We were searching a creek bed about fifteen miles from the mountain when we heard helicopters."

"Military helicopters?"

"That's what we thought. Black Hawks, maybe three or four of them. They came in low, fast, headed for a ravine about half a mile from our position. We figured they were running the same mission we were—looking for survivors, evacuating the injured."

"But they weren't."

"No." Harold's voice caught. "We went to check it out. See if they needed assistance. There were four of us—me, my deputy, and two volunteers from the fire department. We hiked over to where the helicopters had landed."

He stopped. I could hear his labored breathing through the phone.

"Take your time," I said.

"What we found—" He stopped again. Coughed. Started again. "There was a team of men in full hazmat gear. Military, or something like it. They had a perimeter set up, armed guards every twenty feet, and they weren't letting anyone through. But I could see what they were loading onto the helicopters."

"What did you see?"

"Bodies. Big bodies. Too big to be human. Covered in dark hair, even though a lot of it had been burned off by the heat. One of them —" His voice broke completely. "One of them was still moving. Still alive. They had it strapped to a stretcher, and it was trying to get loose. Making these sounds—these awful sounds, like something in terrible pain."

The line went silent except for Harold's labored breathing.

"What happened then?"

"A man in a suit came over. Not military—civilian, but with the kind of authority that says 'don't ask questions.' He told us we'd never been there, never seen anything. Said if we talked about it, there would be consequences. He was very specific about what those consequences would be. He mentioned my wife by name. My daughter. He knew everything about my family."

"Did you report it?"

"To who? The federal government? The same people who were running the operation?" Harold laughed bitterly, the laugh dissolving into another coughing fit. "I went home. I kept my mouth shut. I spent forty years trying to forget what I saw in that ravine. Trying to convince myself it was just the stress, the trauma, the confusion of the disaster."

"But you never forgot."

"You don't forget something like that. For the first few years , every time I closed my eyes, I saw that creature struggling on the stretcher. Heard those sounds it was making. Wondered what happened to it, whether it survived, whether it was still out there somewhere in some government bunker being studied like a lab rat."

"Why are you talking now?"

"Because I'm dying, son. Because I've got maybe three months left, and I'll be damned if I'm going to take this secret to my grave." His voice strengthened, finding reserves of energy from somewhere. "Someone needs to know. Someone needs to tell the truth. And if you're the one doing it—well, I figured I'd help."

Harold Jennings wasn't the only witness Amanda found.

Over the following weeks, she tracked down three more people who'd been in or near the Mount St. Helens blast zone during the recovery operations. Each one had a piece of the puzzle. Each one had been threatened into silence. And each one was willing to talk now, after forty years of carrying secrets that had poisoned their lives.

* * *

John Webb had been an Army National Guard helicopter pilot in 1980. He was seventy-six now, living in a retirement community in Arizona, his flying days long behind him. But he remembered the mission as if it were yesterday.

"They called us in on May 19th," John told me. His voice was clearer than Harold's, his health apparently better, but there was the same weight of long-held secrets in his words. "My unit was based out of Fort Lewis. We'd been doing civilian rescue operations since the eruption—shuttling supplies, evacuating injured, that sort of thing. Standard disaster response."

"What changed?"

"We got new orders. Classified. We were told to report to a staging area about twenty miles from the blast zone. When we arrived, there were already other birds on the ground—Black Hawks, Chinooks, all of them without standard markings. No unit insignia, no tail numbers. Just black paint."

"What was the mission?"

"They called it 'biological recovery.' We assumed it meant bodies —human bodies, victims who'd been killed by the blast. They loaded our bird with body bags and told us to fly to a specific set of coordinates."

"What did you find there?"

John was quiet for a moment. "We landed in what used to be a valley. The eruption had filled it with ash and debris, turned it into a gray wasteland. There were men already on the ground, in full hazmat gear, working with equipment I didn't recognize. And there were bodies."

"Human bodies?"

"No." His voice dropped. "Big. Covered in hair. Some of them were burned so badly you could barely tell what they were, but others —others were more intact. I saw faces. Faces that were almost human but not quite. Hands with fingers. Feet."

"What did you do?"

"We loaded them. Six bodies in our bird, the biggest ones. They barely fit. I could smell them even through the environmental seals— this awful smell, like burned hair and something else, something animal. We flew them to a facility in Nevada. Some kind of underground bunker. Never saw what happened to them after that."

"Did you report what you saw?"

"We were debriefed before we left the staging area. Told that the mission was classified at the highest level. Told that discussing it with anyone—anyone—would result in court-martial and imprisonment.

They made us sign documents. Non-disclosure agreements that would never expire."

"But you're talking now."

"I'm seventy-six years old. I've got grandchildren. Great-grand-children. I've had a good life." He paused. "But I've also spent forty years lying to everyone I love. Pretending I didn't know what I knew. Watching those TV shows about Bigfoot and knowing—knowing—that it was all real, and that the government had proof, and that they were never going to admit it."

* * *

Dr. Elizabeth Warren had been a trauma surgeon at a military hospital in Washington state. In May 1980, she'd been temporarily assigned to something called "Field Hospital Delta"—a facility that, according to official records, had never existed.

"I was young," Elizabeth said. She was seventy-nine now, her voice still sharp, her mind still clear. "Just finished my residency. I was eager to help, to be part of the disaster response. When they asked for volunteers with surgical experience, I raised my hand."

"What did you find at Field Hospital Delta?"

"It wasn't what I expected. We weren't treating human patients. We were treating—" She stopped. Started again. "They called them speci-mens. But they weren't specimens. They were beings. Intelligent beings, injured and dying and scared."

"You treated the survivors from the blast zone?"

"Three of them. Two were already gone by the time I arrived—the trauma was too severe. Burns over most of their bodies, lungs damaged from inhaling superheated gas. There was nothing we could have done."

"And the third?"

"The third lived for three weeks." Her voice softened. "His name—well, we weren't supposed to name them, but one of the nurses started calling him George. Don't ask me why. It stuck."

"What was George like?"

"Remarkable. Despite the pain, despite the fear, he tried to communicate. He'd make these sounds—vocalizations that clearly had meaning, though we couldn't understand them. He'd gesture with his hands, point at things, try to make us understand what he wanted."

"What did he want?"

"To go home, I think. He'd look at the door whenever someone opened it. This longing in his eyes that broke my heart. He knew he was going to die. I could see it in his face. And all he wanted was to die somewhere familiar, somewhere that wasn't a concrete bunker filled with strangers."

"What happened to him?"

"He stopped eating. Stopped responding. The last few days, he just lay there, looking at the wall, making these soft sounds. Like humming. Or singing. I don't know." Her voice caught. "He died at three in the morning. I was holding his hand. I don't know if that mattered to him, but I hope it did."

"And after?"

"They took his body away. I was transferred back to my regular posting and told never to speak of what I'd seen. They gave me a promotion and a commendation for 'classified service.' Blood money, essentially. Payment for my silence."

"You've kept that silence for forty years."

"To my shame, yes. I told myself it was for the best, that the public couldn't handle the truth. But that was a lie. The truth is, I was afraid. Afraid of what they'd do to me if I talked. Afraid of losing everything I'd worked for." She paused. "I'm not afraid anymore. I'm too old to be afraid. And George deserves better than to be forgotten."

* * *

The fourth witness was a Forest Service employee named Robert Collins. He'd been assigned to the Mount St. Helens recovery effort in the weeks following the eruption, helping to assess damage to the national forest lands.

"Most of what we did was routine," Robert told me. He was

seventy-four, still sharp, living in a cabin in Montana that reminded him of his Forest Service days. "Surveying damage, mapping the blast zone, estimating how long it would take for the ecosystem to recover. Scientific work, mostly."

"What wasn't routine?"

"About three weeks after the eruption, I was assigned to escort a team of 'specialists' into a remote area of the blast zone. They didn't say what they were looking for, and I didn't ask. You learned not to ask questions in those days."

"What did you find?"

"A cave. Or what used to be a cave, before the eruption partially collapsed it. The specialists went inside with their equipment while I waited outside. They were in there for maybe four hours."

"What came out?"

"Bodies. They brought out three bodies on stretchers. Big bodies, covered with tarps. And boxes—metal boxes, the kind you'd use for biological samples. They loaded everything onto helicopters and flew away."

"Did you see what was under the tarps?"

"I saw a hand. One of the tarps slipped while they were loading it, and I saw a hand hanging off the stretcher. It was huge—bigger than any human hand I've ever seen. And it wasn't human. The proportions were wrong, the nails were too thick, and it was covered in hair."

"What did you do?"

"What could I do? I reported what I'd seen to my supervisor. He told me to forget about it, that I'd imagined it, that the stress of the disaster was getting to me. A week later, I was transferred to a desk job in Portland. No explanation, no appeal. Just 'thank you for your service, here's your new assignment.'"

"And the cave?"

"Sealed. According to official records, it never existed. I tried to find it again a few years later, after I'd retired. The whole area had been bulldozed and planted with seedlings. No trace of the cave, no trace of anything. Like it had never been there at all."

* * *

Four witnesses. Four pieces of the puzzle. Four voices that had been silent for forty years, now ready to speak.

Amanda filmed their testimonies over the course of three weeks, traveling across the country to sit with each one in person. The interviews were long and detailed, covering every aspect of what they'd seen, what they'd been told, how they'd been threatened into silence.

By the end, we had something unprecedented: eyewitness accounts of a government operation to recover non-human bodies from the Mount St. Helens disaster zone. Accounts that corroborated the documents I'd received. Accounts that proved, beyond any reasonable doubt, that the cover-up was real.

"This is going to change everything," Amanda said, during a video call after the last interview was complete. "The documents were compelling, but they could be dismissed as forgeries. The witnesses make it real. You can't fake that kind of pain, that kind of regret, that kind of relief at finally being able to tell the truth."

"When do we release?"

"March. We're looking at a March release. The network's excited —they think this is going to be the biggest documentary event in years."

I wanted to share her optimism. But I couldn't shake the feeling that we were poking a hornet's nest, and the hornets were about to come swarming out.

"Be careful," I told her. "These people have kept this secret for forty years. They're not going to let it come out without a fight."

"I know. But that's exactly why we have to do this. If we back down now, the secret stays buried forever. And the people who've been seeing these creatures, getting laughed at, called crazy—they deserve better than that."

She was right, of course. We'd come too far to turn back now.

But I still slept with my rifle beside the bed.

And I still checked the locks on the doors every night.

And I still wondered, every time I heard a sound outside, if this was the night they'd finally come for us.

* * *

The Austin Mercer case remained unsolved.

I hadn't forgotten him. The trail camera footage we'd recovered still haunted me—the sound of his screams, the glimpse of something massive chasing him through the trees, the awful silence that followed. Whatever had taken Austin, it hadn't been benevolent. It hadn't been curious. It had been predatory.

I sat down with his parents one cold evening in February. They'd aged years in the months since their son's disappearance. The hope that had sustained them through the early weeks was gone, replaced by a hollow acceptance that was almost worse than grief.

"I need to be honest with you," I said. "Based on everything we've found—the footage, the patterns of other disappearances, the behavior of these creatures—I don't believe Austin is coming home."

His mother's hand went to her mouth. His father sat very still.

"You think he's dead," his father said. Not a question.

"I think there are different types of these creatures. Some of them are curious. Some of them are protective. And some of them are predators." I took a breath. "The footage we recovered suggests Austin encountered the third kind. I'm sorry. I wish I had better news."

"But you never found a body," his mother said. "Without a body, how can you be sure?"

"I can't be sure. And I'll keep looking. I'll never stop looking." I leaned forward. "But I also don't want to give you false hope. Whatever happened to Austin, whatever took him—I don't think it meant him well."

The silence that followed was the hardest I'd ever endured.

Finally, his father spoke. "Thank you for telling us the truth. Even if it's not what we wanted to hear."

"I'm sorry I couldn't do more."

"You did more than anyone else would have. You believed us when no one else did. You searched when everyone else gave up." He reached out and gripped my hand. "Whatever happened to our son, at least we know someone cared enough to look for the truth."

I drove home that night feeling the weight of every missing person, every unanswered question, every family left wondering what had happened to someone they loved. The creatures were real. The cover-up was real. And somewhere in those mountains, Austin Mercer's remains lay hidden, waiting to be found.

I would find them someday. I had to believe that. But until then, all I could do was keep searching. Keep telling the truth. Keep hoping that someday, the answers would come.

17

THE NETWORK FALLS

The documentary was scheduled for release in March. Amanda had managed to get it picked up by a major streaming platform —a company brave enough (or foolish enough) to broadcast what we'd found. The promotion started in February, teasers and trailers that hinted at revelations to come.

The response was immediate and intense.

Some people dismissed it as another conspiracy theory, another piece of sensationalized nonsense from people who'd watched too many X-Files episodes. But others were intrigued. The numbers were good. People wanted to know.

And then, two weeks before the release, everything fell apart.

18

THE EDGE OF EVERYTHING

Amanda called at three in the morning.

"They got to us," she said, her voice shaking. "They got to the network."

"What do you mean?"

"The documentary. They're pulling it. The whole thing. Someone got to the executives, threatened them, bought them off—I don't know. But they're killing it. Two weeks before air, and they're killing it."

I sat up in bed, my heart racing. Daniel stirred beside me, sensing something was wrong.

"Can't you take it somewhere else?"

"I've been trying. Everyone's suddenly not interested. Every network, every platform—they're all backing away. It's like someone flipped a switch and turned off the entire industry."

"The men in black."

"Has to be. They finally made their move." She let out a bitter laugh. "I should have known. All that work, all those months—and they just make a few phone calls and it all disappears."

I got out of bed and walked to the window. Outside, the mountains were dark shapes against a darker sky. Somewhere out there, in the vast wilderness, the creatures waited. The truth waited.

"What about the footage?" I asked. "The files? Do you still have everything?"

"They tried to seize it. Showed up with federal agents and court orders. But I'd already moved the backups. They got some of it, but not everything."

"Then we're not finished."

"Brian, without a platform—"

"We don't need their platform. We have the internet. We have social media. We have a million ways to get this information out that doesn't involve corporate gatekeepers."

"It won't have the same impact. It won't reach the same audience."

"Maybe not. But it'll reach someone. And that someone will tell someone else. And eventually, the truth will spread." I turned away from the window. "They can't stop it, Amanda. They can slow it down, they can make it harder, but they can't stop it. The creatures told me— the time for secrets is ending. Whatever happens, the truth is going to come out."

Amanda was quiet for a long moment. When she spoke again, her voice was stronger. "You really believe that?"

"I have to. Because if I don't, then everything we've done is meaningless. And I'm not willing to accept that."

Another pause. Then: "Okay. Let's do it. Let's put everything online and let the chips fall where they may."

"That's my girl."

* * *

We released the documentary in pieces over the next two weeks.

Each day, a new segment appeared on a new platform. YouTube. Vimeo. BitTorrent. Anywhere and everywhere we could post it without getting immediately taken down. Amanda and her team worked around the clock, uploading and re-uploading as fast as the content was removed.

The response was overwhelming.

The videos went viral. Millions of views in the first few days, tens of millions by the end of the first week. People shared them, discussed them, argued about them. Mainstream media, which had initially ignored us, was forced to respond. Debunkers and skeptics came out of the woodwork, but so did believers. The conversation we'd wanted to start was finally happening.

And then the witnesses started coming forward.

First a handful, then dozens, then hundreds. People who'd had their own encounters. People who'd seen things they couldn't explain. People who'd been silenced, threatened, dismissed—but who now felt empowered to speak.

The dam had broken.

* * *

The men in black tried to stop it. They took down videos. They filed legal actions. They pressured platforms and service providers. They made examples of a few people, hoping to scare the rest into silence.

It didn't work.

For every video they removed, three more appeared. For every witness they intimidated, ten more stepped up. The information was out there now, spreading like wildfire, impossible to contain.

And in the middle of it all, something remarkable happened.

Other researchers started sharing their findings. Scientists who'd been studying these phenomena in secret. Government whistleblowers who'd been waiting for the right moment to speak. Decades of suppressed evidence came flooding out, adding weight and credibility to everything we'd revealed.

The cover-up was crumbling.

* * *

I was sitting on my porch one evening in late March, watching the sun set over the mountains, when I heard it.

A howl. Rising from somewhere deep in the forest. Not threatening. Not territorial.

Celebratory.

Other howls answered it. Dozens of them, echoing across the valleys and ridges, filling the air with a chorus of voices that had been silent for too long.

Daniel came out and stood beside me.

"What is that?" he asked.

"Them," I said. "The creatures. I think they know."

"Know what?"

"That things are changing. That the world is finally ready to see them."

We stood there together, listening to the howls, watching the darkness gather. And for the first time since all of this started, I felt something I'd almost forgotten was possible.

Hope.

* * *

But the story wasn't over. Not even close.

The documentary had started a conversation, but conversations aren't the same as change. There were still powerful forces working against us. Still secrets that hadn't been revealed. Still dangers that lurked in the shadows.

And there was still Austin.

I hadn't forgotten him. Hadn't forgotten the cave, the creatures, the vision they'd given me. He was out there, somewhere, learning things that no human had ever learned before. And someday, he would return.

When that day came, everything would change again.

* * *

The night before this chapter of my life closed, I had a dream.

I was back in the woods behind our house in Lyerly. I was twelve years old again, standing in that clearing, listening to the sounds of something huge moving through the undergrowth.

But this time, I wasn't afraid.

The creature emerged from the trees. The same one I'd encountered all those years ago—or maybe its descendant, its child, its legacy. It stood before me, massive and terrible and beautiful, and it looked at me with eyes that held the wisdom of ages.

"You did well," it said. Not in words, but in that way they had of communicating. "You kept your promise."

"What promise?"

"The promise you made that day, when you were young. When you decided you would find the truth, no matter what it cost."

I remembered. I remembered sitting in my room after the encounter, staring at the wall, telling myself I would figure this out someday. I would understand what was out there. I would make sense of the impossible.

"There's more to come," the creature continued. "More truth. More danger. More change. Are you ready?"

I thought about everything I'd been through. Everything I'd lost and gained. Everything that had led me to this moment.

"Yes," I said. "I'm ready."

The creature nodded. And then it turned and walked back into the trees, disappearing into the darkness it had emerged from.

And I woke up.

* * *

I'm writing this now because I don't know what's coming next.

The documentary changed things, but the change is just beginning. The forces that have been hiding the truth for decades won't give up without a fight. There are battles ahead—legal battles, political battles, maybe even physical battles.

And there's something else. Something about the Mount St. Helens documents that suggests this cover-up goes far deeper than anyone imagined. Project Vulcan wasn't just about one eruption. It was about decades of encounters, of recoveries, of secrets kept from the public.

The truth is coming out. I can feel it.

When it finally does, nothing will ever be the same.

* * *

For now, I'm still the sheriff of Caldwell County. Still protecting the people who elected me. Still investigating the mysteries that lurk in these ancient mountains.

Daniel is still by my side. We've been through hell together, and we've come out stronger. Whatever happens next, we'll face it together.

Zach is still digging. Every day brings new revelations, new pieces of the puzzle. The truth is out there, and he won't stop until he's found it all.

And somewhere, in the deep places where humans rarely go, the creatures watch and wait. They've been patient for millennia. They can be patient a little longer.

But not forever.

The time for secrets is ending.

The time for truth is beginning.

And I'm going to be there when it happens.

* * *

This is where this part of my story ends. But it's also where the next part begins.

Austin's fate remains unknown. The cover-up is still crumbling. The men in black are still watching.

And I have promises to keep.

PART IV

SASQUATCH ODYSSEY

19

THE WEIGHT OF THE BADGE

The months following the documentary release should have been a triumph. The truth was finally out there. People were listening. The cover-up that had hidden these creatures for decades was crumbling, one revelation at a time.

But being sheriff had become unbearable.

It started with the county commissioners who called me in for a "meeting" two weeks after the documentary went viral—which turned out to be three hours of them questioning my judgment, my sanity, and my fitness for office. Did I really believe in Bigfoot? Did I understand how this made the county look? Had I considered the impact on tourism, on property values, on the good reputation of Caldwell County?

I told them the truth. I told them what I'd seen, what I'd experienced, what the evidence showed. They looked at me like I'd sprouted a second head.

"Sheriff Patterson," Commissioner Harold Davis said, leaning back in his chair with that condescending smile politicians perfect over years of practice, "we appreciate your... enthusiasm. But surely you understand that this kind of publicity isn't what our county needs right now."

"What the county needs is the truth," I said.

"The county needs responsible leadership. The county needs a sheriff who focuses on real crimes, not—" he waved his hand dismissively "—monster hunting."

I wanted to tell him about the forty-seven people who'd disappeared in the Pisgah over the past twenty years. I wanted to tell him about Austin Mercer, whose screams still echoed in my nightmares. I wanted to tell him about the Mount St. Helens documents, about the government cover-up, about everything we'd uncovered.

But I didn't. Because I knew it wouldn't matter. He'd already made up his mind. They all had.

"Is there anything else?" I asked.

"Just a friendly warning, Sheriff. Elections are coming up. The people of this county expect certain things from their law enforcement. It would be a shame if your... outside interests... interfered with your ability to serve them."

I stood. "I appreciate the advice, Commissioner. I'll take it under consideration."

I walked out of that meeting knowing that my days as sheriff were numbered. Not because they'd fire me—they couldn't, not without cause—but because I was tired. Tired of the politics. Tired of the bureaucracy. Tired of pretending that catching speeders and breaking up bar fights was the most important work I could be doing.

There was something bigger out there. Something that needed my attention. And I couldn't give it the attention it deserved while I was wearing this badge.

* * *

The hate mail started arriving around the same time.

Not a lot at first—just a few letters from people who thought I was either crazy or a fraud. But as the documentary spread, as more and more people learned about the sheriff in North Carolina who believed in Bigfoot, the volume increased. Some of it was angry. Some of it was threatening. Some of it was just sad—people who felt betrayed by someone in a position of authority who'd gone off the deep end.

But there was other mail too. Letters from people who'd had their own experiences. People who'd seen things, heard things, encountered things they couldn't explain. People who'd been laughed at, dismissed, told they were crazy—and who now felt validated because someone with a badge was finally telling the truth.

Those letters piled up on my desk. Dozens of them, then hundreds. Each one a story. Each one a piece of the puzzle. Each one a person who deserved to be heard.

I started responding to them. Writing back, asking for details, collecting information. It wasn't official sheriff's business—I did it on my own time, late at night after Daniel had gone to bed. But the more I read, the more I realized how big this really was.

These encounters weren't isolated incidents. They were happening everywhere. In every state. In every country. People from all walks of life, with nothing to gain and everything to lose, were reporting the same things. The same creatures. The same sounds. The same experiences.

The world was full of witnesses. And nobody was listening to them.

Until now.

* * *

The idea for the podcast came to me on a rainy Tuesday night in June.

I was sitting at the kitchen table, reading through another stack of letters, when Daniel came in and set a cup of coffee beside me.

"You're going to wear yourself out," he said, sitting down across from me. "You can't save everyone, Brian."

"I'm not trying to save them. I'm trying to listen to them." I held up one of the letters. "This woman, Rebecca, she had an encounter in Florida back in 1987. She's never told anyone about it because she was afraid people would think she was crazy. Thirty-five years of carrying this secret, and she finally feels like she can share it because of what we did."

"That's good. That's important. But you can't personally respond to every person who writes to you."

"I know." I set down the letter and rubbed my eyes. "But there has to be some way to reach them. Some way to let them know they're not alone. Some way to collect all these stories and share them with the world."

Daniel was quiet for a moment. Then he said, "What about a podcast?"

"A what?"

"A podcast. You know, like a radio show, but on the internet. You could interview these people, let them tell their stories in their own words. Build a community of believers and witnesses."

I thought about it. I'd listened to a few podcasts over the years— true crime stuff, mostly, during long drives through the county. The format made sense. It was accessible, personal, intimate. Just two people talking, sharing experiences, connecting over something that mattered to them.

"I wouldn't know the first thing about how to start something like that," I said.

"Then learn. You learned how to be a cop. You learned how to run a juvenile facility. You learned how to be sheriff. You can learn how to talk into a microphone."

I looked at the stack of letters on the table. At all those stories waiting to be told. At all those people waiting to be heard.

"*Sasquatch Odyssey*," I said.

"What?"

"That's what I'd call it. *Sasquatch Odyssey*. Because that's what this is—a journey. An odyssey through all these encounters, all these experiences. A search for the truth that never really ends."

Daniel smiled. "I like it."

"You think I could really do this?"

"I think you can do anything you set your mind to. I've seen you do it."

I reached across the table and took his hand.

"Alright then," I said. "Let's see how this goes."

* * *

The first episode of *Sasquatch Odyssey* went live on August 15th.

It wasn't much to look at—just me, sitting in the spare bedroom we'd converted into a makeshift studio, talking into a decent microphone I'd bought on Amazon. The audio quality was rough. My delivery was awkward. I stumbled over my words more times than I could count.

But the content was real. I told my own story—the encounter in Lyerly, the years of searching, the investigation that had led me here. I explained what I was trying to do with the podcast: create a space where people could share their experiences without fear of ridicule. A community of witnesses. A record of the truth.

I uploaded it to all the podcast platforms I could find and waited.

For the first few days, nothing happened. A handful of downloads, mostly from friends and family who were humoring me. I started to wonder if Daniel had been wrong, if this whole thing was a waste of time.

And then the messages started coming.

At first, it was just a trickle. People who'd heard the documentary, who'd seen the news coverage, who'd somehow found their way to this little podcast from a sheriff in North Carolina. But the trickle became a stream, and the stream became a flood.

By the end of the first week, *Sasquatch Odyssey* had been downloaded over ten thousand times.

By the end of the first month, it was over fifty thousand.

And the emails—Lord, the emails. More stories than I could ever tell. More witnesses than I could ever interview. A whole world of people who'd been waiting for someone to listen.

I started scheduling interviews. One a week at first, then two, then three. Each episode featuring someone new, someone with a story to tell, someone who'd encountered something they couldn't explain and had carried that experience with them for years or decades.

The podcast was growing. And so was I.

But I was still sheriff. Still wearing the badge. Still trying to serve two masters.

Something had to give.

20

VOICES FROM THE SOUTH

My first interview was with a man named Earl Hutchins from Rabun County, Georgia.

Earl was seventy-three years old, a retired logger who'd spent fifty years working in the forests of northeast Georgia. He'd contacted me through the website Daniel had helped me set up, sending a long email that described an encounter he'd had back in 1978.

"I ain't never told nobody about this," he said, when I called him to set up the interview. "My wife thinks I'm crazy as a sprayed roach for even considering it. But I seen what I seen, and I reckon it's time somebody knew."

We recorded the interview over the phone—I hadn't figured out video yet, and Earl didn't have a computer anyway. His voice was rough, weathered by decades of cigarettes and mountain air, but there was something solid about it. Something that told you this man wasn't lying.

"It was October of '78," Earl began. "I was working a timber contract up near Clayton, cutting white pine for a lumber company out of Gainesville. We'd been working that stand for about three weeks, me and a crew of five other boys. Hard work, but good work. The kind of work that makes you sleep like the dead every night."

"What happened that day?" I asked.

"Well, we'd finished up early on account of the rain. The other boys had gone back to camp, but I stayed behind to sharpen my saw. I was sitting on a stump, running the file along the chain, when I heard something moving in the brush about fifty yards out."

"What kind of movement?"

"Heavy. Real heavy. Like a bull walking through the woods, except bulls don't walk on two legs." Earl paused, and I could hear him take a deep breath. "I looked up, and there it was. Standing right there at the edge of the clearing, plain as day."

"Can you describe what you saw?"

"Biggest damn thing I ever seen in my life. Eight feet tall, maybe more. Shoulders wider than a doorway. Covered in dark brown hair, kind of reddish in places where the sun hit it. And the face—" He stopped again. "The face was like nothing I can describe. Almost human, but not. Like looking at something that was human a million years ago and went a different direction."

"What did it do?"

"Just stood there. Watching me. I was frozen solid—couldn't move, couldn't breathe, couldn't do nothing but sit there and stare back at it. We must have stayed like that for two, three minutes. Longest minutes of my life."

"How did the encounter end?"

"It turned and walked away. Didn't run, didn't hurry. Just turned around and walked into the trees like it had somewhere to be. I heard it moving for another minute or so, and then nothing. Just the rain starting up again and my own heart trying to beat its way out of my chest."

"Did you tell anyone at the time?"

"Hell no. I went back to camp, drank half a bottle of whiskey, and didn't say a word. Who was gonna believe me? The boys would've thought I'd lost my mind. My wife would've had me committed. So I kept it to myself. Forty-five years, and you're the first person I've ever told."

"Why are you telling me now?"

Earl was quiet for a moment. When he spoke again, his voice was softer.

"Because I'm seventy-three years old, and I ain't gonna be around forever. And I figure if I don't tell somebody while I still can, that story dies with me. And that don't seem right. What I saw was real. It deserves to be remembered."

* * *

The episode with Earl Hutchins was downloaded more than anything I'd done before.

People responded to his authenticity, to the rawness of his story, to the emotion in his voice when he talked about carrying this secret for nearly half a century. Comments flooded in—some from skeptics, but most from people who'd had similar experiences. People who knew what it was like to see something impossible and have no one to tell.

I started getting more emails from Georgia. It turned out the Peach State was a hotbed of Sasquatch activity, with reports going back centuries. The Cherokee had called them Tsul 'Kalu—the slant-eyed giant. Modern witnesses described encounters throughout the Appalachian foothills, from the Cohutta Wilderness to the Okefenokee Swamp.

My next interview was with a woman named Patricia Nolan from Ellijay.

Patricia was a retired schoolteacher, soft-spoken and precise in the way that teachers often are. Her encounter had happened in 1994, while she was hiking in the Chattahoochee National Forest with her sister.

"We were on the Benton MacKaye Trail," she told me. "About six miles in, near the Toccoa River. It was early morning, maybe seven o'clock. The sun was just coming up through the trees, and everything was quiet. That perfect kind of quiet you only get in the deep woods."

"And then?"

"We heard something screaming. That's the only word for it— screaming. But not like any animal I'd ever heard. It was loud and deep, and it went on for what felt like forever. My sister grabbed my arm so hard she left bruises."

"Did you see anything?"

"Not at first. We just stood there, frozen, trying to figure out what direction it was coming from. And then we heard footsteps. Heavy footsteps, coming toward us through the brush. I remember thinking we should run, but my legs wouldn't work. It was like being stuck in a nightmare."

"What happened next?"

"It came out of the trees about thirty feet from us. A massive creature, covered in black hair. It was walking upright, like a man, but there was nothing human about the way it moved. So fluid. So powerful. Like watching a machine made of muscle."

"Did it approach you?"

"No. It stopped when it saw us, like it was surprised we were there. We stared at each other for maybe ten seconds. I could see its eyes—they were dark, intelligent, watching us like it was trying to figure out what we were. And then it made this sound, like a bark or a grunt, and it turned and disappeared into the forest. We never saw it again."

"What did you do afterward?"

"We ran. All six miles back to the trailhead, faster than I've ever moved in my life. By the time we got to the car, we were both hyperventilating. My sister wanted to call the police, but I talked her out of it. What were we going to say? 'Officer, we saw Bigfoot'? They would have laughed us out of the station."

"Did you ever go back to that area?"

"Never. I haven't been hiking since. That one experience was enough to last me a lifetime."

Patricia's story struck a chord with listeners. Here was an educated, articulate woman with no reason to lie, describing an encounter that had fundamentally changed her relationship with the natural world. The comments section filled with people sharing similar experiences— encounters that had made them afraid to return to places they'd once loved.

* * *

Florida was next.

I hadn't expected Florida to be a hotspot, but the emails proved me wrong. The state had a long history of Sasquatch sightings, particularly in the vast wilderness areas of the interior—the Green Swamp, the Big Cypress, the Ocala National Forest. The creatures there even had their own name: the Skunk Ape, so called because of the overwhelming stench that often accompanied sightings.

My first Florida interview was with a man named Miguel Santos, a fishing guide from Everglades City.

Miguel was fifty-two years old and had spent his entire life on the water. His encounter had happened five years earlier, during a late-night fishing trip in the Ten Thousand Islands.

"I was anchored up in a little bay, maybe two miles from the nearest land," Miguel said. His accent was thick, a mix of Cuban and Southern that made his words roll together. "It was around midnight, dead calm, no moon. I was waiting for the tarpon to start rolling."

"What happened?"

"I started smelling something. At first I thought maybe a manatee had died nearby—you know, that rotting smell you get sometimes. But this was different. Stronger. Like a wet dog mixed with sulfur and garbage. It was so bad I almost threw up."

"Did you see anything?"

"I grabbed my spotlight and started scanning the mangroves. And that's when I saw eyes. Two eyes, reflecting back at me, maybe seven or eight feet off the ground. Way too high for any animal I knew of. They just stared at me, not blinking, not moving. Just watching."

"What did you do?"

"I pulled anchor and got the hell out of there. Started the motor and didn't stop until I was back at the dock. The whole way back, I could feel those eyes on me. Like whatever it was could see me even in the dark. Like it was tracking me across the water."

"Did you ever go back to that spot?"

"Once. During the day, with two other guides. We found tracks in the mud near where I'd been anchored. Big tracks, like human feet but twice the size. And there was hair caught on some of the mangrove roots—long, reddish-brown hair that didn't match any animal we could think of."

"What do you think you saw?"

"I think I saw a Skunk Ape. I've been on this water my whole life, and I've seen things that would make most people's hair stand up. But nothing like that. Whatever was watching me that night, it wasn't natural. It wasn't something that's supposed to exist. But it does. I know it does."

* * *

The Florida episodes brought in a new audience—people who'd assumed Sasquatch was strictly a Pacific Northwest phenomenon. They were surprised to learn that these creatures were being spotted throughout the Southeast, in swamps and forests and wilderness areas that most people never visited.

I started receiving emails from South Carolina, Tennessee, Arkansas. Each state had its own stories, its own witnesses, its own history of encounters that had been dismissed and forgotten.

The podcast was growing. And so was my reputation.

Not all of it was positive.

21

ACROSS THE CAROLINA LINE

The South Carolina interviews taught me something important: these creatures didn't respect state lines.

My first witness from the Palmetto State was a woman named Delores Freeman from Oconee County, right on the border with Georgia. Her encounter had happened in 1983, but she remembered every detail like it was yesterday.

"I was seventeen years old," Delores said. Her voice was gentle, melodic, with that distinctive Lowcountry lilt even though she'd lived in the mountains her whole life. "My family had a cabin up near Stumphouse Tunnel, and we'd go there every summer. That July, I was out walking the property line with my daddy's hound dog, a bluetick named Chester."

"Tell me about the encounter."

"Well, Chester was a good dog. Didn't spook easy. He'd treed bears before, faced down wild boar, never showed fear of anything. But that afternoon, he started whimpering. Just stopped dead in his tracks and started making this pitiful sound, like he wanted to be anywhere else in the world."

"What did you see?"

"At first, nothing. I was looking around, trying to figure out what had gotten into him. And then I noticed the smell. Like someone had left meat out to rot in the sun. It was coming from this thicket of rhododendrons about twenty yards up the hill."

"Did something emerge from the thicket?"

"Not emerge, exactly. More like... unfolded. This massive shape just rose up out of the bushes, like it had been crouching there waiting for us. It was at least seven and a half feet tall, covered in grayish-brown hair. The face was flat, with a heavy brow and deep-set eyes. And it was looking right at me."

"How did you react?"

"I couldn't react. I was paralyzed. My whole body locked up, like my brain had just shut down. Chester was pressed against my leg, shaking so hard I could feel it through my jeans. We just stood there, me and that creature, staring at each other."

"How long did the encounter last?"

"Maybe thirty seconds. Felt like an hour. And then it made this sound—this deep, rumbling grunt—and it turned and walked into the woods. Didn't run. Just walked. Like it had decided we weren't worth its time."

"Did you tell anyone?"

"I told my daddy when I got back to the cabin. He didn't believe me, of course. Said I'd probably seen a bear standing up. But I know what I saw, Sheriff Patterson. I've seen bears. That wasn't a bear."

"What happened to Chester?"

Delores was quiet for a moment. "He was never the same after that. Wouldn't go in the woods anymore. Wouldn't leave the porch. It was like that encounter broke something in him. He died about a year later—the vet said it was just old age, but I think he died of fear. I think that thing scared the life right out of him."

* * *

The interviews kept coming, each one adding another thread to the tapestry I was weaving.

From South Carolina, I spoke with a deer hunter named Terrance Washington who'd had a rock thrown at his tree stand in the Francis Marion National Forest. The rock was the size of a grapefruit and had come from at least fifty yards away. When Terrance climbed down to investigate, he found footprints in the mud—sixteen inches long, with a distinct heel and five toes.

"I've been hunting those woods for thirty years," Terrance told me. "I know every animal that lives there. And I'm telling you, whatever threw that rock wasn't any animal I've ever seen. It was watching me. Testing me. Seeing what I'd do."

From Tennessee, I interviewed a family of four who'd had an encounter while camping in the Cherokee National Forest. The Hendersons—Tom, Lisa, and their two teenage sons—had been awakened in the middle of the night by something shaking their tent.

"At first I thought it was a bear," Tom said. "I grabbed my flashlight and unzipped the door, ready to scare it off. But when I shined the light outside, there was nothing there. Just this... presence. This feeling that something was watching us from the trees."

"Then we heard the howl," Lisa added. "It started low, like a moan, and then rose up into this piercing scream. It was the most terrifying sound I've ever heard. The boys were crying. I was crying. Even Tom was shaking."

"We packed up and left," Tom said. "Three in the morning, we loaded everything into the car and drove straight home. We've never been camping since."

From Virginia, I spoke with a state trooper named Marcus Cole who'd had a sighting while on patrol near Shenandoah National Park. He'd asked to remain anonymous at first, afraid of the professional repercussions, but eventually agreed to let me use his real name.

"I was working the night shift, driving along Skyline Drive around two AM," Marcus said. "It was a quiet night—no other cars, no calls, just me and the road. And then something stepped out of the trees about a hundred yards ahead."

"Can you describe it?"

"Tall. Massive. Covered in dark hair. It crossed the road in three strides—three strides to cover a two-lane highway. By the time I got to where it had been, there was no sign of it. Just that smell. Like a wet animal, but stronger. Ranker."

"Did you report the sighting?"

"Hell no. I've got a family to support. If I'd told my sergeant I'd seen Bigfoot, I'd have been assigned to a desk or worse. So I kept my mouth shut. But I've never forgotten it. And I've never driven that stretch of road at night since."

* * *

Each interview taught me something new about these creatures.

They were everywhere—not just in the Pacific Northwest, not just in remote wilderness areas, but throughout the Eastern United States. They lived in forests and swamps and mountains, adapting to different environments while maintaining their essential nature. They were intelligent, cautious, aware of human presence and careful to avoid contact. When they did reveal themselves, it was usually by accident or by choice—and when it was by choice, there was always a reason.

They weren't monsters. They weren't animals. They were something in between, something that didn't fit into any category science had created.

And they'd been here all along, watching us from the shadows, waiting for the world to be ready to see them.

* * *

The Arkansas interviews brought a new dimension to the podcast.

Arkansas had one of the highest concentrations of Sasquatch sightings in the country, particularly in the Ouachita Mountains and the Ozarks. The legends there went back centuries, with indigenous peoples speaking of tall, hairy creatures that lived in the deep hollows and remote valleys.

My first Arkansas witness was a man named Bobby Dean Carver from Polk County.

Bobby Dean was a character—a sixty-eight-year-old retired coal miner with a voice like gravel and a laugh that could shake windows. His encounter had happened in 1991, but he told the story like it had been that morning.

"I was coon hunting with my cousin Earl up near Mena," Bobby Dean began. "We had a good pack of dogs—six walkers and a redbone —and they'd treed something about a quarter mile into the timber. We could hear them baying, so we grabbed our lanterns and headed in."

"What did you find?"

"The dogs were going crazy, all six of them standing at the base of this big oak, barking their fool heads off. Earl and I figured they'd treed a big coon, maybe even a bobcat. So I shined my lantern up into the branches, expecting to see eyes reflecting back."

"Did you see a raccoon?"

"Brother, I wish I had. What I saw was a face. A human face, or close to it. Except it was covered in hair and had these eyes that glowed yellow in the light. It was sitting on a branch about twenty feet up, watching us like we were the most interesting thing it had ever seen."

"How did you react?"

"Earl screamed like a little girl. I probably did too—I don't remember much of the next few seconds. What I do remember is the thing jumping out of that tree and landing on the ground between us and the dogs. It must have dropped fifteen feet, and it landed like a cat. Didn't make a sound."

"What happened then?"

"It stood up. And up. And up. Must have been eight feet tall, easy. It looked at me, looked at Earl, looked at the dogs. And then it made this sound—this deep, rumbling growl that I felt in my chest. The dogs shut up immediately. Six hunting dogs that had never backed down from anything, and they went silent like someone had flipped a switch."

"Did it attack?"

"No. It just turned and walked into the woods. Didn't run, didn't hurry. Just walked away like it had somewhere better to be. We stood there for maybe five minutes, too scared to move. Then we gathered up the dogs and went home. Never told nobody about it until now."

"Why are you telling me?"

"Because I'm sixty-eight years old and I ain't got much time left. And I figure somebody ought to know the truth. Those things are out there, Sheriff. They've always been out there. And if folks keep pretending they don't exist, somebody's gonna get hurt."

* * *

The Bobby Dean episode became one of the most popular in the podcast's history.

There was something about his storytelling—the rough authenticity, the humor mixed with genuine fear—that resonated with listeners. Comments poured in, many from people who'd had their own experiences in Arkansas. The Ouachitas, it turned out, were a hotbed of activity.

I scheduled a dozen more interviews from the state. Each one added new details, new perspectives, new pieces of the puzzle.

A timber cruiser named Henry Wallace described finding a structure deep in the forest—branches woven together in a way that suggested intelligent design. "It wasn't a beaver dam," he insisted. "It wasn't a bird's nest. It was something else. Something built by hands."

A park ranger named Carly Blackwell shared stories of hikers who'd reported being followed, of campers who'd fled in the middle of the night, of footprints that appeared on remote trails and disappeared just as mysteriously.

A grandmother named Ethel May Robinson described an encounter from 1962, when she was just a girl. She'd seen a creature watching her family's farm from the edge of the woods. "It came back every evening for a week," she said. "Just stood there in the tree line, watching. My daddy finally went out there with his shotgun, and it never came back. But I still dream about it sometimes. Those eyes. Those sad, intelligent eyes."

The podcast was growing beyond anything I'd imagined. Downloads were climbing into the hundreds of thousands. Sponsors were starting to reach out. What had started as a hobby, a way to give voice to people who'd been silenced, was becoming something bigger.

Something that might actually change things.

22

THE NATION LISTENS

By the end of my first year hosting *Sasquatch Odyssey*, I'd interviewed over one hundred and fifty witnesses.

They came from every corner of the country. Loggers from Oregon. Fishermen from Louisiana. Teachers from Ohio. Nurses from Michigan. Soldiers from Texas. Retirees from Maine. Rich and poor, young and old, educated and not—the only thing they had in common was that they'd seen something they couldn't explain.

And they all told essentially the same story.

Large bipedal creatures, covered in hair, moving through the wilderness with intelligence and purpose. Some were aggressive, throwing rocks or charging at intruders. Others were curious, watching from a distance without threat. A few were even playful, seemingly toying with humans who'd wandered into their territory.

But all of them were real. All of them had left marks on the people who'd encountered them—psychological scars that never fully healed, questions that never got answered, secrets that weighed heavier with every passing year.

The podcast gave them a place to unburden themselves. And in doing so, it created something I hadn't anticipated: a community.

* * *

The *Sasquatch Odyssey* community grew organically, without any real effort on my part.

It started with the comment sections on the podcast platforms—people sharing their own stories, connecting with others who'd had similar experiences. Then someone set up a Facebook group. Then a Discord server. Then a forum on the website that Daniel had built for me.

Within months, there were thousands of people participating. They shared sightings, analyzed evidence, debated theories about what these creatures were and where they came from. They organized expeditions into areas with high concentrations of reports. They collected data, mapped encounters, built databases of information that would have taken a single researcher decades to compile.

And they found each other.

That was the most important thing, I think. People who'd spent years—sometimes decades—feeling isolated and crazy suddenly discovered they weren't alone. There were others out there who'd seen what they'd seen. Others who understood. Others who believed.

The community became a support network. When a new witness came forward, there were people ready to listen, to validate, to help them process what they'd experienced. When someone faced ridicule from family or friends, there were others who'd been through the same thing and could offer advice. When the doubt crept in—as it always did, that nagging voice asking if maybe you imagined it—there were hundreds of voices ready to remind you that what you saw was real.

I hadn't set out to build a community. I'd just wanted to tell stories. But the community had built itself around those stories, and it had become something bigger than any of us could have predicted.

* * *

The national interviews brought new challenges.

The Southeast had been comfortable territory—states I knew,

accents I understood, landscapes I could picture in my mind. But as the podcast expanded, I found myself talking to people from places I'd never been, hearing stories from environments I couldn't imagine.

From Washington State, I interviewed a man named James Clearwater, a member of the Lummi Nation whose people had been living alongside these creatures for thousands of years.

"We call them Ts'emekwes," James explained. "The wild men of the woods. They've always been here. Our grandparents knew them. Our great-grandparents knew them. They're not monsters—they're neighbors. Just neighbors who like to keep to themselves."

"Has your tribe had recent encounters?"

"All the time. But we don't talk about it much, not to outsiders. The creatures value their privacy, and we respect that. We leave offerings sometimes—fish, berries, things like that. And they leave us alone. It's an understanding that goes back generations."

"What do you think of all the people who claim Sasquatch doesn't exist?"

James laughed—a warm, genuine sound. "I think they haven't been paying attention. The evidence is everywhere, if you know how to look. Tracks, scat, hair, structures. The creatures leave signs of their presence all over the forest. Most people just don't know how to see them."

"Why do you think they've remained hidden for so long?"

"Because they're smarter than us. Smarter about the things that matter, anyway. They know how to live in harmony with the land. They know how to avoid detection. They've watched us build cities and highways and shopping malls, and they've decided they want no part of it. Can you blame them?"

* * *

From Ohio, I interviewed a woman named Sandra Mitchell who'd had a terrifying encounter in the Hocking Hills region.

"It was June of 2018," Sandra said. Her voice was steady, but I could hear the tension underneath. "I was hiking alone on a trail near

Old Man's Cave. It was midday, broad daylight. I wasn't worried about anything—it's a popular trail, lots of foot traffic. But I'd wandered off the main path to take some photos of wildflowers, and that's when I heard it."

"What did you hear?"

"Breathing. Heavy breathing, like a large animal. I looked up, and there it was, maybe fifteen feet away. Standing between two trees, just watching me."

"Can you describe it?"

"Enormous. At least seven feet tall, probably more. Covered in dark brown hair, almost black. The face was... not human, but not animal either. Something in between. And the eyes—God, the eyes. They were looking right into me, like they could see everything I was thinking."

"What happened next?"

"I don't remember much. I think I screamed. I think I ran. The next clear memory I have is being back on the main trail, surrounded by other hikers who were asking if I was okay. I must have looked terrible —I was crying, shaking, couldn't catch my breath."

"Did you report the encounter?"

"I tried. I called the park office, tried to explain what I'd seen. The ranger was polite but clearly didn't believe me. Said it was probably a bear, that the light can play tricks on you in the forest. But I know what I saw. It wasn't a bear. It was something else."

"How has the experience affected you?"

Sandra was quiet for a moment. "I don't hike anymore. I don't go in the woods. I have nightmares sometimes—not scary ones, exactly. Just dreams where it's watching me. Always watching. Like it's still out there, keeping track of me. Making sure I remember."

* * *

The interviews kept coming. Michigan, Minnesota, Montana. California, Colorado, Connecticut. States I'd heard of and states I'd barely thought about.

From Louisiana, I spoke with a Cajun fisherman named Pierre Boudreaux who'd seen something in the Atchafalaya Basin—"A tall, hairy devil," he called it, "standing in the cypress knees like it owned the place."

From Alaska, I interviewed a bush pilot named Karen Hendricks who'd spotted a creature crossing a glacier at high altitude—"Moving fast, faster than anything that big should be able to move. And leaving tracks in the snow that I could see from five hundred feet up."

From Hawaii—Hawaii, of all places—I talked to a park ranger named David Akana who described encounters on the Big Island. "We call them the Menehune," he said. "Little people, supposedly. But some of the stories describe something bigger. Something that lives in the rainforest and comes out at night."

Each story added another piece to the puzzle. Each witness added another voice to the chorus. The picture that was emerging was bigger than I'd ever imagined—a phenomenon that spanned the entire country, that had been happening for centuries, that millions of people had experienced but never felt safe enough to discuss.

Until now.

* * *

The sponsors started calling around month ten.

I'd resisted advertising at first—it felt wrong somehow, monetizing these stories of fear and wonder. But Daniel pointed out that running the podcast cost money. Equipment, hosting, website maintenance, phone bills for all those long-distance interviews. If we wanted to keep doing this, we needed income.

The first sponsor was an outdoor gear company. Then a survival food supplier. Then a night vision equipment manufacturer. The ads were unobtrusive—just brief mentions at the beginning and end of episodes—but they added up. By the end of the first year, *Sasquatch Odyssey* was generating enough revenue to cover its costs and then some.

It wasn't a fortune. But it was a start.

And it made me think about the future.

* * *

The conversation happened on a Sunday evening in October.

Daniel and I were sitting on the back deck, watching the sunset paint the mountains in shades of gold and orange. It was our favorite time of day, the quiet hour when the world seemed to slow down and anything felt possible.

"I've been thinking," I said.

"That's usually dangerous," Daniel replied with a smile.

"The election is next year. And I don't think I want to run again."

Daniel turned to look at me. "You're serious?"

"I'm serious. The podcast is growing. The community is growing. There's so much more I could be doing if I wasn't spending forty hours a week on sheriff business. And honestly—" I shook my head "—I'm tired of the politics. Tired of the commissioners looking at me like I've lost my mind. Tired of pretending to care about speeding tickets and property disputes when I know what's really out there."

"What would you do instead?"

"Focus on *Sasquatch Odyssey*. Full time. Expand the podcast, conduct more research, build the community. Maybe even write a book." I looked at him. "I know it's a risk. The podcast is doing well, but it's not guaranteed income. We'd have to be careful, budget tighter, maybe make some sacrifices. But I think it's worth it."

Daniel was quiet for a long moment. Then he said, "I've been thinking too."

"About what?"

"About what I want to do with my life. I've been worrying about you being in law enforcement for years now. The danger, the stress, the toll it takes. If you're stepping back, maybe it's time for me to step back too."

"Step back from what?"

"From everything. Start fresh." He smiled. "There's a new pizza place opening up a few miles down the road. Family-owned, locally sourced ingredients. They're looking for a manager. The pay isn't great, but it's stable, and it would get me out of the house without putting me in danger."

"Pizza?"

"I like pizza. And I like the idea of doing something simple for a while. Something that doesn't involve creatures in the woods or government conspiracies or men in black showing up at our door in the middle of the night."

I reached over and took his hand. "Are we really doing this? Walking away from everything we've built?"

"We're not walking away. We're walking toward something. Something new. Something that might actually make us happy."

I looked out at the mountains, at the endless forest that surrounded our little home. Somewhere out there, in the deep places where humans rarely ventured, creatures watched and waited. Creatures I'd dedicated my life to understanding. Creatures who'd been calling to me since I was twelve years old.

"Okay," I said. "Let's do it."

Daniel squeezed my hand. "No regrets?"

"No regrets."

We sat there together, watching the last light fade from the sky, dreaming of the future that was waiting for us.

It was going to be a hell of a ride.

23

INTERNATIONAL VOICES

T he decision not to seek re-election was easier than I'd expected.

I made the announcement in January, six months before the primary. The commissioners were relieved—they'd been dreading another term of "the Bigfoot sheriff," as some of the local papers had taken to calling me. My deputies were more understanding. Most of them had come to respect what I was doing, even if they didn't fully believe.

"You're doing important work," my chief deputy said on my last day. "I may not understand it, but I can see it matters to you. And it matters to a lot of people out there. Don't let the bastards get you down."

The transition was surprisingly smooth. I handed over my badge, cleaned out my office, said goodbye to the job that had defined me for the past several years. And then I went home, sat down at my microphone, and got to work.

Full-time podcasting was different than I'd imagined. Without the structure of the sheriff's office—the schedules, the routines, the constant demands on my time—I found myself with more freedom than I knew what to do with. I could interview witnesses at any hour. I could spend days researching a single case. I could travel to locations, meet people in person, see the places where encounters had happened.

And I could expand beyond the borders of the United States.

* * *

The international interviews started with Canada.

It made sense—the creatures didn't respect the border, and neither should my research. British Columbia, in particular, was a hotbed of activity, with hundreds of documented sightings going back to the earliest European settlement.

My first Canadian interview was with a man named William Redfeather, a member of the Sts'ailes First Nation whose traditional territory included some of the most active Sasquatch habitat on the continent.

"We call them Sasquatch," William explained. "That's actually our word—it comes from the Halkomelem language. It means 'wild man' or 'hairy man.' The anthropologists and scientists, they think they invented the term, but our people have been using it for thousands of years."

"Tell me about your people's relationship with these creatures."

"It's complicated. They're not animals to us—they're people. Different from us, living in a different way, but people nonetheless. We have stories about them that go back to the beginning of time. Stories about interactions, about conflicts, about cooperation. They're part of our world, just like the bears and the salmon and the cedar trees."

"Have you had personal encounters?"

"Many times. Most of them I can't talk about—they're sacred, part of my spiritual journey. But I can tell you that when you meet one of these beings in the forest, you understand immediately that you're in the presence of something ancient. Something that knows things we've forgotten. Something that carries the wisdom of ages."

"What do you think of the scientific community's dismissal of Sasquatch evidence?"

William laughed, but there was no humor in it. "Science is young.

Our knowledge is old. The scientists will catch up eventually. They always do. In the meantime, we'll keep living alongside our neighbors, the way we always have."

* * *

From Canada, I expanded to other countries.

Russia had its own version of Sasquatch—the Almas, reported throughout Siberia and the Caucasus Mountains. I interviewed a researcher named Dr. Dmitri Ivanov who'd spent decades collecting accounts from remote villages.

"The peasants know," Dr. Ivanov said, his English heavily accented but precise. "In the villages, far from Moscow, far from the universities, they tell stories of the wild men. They've seen them for generations. They leave offerings, same as your Native Americans. They understand what the scientists refuse to accept."

"Have you seen one yourself?"

"Once. In the Pamir Mountains, 1987. A shape in the snow, moving across a valley at dusk. Too large to be a man, too upright to be a bear. I watched it for perhaps ten minutes before it disappeared into a ravine. That ten minutes changed my life. That ten minutes is why I do this work."

Australia had the Yowie—a creature described by Aboriginal peoples for thousands of years and reported by European settlers since the early colonial period. I interviewed a man named Stuart Connelly from Queensland who'd had an encounter while prospecting in the outback.

"It was standing by a waterhole at sunset," Stuart said. "Biggest thing I've ever seen. Had to be eight feet tall, covered in reddish-brown hair. I'd been in the bush my whole life, seen every animal Australia has to offer. This wasn't any of them. This was something else entirely."

"How did the encounter end?"

"It saw me watching and just... vanished. One moment it was there, the next it was gone. No sound, no movement I could track. Just gone.

Like it had never been there at all. Except I had the smell in my nose for hours afterward—this rank, musky smell that I'll never forget."

* * *

The international episodes brought new listeners to the podcast.

People from around the world started tuning in, sharing their own stories, connecting with the community. The phenomenon, it turned out, was truly global. Every continent except Antarctica had reports. Every culture had legends. Every remote wilderness area had witnesses who'd seen things they couldn't explain.

From Nepal, I interviewed a sherpa named Tenzin Dorje who'd had multiple encounters with the Yeti at high altitude. "They live in the places where no one goes," he said. "The valleys between the peaks, the glaciers where the air is too thin for most humans. They've adapted to the cold in ways we can't imagine. And they watch. They always watch."

From China, I spoke with a researcher named Dr. Zhang Wei who'd been studying the Yeren—the "wild man" of the Hubei province —for over thirty years. "We have thousands of reports," she told me. "Scientific expeditions, government investigations, eyewitness accounts from people of all backgrounds. The evidence is overwhelming. But the political situation makes official acknowledgment... difficult."

From Brazil, I interviewed a guide named Marco Silva who led expeditions into the Amazon. "The Mapinguari," he said. "That's what the indigenous people call it. A giant sloth that walks on two legs, with fur like fire and claws that can tear through anything. I've never seen one myself, but I've seen the tracks. I've heard the calls. I know they're out there."

Each interview added to my understanding. These weren't isolated populations of creatures—they were a global phenomenon, a species (or perhaps multiple species) that had survived alongside humanity for millennia. They'd adapted to different environments, developed different behaviors, accumulated different cultural significance. But at their core, they were the same. Wild men of the woods. Neighbors who lived in the shadows.

And they'd been hiding in plain sight all along.

* * *

The podcast hit one million downloads in February.

I remember the moment I saw the number on the analytics dashboard. One million people had listened to these stories. One million people had heard witnesses share their experiences. One million people had been exposed to the truth.

Daniel found me sitting at my desk, staring at the screen.

"What's wrong?" he asked.

"Nothing's wrong. Look at this."

He leaned over my shoulder and saw the number. "Holy shit."

"Yeah."

"Brian, this is incredible. A million people?"

"A million downloads. Probably means half a million actual listeners, maybe more. But still." I shook my head. "When I started this, I figured maybe a few thousand people would care. A niche audience, believers and enthusiasts. I never imagined..."

"You never imagined changing the world?"

"I'm not changing the world. I'm just letting people tell their stories."

Daniel put his hand on my shoulder. "That's exactly how you change the world. One story at a time."

He was right, of course. He usually was. The podcast wasn't just entertainment—it was building something. A record of the truth. A community of witnesses. A movement that was slowly but surely shifting the way people thought about these creatures and the world they lived in.

One million downloads was just the beginning.

24

THE DEEP ENCOUNTERS

Not all encounters were created equal.

Most of the stories I collected were brief—glimpses, sounds, moments of terror or wonder that lasted seconds before dissolving into memory. Important, all of them. Valid, all of them. But some encounters went deeper. Some witnesses had experienced things that defied easy explanation, things that suggested these creatures were far more than simple animals hiding in the woods.

These were the stories that haunted me. The ones that kept me up at night, wondering what else we didn't understand about the world we lived in.

* * *

One of the most profound interviews I conducted was with a woman named Mary Catherine O'Brien from rural Kentucky.

Mary Catherine was seventy-one years old, a retired hospice nurse who'd spent her life caring for the dying. Her voice was gentle, measured, with the calm authority of someone who'd seen things most people only feared.

"I need to tell you something before we start," she said. "What I'm about to describe—it's not a typical encounter. It's not a sighting in the woods or a sound in the night. It's something different. Something I've never told anyone because I knew they wouldn't believe me. But I've listened to your show, Sheriff Patterson, and I think you might understand."

"I'm listening," I said.

Mary Catherine took a deep breath. "In 1989, my husband Ray was dying of cancer. Pancreatic. By the end, he was bedridden, barely conscious, waiting for the release that we both knew was coming. I stayed with him day and night, holding his hand, talking to him even when I wasn't sure he could hear."

"I'm sorry for your loss."

"Thank you. But this story isn't about Ray, not really. It's about what happened the night before he died."

She paused, gathering herself.

"Our cabin was at the end of a long holler, backed up against national forest land. Isolated. Peaceful. The kind of place where you could hear a deer walking a hundred yards away. That night, I was sitting by Ray's bed, half-asleep, when I heard something outside. Footsteps. Heavy footsteps, circling the house."

"What did you think it was?"

"I didn't know. A bear, maybe. We got bears sometimes. I was scared, but I couldn't leave Ray. So I just sat there, listening, watching the windows. And then—" She stopped. When she continued, her voice was thick with emotion. "And then something appeared at the window."

"What did you see?"

"A face. A massive face, covered in hair, with eyes that seemed to glow in the moonlight. It was looking through the glass at Ray. Just looking. And there was something in those eyes, Sheriff Patterson. Something I've only ever seen in one other place."

"Where?"

"In the eyes of people who are dying. That look of... knowing. Of understanding something beyond what the rest of us can perceive. This creature was looking at my husband with that same awareness. Like it knew he was passing. Like it had come to... I don't know. Bear witness. Pay respects. Something."

"How long did the encounter last?"

"Maybe five minutes. It just stood there, watching, that face filling the window. And then it made a sound—not a howl, not a growl. More like a hum. A low, resonant hum that I could feel in my bones. And Ray—Ray, who hadn't responded to anything in days—Ray opened his eyes. He looked at that creature, and he smiled. He smiled, Sheriff Patterson. The first peace I'd seen in his face in months. And then the creature was gone. And the next morning, Ray was gone too."

"I don't know what to say, Mary Catherine."

"You don't have to say anything. I just needed to tell someone. I've carried this story for thirty years, wondering what it meant. Wondering if these creatures are more than we think they are. If they understand things about life and death that we've forgotten. I don't have answers. But I know what I saw. And I know it changed me."

$$* * *$$

Mary Catherine's story opened a floodgate.

After that episode aired, I received hundreds of emails from people who'd had similar experiences. Encounters that went beyond the physical, that suggested some kind of connection between these creatures and the deeper mysteries of existence.

A hospice worker from Oregon wrote about a creature she'd seen outside a dying patient's room. "It stayed for hours," she said. "Just watching. And when the patient passed, it let out this cry—this mournful, beautiful cry—and disappeared into the night."

A man from Montana described an encounter that had happened during a near-death experience. "I was drowning," he said. "Fell through the ice on a frozen lake. And while I was under, while my life was fading, I saw something. A creature, watching me from the ice.

And it reached down—reached through the water—and pulled me out. Saved my life. And then it was gone."

A woman from Quebec told me about a creature that had visited her grandmother on her deathbed. "Grand-mère called it 'le gardien'— the guardian. She said it had come to guide her home. She wasn't afraid. If anything, she was grateful."

These stories were harder to process than the typical sightings. They suggested something profound about the nature of these creatures —something that went beyond biology, beyond zoology, beyond any scientific framework we had.

Were they simply animals? Or were they something more? Something spiritual? Something that existed at the intersection of the physical and the metaphysical?

I didn't have answers. But the questions kept me searching.

* * *

Another category of deep encounters involved communication.

Standard Sasquatch lore held that these creatures were intelligent but non-verbal—they could vocalize, could use body language, could perhaps even understand human speech. But they couldn't talk. Couldn't communicate in any meaningful way.

The interviews I conducted told a different story.

A woman named Elena Vasquez from New Mexico described an encounter in the Gila Wilderness that had changed her understanding of reality.

"I was hiking alone," Elena said. "Something I'd done hundreds of times. But this time, I got lost. Really lost. Wandered off the trail and couldn't find my way back. By nightfall, I was panicking. No cell service, no compass, no idea which direction was out."

"What happened?"

"I found a small clearing and decided to stay there for the night. Build a fire, wait for morning, try to retrace my steps. I was sitting by the fire, trying not to cry, when I felt... something. A presence. I looked up, and there was a creature standing at the edge of the firelight. Watching me."

"What did you do?"

"I froze. I was terrified. But the creature didn't approach. Didn't seem aggressive. It just stood there, and then—this is the part that's hard to explain—I started getting these images in my head. Pictures. A trail I recognized. A river crossing. The parking lot where I'd left my car. It was like the creature was... showing me the way out."

"You're saying it communicated telepathically?"

"I know how that sounds. Believe me, I know. But that's what happened. The images were clear, detailed, specific. And the next morning, I followed them. Every landmark the creature had shown me was exactly where I expected it to be. Four hours later, I was back at my car. Safe. Alive."

"Did you ever see the creature again?"

"No. But I think about it every day. I think about what it means that this creature—this supposedly primitive animal—was able to reach into my mind and give me the information I needed to survive. What does that say about what they really are? What does that say about what we might be capable of, if we just knew how?"

* * *

Elena's story was echoed by others.

A hunter from Wyoming described a creature that had "spoken" to him without words, warning him away from an area where he later learned an avalanche had occurred.

A child from Maine—interviewed with her parents' permission—talked about a "big friend" who had communicated with her through feelings and pictures, who had played with her at the edge of the woods, who had been real even though no one else could see him.

A Native American elder from Arizona shared stories from his tradition about the "mind talkers"—creatures who could project thoughts across great distances, who served as messengers between the physical world and the spirit realm.

The evidence was anecdotal, of course. Impossible to verify. Easy to dismiss as imagination, wishful thinking, mental illness. But there were too many stories, from too many different sources, describing too many similar experiences.

Something was happening. Something beyond simple sightings. These creatures were reaching out to us, communicating in ways we were only beginning to understand.

And if that was true, what else might be possible?

* * *

The most disturbing deep encounter I documented came from a man named Robert Sullivan, a former Army Ranger from Texas.

Robert was not the kind of person you'd expect to believe in Bigfoot. He was hard, practical, deeply skeptical of anything he couldn't verify with his own senses. His military career had taught him to trust facts over feelings, evidence over instinct.

But what he'd experienced had shaken him to his core.

"I was on a solo expedition in the Big Thicket," Robert said. His voice was controlled, precise, military in its economy. "National preserve in East Texas. Dense forest, lots of swamp. The kind of place where you could get lost and never be found."

"Why were you there?"

"Looking for evidence. I'd heard stories—everyone around there has heard stories—and I wanted to see for myself. Set up camp, planned to spend a week surveying the area, collecting data."

"What happened?"

"The first three nights, nothing. Some sounds in the distance, but nothing I couldn't explain. Then, on the fourth night, everything changed."

Robert paused. I could hear him breathing through the phone, steeling himself.

"I woke up around two in the morning. Don't know what woke me —there was no sound, no movement. Just this feeling that I wasn't alone. I reached for my flashlight, and that's when I realized I couldn't move."

"Couldn't move?"

"Paralyzed. My whole body was locked in place. I could breathe, I could blink, but everything else was frozen. And standing over me—" He stopped. Started again. "Standing over me was a creature. Not like the ones you hear about. This one was smaller, maybe six feet tall. Thinner. And the face... the face was different. More human. More expressive."

"What did it do?"

"It looked at me. Just looked. And then I felt this... intrusion. Like something was pushing into my mind, rifling through my thoughts, examining my memories. It wasn't painful, exactly. But it was violating. Like being mentally frisked by something that didn't need your permission."

"How long did this last?"

"I don't know. Could have been minutes, could have been hours. Time didn't work right while it was happening. And then, just as suddenly as it started, it stopped. The creature stepped back, and I could move again. It made this sound—this clicking, chattering sound —and then it was gone. Vanished into the night."

"What do you think happened?"

"I think I was scanned. Examined. Catalogued. I think that creature wanted to know who I was, what I was doing there, whether I was a threat. And once it had the information it needed, it left."

"That's a terrifying thought."

"It is. And it changed my understanding of what we're dealing with. These aren't just animals, Sheriff Patterson. They're intelligent. Technologically advanced, maybe—or psychically advanced, I don't know which. But they're watching us. Studying us. Learning about us. And I don't think we have any idea what they're planning to do with that information."

Robert's interview was one of the most listened-to episodes in the podcast's history. It sparked debates, discussions, arguments that persisted for weeks. Some people believed every word. Others dismissed it as a fever dream or fabrication.

But Robert's voice, when he told that story—the suppressed fear, the careful precision, the obvious reluctance to share something that made him sound crazy—convinced me that whatever had happened to him in the Big Thicket, he believed it was real.

And if it was real, what did that mean for all of us?

25

PATTERNS IN THE NOISE

B y my second year of full-time podcasting, I'd conducted over three hundred interviews.

The stories had come from every corner of the globe. Encounters spanning decades. Witnesses of every age, every background, every level of education. Some were brief and terrifying. Others were prolonged and profoundly strange. A few defied any attempt at categorization.

But patterns were emerging. The more I listened, the more I began to see connections between the stories. Recurring elements. Common threads. A picture slowly forming from thousands of individual data points.

* * *

The first pattern was behavioral.

Regardless of location or era, the creatures seemed to follow certain rules. They avoided direct contact with humans whenever possible. They became aggressive only when cornered, threatened, or surprised. They were curious about human activity but careful to observe from a distance.

Most encounters happened at dawn or dusk—the liminal hours when visibility was reduced. Most sightings occurred in transitional zones between different types of habitat—the edge of a forest, the border between swamp and dry land, the confluence of two streams. Most witnesses reported a sense of being watched before the actual encounter, as if the creatures were assessing them before deciding whether to reveal themselves.

This suggested intelligence. Planning. The ability to evaluate risk and make decisions based on complex factors. These weren't random animals blundering into human territory. They were careful observers who chose when and how to interact with us.

* * *

The second pattern was physical.

Descriptions varied, of course. Some witnesses reported creatures over nine feet tall; others described beings closer to six feet. Hair color ranged from black to brown to reddish to gray. Faces were sometimes flat and ape-like, sometimes more human in appearance.

But certain features remained consistent. Massive shoulders. Long arms that hung past the knees. A pronounced brow ridge. Eyes that reflected light, sometimes described as glowing. A distinct smell— musky, rank, often compared to rotting garbage or wet dog.

And one more thing: they all walked upright. Not with the shuffling gait of an ape trying to imitate human locomotion, but with a smooth, natural stride that suggested this was their primary means of movement. Whatever these creatures were, they'd been bipedal for a very long time.

* * *

The third pattern was geographic.

The creatures weren't distributed randomly across the landscape. They clustered in certain areas—areas characterized by dense forest cover, reliable water sources, abundant wildlife, and limited human presence. In the Pacific Northwest, they concentrated in the old-growth forests of the Cascades. In the Southeast, they favored the deep swamps and mountain hollows. In the Midwest, they stuck to the river bottoms and the remnant woodlands that had escaped the plow.

More interestingly, the distribution seemed to follow corridors. Long, narrow pathways of suitable habitat that connected larger wilderness areas. The Appalachian chain. The Rocky Mountain spine. The network of national forests and wildlife refuges that crisscrossed the country.

This suggested migration. Movement. The creatures weren't static populations trapped in isolated refugia. They were travelers, moving across the landscape along routes that humans rarely used. Appearing in one area for a season or a year, then vanishing. Showing up somewhere else months later, a hundred miles away.

They were nomads, I realized. Nomads following patterns we couldn't yet perceive.

* * *

The fourth pattern was temporal.

Sightings weren't evenly distributed throughout the year. They peaked in spring and fall, during the transitional seasons when the forest was changing. They dropped during the deep winter and the height of summer. They increased during periods of heavy rain, when human outdoor activity was reduced.

More intriguingly, there seemed to be longer cycles as well. Decades when sightings were common, followed by decades when they were rare. As if the creatures went through periods of activity and dormancy, revealing themselves to humans and then retreating back into the shadows.

Some researchers had speculated that these cycles correlated with prey populations, with climate patterns, with phases of the moon. Others suggested they were tied to human activity—that the creatures became more cautious when hunting pressure increased, bolder when wilderness areas expanded.

I didn't know which explanation was correct. But I was certain that the patterns were real. Too consistent across too many data points to be coincidence.

* * *

The fifth pattern was the hardest to accept.

A significant minority of encounters—perhaps fifteen percent—included elements that went beyond the physical. Telepathic communication. Apparent healing or harm at a distance. Connections to UFO sightings, to missing time, to phenomena that seemed to belong in a different category entirely.

I'd dismissed these accounts at first. They seemed too outlandish, too incompatible with the more straightforward sightings that made up the bulk of my data. But the witnesses who reported them were no less credible than the others. They came from the same backgrounds, described the same creatures, experienced the same fear and wonder.

Either they were all lying or delusional—a statistical impossibility, given the numbers—or there was something more going on here. Something that our current understanding of reality couldn't explain.

I thought about the Mount St. Helens documents. The evidence of government programs going back decades. The suggestion that these creatures had been studied, catalogued, perhaps even communicated with. A systematic cover-up of phenomena that humanity wasn't supposed to know existed.

Maybe the strange encounters weren't outliers. Maybe they were glimpses of a deeper truth that most witnesses weren't equipped to perceive.

Maybe the creatures were stranger than any of us could imagine.

* * *

I shared my analysis with Zach one evening, sitting on my back porch while the sun set over the mountains.

He'd continued his research after I left the sheriff's office, digging deeper into government files, connecting with other investigators, building a network of information that rivaled anything the authorities had compiled. We talked regularly, comparing notes, sharing theories.

"The patterns are real," he agreed, studying the charts and maps I'd spread out on the table. "I've seen the same things in my data. But there's something you're missing."

"What?"

"The human element." He pointed to a cluster of sightings on the map. "Look at where these encounters are happening. Not just wilderness areas—areas where the wilderness meets human settlement. Where our world and their world overlap."

"You think they're attracted to us?"

"I think they're interested in us. They've been living in the shadows for millennia, watching us develop, watching us change the world. And now—" He leaned back, staring at the mountains. "Now something's different. The sightings are increasing. The encounters are getting more frequent. It's like they're preparing for something."

"A revelation. Some kind of... disclosure."

"Whatever you want to call it. Something's coming, Brian. Something that's going to change the relationship between us and them. And I think they know it. I think they've known it for a long time."

We sat in silence, watching the darkness gather. Somewhere in the distance, a howl rose—that familiar, eerie sound that I'd come to associate with everything I'd learned, everything I'd experienced, everything I still didn't understand.

"What do we do?" I asked.

"We keep searching. We keep documenting. We keep preparing." Zach smiled grimly. "And we wait for the world to catch up with what we already know."

It wasn't much of a plan. But it was all we had.

And the podcast was doing its part. One interview at a time, one story at a time, one million listeners at a time, the truth was spreading. Slowly but surely, the world was waking up.

I just hoped we'd be ready when the revelation finally came.

26

HOME FIRES

Daniel settled into his new life with the contentment of a man who'd found his calling.

The pizza place—a family-owned joint called Mountain Pies—had opened in March, about six miles down the road from our property. It was a small operation, just a kitchen and a few tables, but the food was good and the owners were good people. The Hartley family had moved up from Georgia a few years back, looking for a quieter life, and they'd poured everything they had into making the restaurant work.

Daniel started as assistant manager but quickly became indispensable. He handled the books, managed the staff, dealt with suppliers. He came home smelling of dough and tomato sauce, tired but happy, talking about the day's challenges with an enthusiasm I hadn't seen in years.

"You know what I love about this?" he said one evening, as we sat on the porch watching the sunset. "Nobody's trying to kill me. Nobody's threatening us. Nobody's making mysterious phone calls in the middle of the night. I just make pizza and go home."

"Sounds boring," I teased.

"Boring is underrated. After everything we've been through, boring is exactly what I needed."

He was right. The intensity of the investigation, the threats, the constant sense of danger—it had taken a toll on both of us. We'd been living on adrenaline for so long that we'd forgotten what normal felt like. Now, finally, we had a chance to remember.

Our life had found a rhythm. I spent my mornings researching, my afternoons interviewing, my evenings editing and preparing episodes. Daniel worked his shifts at the restaurant, came home, cooked dinner. We talked about our days, about the stories I was collecting, about the funny things that happened at the pizza place. We went to bed together, slept soundly, woke up ready to do it all again.

It was simple. It was peaceful. It was everything we'd dreamed of when we'd first moved to these mountains.

But the work continued. The work always continued.

* * *

The podcast had become something bigger than I'd ever imagined.

By the end of my second year, *Sasquatch Odyssey* had been downloaded over five million times. The community had grown to tens of thousands of active members. I'd been featured in magazines, interviewed on radio shows, invited to speak at conferences.

The money was coming in too—enough to cover our expenses, enough to invest in better equipment, enough to feel secure for the first time in years. We weren't rich by any means, but we weren't struggling either. The podcast was working.

And more importantly, it was making a difference.

I knew this because of the emails I received. Hundreds of them, every week, from people who'd found the podcast and felt validated for the first time in their lives. People who'd been carrying their encounters in secret, afraid to speak, convinced they were alone. People who'd finally found a community that understood.

One email in particular stood out.

It came from a woman named Margaret, seventy-eight years old, living in a nursing home in rural Pennsylvania. She'd had an encounter in 1952—she was a young girl, walking home from school through the woods, when she'd seen a creature watching her from behind a fallen tree.

"I've never told anyone," Margaret wrote. "Seventy years I've kept this secret. My husband didn't know. My children don't know. I was always afraid they'd think I was crazy. But I'm old now, and I don't have much time left, and I needed to tell someone before I die. I needed someone to know that what I saw was real."

"Thank you for creating a space where people like me can finally speak. Thank you for believing us. Thank you for carrying our stories forward."

I read that email with tears in my eyes.

This was why I did this work. Not for the money, not for the recognition. For Margaret. For all the Margarets out there, carrying secrets they were afraid to share. For the witnesses who deserved to be heard. For the truth that had been hidden for too long.

The podcast was giving them a voice. And I would keep doing it for as long as there were stories to tell.

* * *

The third year brought new challenges.

As the podcast grew, so did the scrutiny. Skeptics came out in force, attacking my credibility, dismissing my witnesses, demanding scientific proof that I couldn't provide. Some of them were genuine debunkers, committed to rational inquiry. Others were trolls, looking to stir up trouble. A few, I suspected, were more sinister—part of the same apparatus that had tried to shut us down before.

I learned to handle them. To respond calmly, to present the evidence without getting defensive, to acknowledge the limits of what I could prove while standing firm on what I knew to be true. It wasn't easy. But it was necessary.

The bigger challenge was maintaining quality as the volume of potential interviews exploded. I was receiving dozens of requests every day—too many to possibly accommodate. I had to develop systems for screening, for prioritizing, for identifying the stories that were most worth telling. I hired a part-time researcher to help with the workload. Then a second one.

The podcast was becoming a business. And while that brought benefits, it also brought complications I hadn't anticipated.

* * *

One of those complications arrived in April, in the form of a phone call from a producer in Los Angeles.

"Mr. Patterson, my name is Amanda Gardener. I'm with Meridian Productions. We've been following your podcast for some time, and we'd like to discuss a potential partnership."

"What kind of partnership?"

"A television series. Documentary style, based on *Sasquatch Odyssey*. We'd feature your interviews, recreate some of the encounters, add production value that you can't achieve with a podcast alone. It would reach millions of viewers who've never heard of your show."

I was skeptical. Television meant giving up control. It meant letting other people make decisions about how the stories were told. It meant the kind of sensationalism that I'd always tried to avoid.

But it also meant exposure. It meant reaching people who wouldn't find the podcast on their own. It meant amplifying the voices of witnesses who deserved to be heard.

"I'll think about it," I said.

"Take all the time you need. But Mr. Patterson—I want you to know that we're committed to doing this right. We've seen too many shows exploit this subject for cheap thrills. That's not what we're interested in. We want to tell these stories with the respect and authenticity they deserve."

I told Daniel about the offer that evening.

"What do you think?" I asked.

"I think you should be careful," he said. "Television changes things. It's not like the podcast, where you control everything. Once you sign a contract, you're playing by their rules."

"I know. But the reach..."

"The reach is tempting. But is it worth it if they turn these stories into a freak show?"

I didn't have an answer. Not yet. But the question stayed with me, turning over in my mind as I continued the work that had become my life's calling.

* * *

The four hundred and fiftieth interview happened on a rainy Tuesday in September.

The witness was a man named Jacob Whitehorse, a Navajo elder from Arizona. He'd reached out to me through the community forum, asking to share stories from his people's tradition.

"We call them the Ye'iitsoh," Jacob said, his voice carrying the weight of centuries. "The big giant. They've been part of our stories since the beginning. Not as monsters to be feared, but as neighbors to be respected. Different from us, living by different rules, but part of the same world."

"Tell me about your personal experiences."

"I've seen them three times in my life. Once as a child, once as a young man, once as an elder. Each time, the encounter taught me something. Something about respect, about humility, about our place in the web of life."

"What did you learn?"

Jacob was quiet for a moment. When he spoke again, his voice was soft.

"I learned that we are not alone. I learned that the world is bigger than we think, full of beings and forces that we can't fully understand. And I learned that our job—the job of humans—is not to conquer or control, but to live in balance. To take what we need and give back what we can. To be good neighbors to all the creatures who share this earth with us."

"Do you think these creatures are spiritual beings?"

"I think the line between physical and spiritual is thinner than you Westerners believe. These beings walk in both worlds. They have bodies you can see and touch, but they also have spirits that can reach across the divide. They are teachers, if we're willing to learn. Guides, if we're willing to follow."

"What do you think is happening now? Why are the sightings increasing?"

"Because the balance is broken. Humanity has taken too much, destroyed too much, forgotten too much. The old ways are dying. The web of life is fraying. And the Ye'iitsoh are concerned. They've watched us for millennia, hoping we would find our way. But time is running out. The world is changing, and not for the better."

"What can we do?"

"Listen. Learn. Remember what our ancestors knew. These beings are trying to tell us something—through their appearances, through their communications, through the very fact of their existence. They're reminding us that we're not the only ones who matter. That the world doesn't belong to us alone. That we have responsibilities we've been ignoring for too long."

Jacob's interview stayed with me long after we hung up. His words echoed through my mind as I edited the episode, as I fell asleep that night, as I woke up to another day of searching for truth.

A reckoning was coming. I didn't know when, didn't know how. But I knew that Jacob was right.

We had responsibilities. We had lessons to learn. And the creatures in the shadows were waiting to see if we'd finally pay attention.

* * *

As the third year drew to a close, I took stock of everything I'd built.

Four hundred and fifty interviews. Five million downloads. A community spanning dozens of countries. Witnesses validated. Secrets shared. Truth spread.

And yet it felt like we were just beginning.

The creatures were still out there, watching from the darkness. The cover-up was crumbling but not yet collapsed. The truth was emerging but had not yet been fully revealed.

There was so much more to do. So many more stories to tell. So many more people to reach.

I looked out at the mountains, at the endless forest that surrounded our home, and I made a promise to myself.

I would keep going. No matter how long it took. No matter what obstacles appeared. I would keep searching for the truth, keep giving voice to the witnesses, keep preparing the world for what was coming.

Because that's what I'd been called to do. That's what I'd been preparing for my whole life, since that day in the woods behind our house in Lyerly when I was twelve years old.

The odyssey continued. And I was ready for whatever came next.

27

SEPARATING WHEAT FROM CHAFF

Not every interview was a gem.

In fact, as the podcast grew and more people reached out, I found myself spending increasing amounts of time filtering through stories that ranged from the dubious to the outright absurd. For every Earl Hutchins or Mary Catherine O'Brien—witnesses whose sincerity and detail convinced me of their authenticity—there were a dozen others whose accounts raised red flags.

Some were obvious hoaxers, looking for attention or trying to capitalize on the podcast's growing audience. These were usually easy to spot: inconsistent details, borrowed elements from famous cases, an eagerness to be featured that felt more like self-promotion than truth-telling.

Others were harder to categorize. People who genuinely believed what they were saying but whose stories didn't hold up under scrutiny. People who'd conflated dreams with reality, who'd embellished mundane experiences into extraordinary ones, who'd convinced themselves of encounters that had never actually happened.

And then there were the ones that made me question whether I was wasting my time entirely.

* * *

The interview that nearly broke me came in the spring of my third year.

His name was Derek Fontaine, a forty-two-year-old construction worker from British Columbia. He'd reached out through the website, claiming to have had an encounter unlike any I'd documented before. His initial email was vague but intriguing, promising details that would "change everything I thought I knew about these creatures."

I should have known better. The vague promises, the grandiose claims—these were warning signs I'd learned to recognize. But I was tired, stretched thin by the volume of requests, and his location in the Pacific Northwest—prime Sasquatch territory—made me give him the benefit of the doubt.

We scheduled a video call for a Tuesday evening. Derek appeared on screen looking exactly like I'd expected: a stocky, bearded man in a flannel shirt, sitting in what appeared to be a basement rec room. He seemed nervous, fidgeting with something off-camera, avoiding eye contact.

"Thanks for taking the time, Derek," I said. "Why don't you start by telling me about your encounter?"

"Well, it happened back in 2015," he began. "I was on this camping trip up near Harrison Lake. A men's retreat, you know? Bunch of guys from my church, getting back to nature, doing the whole bonding thing."

"How many people were on the trip?"

"About fifteen, I think. We had a base camp set up, tents all around, fire pit in the middle. Real nice setup."

"And what happened?"

Derek shifted uncomfortably. "Well, the first couple nights were normal. Hiking, fishing, sitting around the fire telling stories. But on the third night, something changed."

"Changed how?"

"I couldn't sleep. It was hot, and I'd had too much coffee after dinner. So I was just lying there in my tent, staring at the ceiling, when

I heard something outside. Footsteps. Heavy footsteps, circling the camp."

This was familiar territory. I nodded encouragingly.

"I didn't think much of it at first. Figured it was a bear, maybe one of the other guys going to take a leak. But then my tent flap opened."

"Someone came into your tent?"

"Something came into my tent." Derek's voice dropped to a near-whisper. "It was... it was a Sasquatch. A female. I could tell because—well, I could tell."

I felt a knot forming in my stomach. I'd heard stories like this before—claims of intimate encounters with these creatures that stretched credulity beyond the breaking point.

"What happened next, Derek?"

He wouldn't meet my eyes. "She... we... look, I know this sounds crazy. But she came into my tent, and she... we had relations. Sexual relations. She wanted it, I could tell. The way she looked at me, the way she touched me—"

I held up my hand. "Hold on. You're telling me that a Sasquatch entered your tent while you were surrounded by fourteen other men, and you had sexual intercourse with it?"

"Her. With her. And yes, that's what I'm saying."

"Did anyone else see this creature? Did anyone hear anything?"

"No. She was quiet. Real quiet. And it was... it was over pretty quick."

"Derek." I tried to keep my voice level, professional. "I've interviewed hundreds of witnesses. I've heard stories that would make most people's hair stand up. But this—this is not consistent with anything we know about these creatures' behavior."

"I knew you wouldn't believe me. Nobody believes me."

"It's not about belief. It's about evidence. It's about patterns. In all the documented encounters, across decades of research, there's never been a credible report of this kind of interaction. These creatures avoid human contact. They don't seek out intimate encounters with strangers in tents."

"Maybe I'm special. Maybe she saw something in me—"

"Derek." My patience was wearing thin. "Did you report this to anyone at the time? Did you tell the other men on the retreat?"

"No. I was embarrassed. I didn't know what to say."

"Are there any physical traces? Any evidence at all that this happened?"

"Well, no. But I know what I experienced. It was real. It was the most real thing that's ever happened to me."

I took a deep breath. "I appreciate you reaching out, Derek. But I'm not going to be able to feature this story on the podcast. The lack of corroborating evidence, the inconsistency with known behavior patterns, the—" I stopped myself. "It just doesn't meet the standards I've set for the show."

Derek's face hardened. "You're just like all the others. You say you want the truth, but when someone gives it to you, you can't handle it."

"I want credible truth. I want verifiable experiences. What you're describing—"

"Is what happened. Whether you believe it or not."

The call ended shortly after that, with Derek hanging up in obvious frustration. I sat in my studio, staring at the blank screen, wondering for the hundredth time if I was doing this right.

* * *

Daniel found me on the porch an hour later, nursing a beer and watching the stars come out.

"Rough interview?" he asked, sitting down beside me.

"You could say that." I told him about Derek, about the story, about my frustration. "The thing is, he seemed to genuinely believe it. He wasn't lying, exactly. He was just... I don't know. Deluded? Fantasizing?"

"Does it matter? You can't put every story on the show."

"I know. But it's getting harder to sort through them all. For every legitimate witness, there are five Derek Fontaines. People who've convinced themselves of experiences that never happened. People who want attention, or validation, or just someone to listen to their fantasies."

"That's the price of success," Daniel said. "The bigger the platform, the more noise you have to filter out."

"I just don't want to become one of those shows. The ones that'll put anything on air as long as it's sensational. That's not what this is supposed to be about."

"Then don't let it become that. You've built something real here, Brian. Something that helps people. Don't let the Derek Fontaines of the world make you forget that."

He was right, of course. He usually was. But the frustration lingered, a reminder that this work—this calling—wasn't always easy. Sometimes it meant disappointing people. Sometimes it meant being the bad guy.

But if I didn't maintain standards, if I didn't filter the wheat from the chaff, the podcast would become worthless. Just another collection of tall tales and wishful thinking. And that would help no one.

So I kept filtering. Kept sorting. Kept searching for the real stories buried under the mountain of noise.

* * *

The next interview couldn't have been more different.

Her name was Gloria Reyes, a sixty-four-year-old retired nurse from rural New Mexico. She'd been hesitant to reach out, her email full of apologies and disclaimers, convinced that no one would take her seriously.

"I've never told anyone about this," she said, when we connected. "Not my husband, not my children. I was afraid they'd think I'd lost my mind."

"Tell me what happened, Gloria."

"It was 1992. I was working at a small hospital in Las Vegas— that's Las Vegas, New Mexico, not Nevada. We served a lot of the outlying communities, ranches and pueblos that didn't have their own medical facilities."

"What happened that year?"

"A young man was brought in late one night. A Navajo boy, maybe nineteen or twenty. He'd been found wandering on the highway, dehydrated, confused, covered in scratches and bruises. The people who found him thought he'd been in an accident, but there was no damaged vehicle anywhere nearby."

"What was his condition?"

"Physically, he was okay—dehydrated and scraped up, but nothing serious. But mentally, he was... somewhere else. He kept mumbling about 'the big people.' About being taken, being held, being examined. We assumed he was delirious, maybe on drugs, maybe suffering from heatstroke."

"What did he describe?"

"As his condition stabilized, the story became clearer. He said he'd been camping in the mountains when something grabbed him. Something big and hairy, walking on two legs. Multiple creatures, actually— he said there were at least three of them. They'd carried him to a cave, held him there for what he thought was several days, and then released him near the highway."

"Did you believe him?"

"At the time? I didn't know what to believe. His story was consistent, detailed, specific in ways that didn't seem like fabrication. But it was also impossible. Creatures like that didn't exist—that's what I told myself."

"What made you change your mind?"

"The physical evidence." Gloria's voice grew quieter. "When we examined him more thoroughly, we found things we couldn't explain. Hair caught in his clothing that didn't match any known animal. Bruises on his arms in patterns that suggested large, humanoid hands. And his feet—his feet were injured in a way that suggested he'd been carried for miles, not walked."

"What happened to the evidence?"

"That's the strangest part. The next morning, two men showed up at the hospital. Federal agents, they said, though they never showed proper ID. They took all the physical evidence—the hair samples, the photographs we'd taken of the bruises. They interviewed the young man for hours, and when they were done, he signed a statement saying he'd been confused and didn't remember what had happened to him."

"He recanted?"

"He was terrified. I saw his face when those men were done with him. He'd been threatened, I'm sure of it. They made him afraid to tell the truth."

"And you've kept this secret for thirty years?"

"What choice did I have? I was a nurse at a small hospital. Those men made it clear that talking about what happened would have consequences. And I had a family to think about, a career to protect." She paused. "But I'm retired now. My husband passed two years ago. And I'm tired of carrying this secret. That boy—that young man—he deserved to be believed. And I need someone to know what really happened."

Gloria's story was everything Derek Fontaine's wasn't: specific, verifiable, consistent with known patterns. The involvement of mysterious federal agents, the confiscation of evidence, the intimidation of witnesses—it all fit with what I'd learned about the cover-up.

And unlike Derek's fantasy, Gloria's account came with something else: corroboration. The young Navajo man she'd treated—she still remembered his name. And with some digging, I might have been able to find him.

This was why I did this work. This was why I pushed through the Derek Fontaines and the hoaxers and the attention-seekers. Because buried under all that noise were stories like Gloria's—real experiences, real witnesses, real pieces of the truth.

The wheat among the chaff.

28

GHOSTS FROM THE PAST

The men in black returned on a Thursday evening in October.

I hadn't thought about them in months. The podcast had become my life, the community had become my focus, and the threats that had once kept me up at night had faded into memory. Maybe I'd grown complacent. Maybe I'd convinced myself that they'd given up, that the information was too far out of their control to contain anymore.

I was wrong.

Daniel was at the restaurant, working the dinner shift. I was in my studio, editing an episode, when the driveway alarm chimed. We got false alarms sometimes—deer, mostly, occasionally a black bear wandering through—so I almost ignored it. But something made me check the monitor.

Two black SUVs were rolling up the drive.

My heart rate spiked. I watched as the vehicles stopped in front of the house, as four men in dark suits emerged. They moved with the same choreographed precision I remembered from years ago, spreading out to cover the approaches to the house while two of them walked toward the porch.

I grabbed my rifle—still kept by the door, still loaded—and stepped outside.

"That's far enough," I said.

The lead man stopped. He was different from the ones who'd visited before—younger, with a harder edge to his features. But the look in his eyes was the same. The cold certainty of someone operating with authority they didn't have to explain.

"Mr. Patterson. We're not here to cause trouble."

"Then why are you here?"

"To deliver a message. And to make a request."

"I'm listening."

The man reached inside his jacket—slowly, making sure I could see his hands. He pulled out a manila folder and held it up.

"You've been busy these past few years. The podcast, the community you've built, the attention you've brought to this subject. It's been... impressive."

"Thank you. Now get to the point."

"The point is that you've reached a crossroads, Mr. Patterson. The work you've been doing—documenting encounters, collecting testimony, building a public record—it's had consequences. Some of them intended. Some of them... less so."

"What consequences?"

"People are asking questions. People in positions of power. Congressional staffers, journalists, academics. The pressure is building for official acknowledgment of what you've been documenting. And that puts certain interests in a difficult position."

"Good. That's what I was hoping for."

The man smiled, but there was no warmth in it. "We anticipated you'd say that. Which is why we're offering an alternative." He extended the folder toward me.

"What is that?"

"Information. The kind of information you've been seeking for years. Details about the creatures. About the research that's been conducted. About what we really know and how long we've known it."

"And what's the catch?"

"No catch. Just a request. You take this information, you add it to your research, but you don't identify where it came from. And you stop pushing for official disclosure. Let the information speak for itself, without forcing the government's hand."

I stared at him. "You want me to become your mouthpiece."

"We want you to become a partner. Someone who helps manage the transition, rather than forcing it to happen on an uncontrolled timetable."

"And if I refuse?"

The man's expression didn't change. "Then we continue as we have been. Monitoring. Containing. Doing what's necessary to maintain order."

"You mean threatening people. Suppressing evidence. Covering up the truth."

"Maintaining order," he repeated. "Mr. Patterson, you've seen a fraction of what's out there. The creatures you've been documenting—they're just one piece of a much larger picture. There are things in this world that would break most people's minds if they knew about them. We're not the villains you've made us out to be. We're the ones holding back the tide."

I thought about the Mount St. Helens documents. The evidence of government programs studying these creatures for decades. The pattern of cover-ups and silencings that stretched back generations.

"I've seen more than you think," I said.

Something flickered in the man's eyes. Surprise, maybe. Or recognition.

"Then you understand why we're concerned."

"What I understand is that you've been lying to people for decades. Hiding the truth because you thought we couldn't handle it. And now that the truth is coming out anyway, you want to control the narrative."

"We want to prevent panic. We want to ensure a stable transition. Is that so unreasonable?"

"It's not your decision to make. The people deserve to know the truth. All of it, not just what you think they can handle."

The man sighed. "I was afraid you'd say that." He set the folder on the porch railing. "The offer stands. Take some time, think it over. Read what's in that folder. Maybe it will change your perspective."

"And if it doesn't?"

"Then I suppose we'll see who's right about what's best for humanity. I hope, for everyone's sake, that it's not you."

He turned and walked back to the SUVs. The other men followed, moving with that same eerie precision. Within moments, they were gone, disappearing down the driveway and into the night.

I stood on the porch for a long time, the folder in my hands, wondering what I'd just agreed to.

Or refused.

* * *

The folder contained exactly what the man had promised: information.

Pages and pages of it. Documents I'd never seen before, with classification stamps and agency headers and detailed research findings. Studies on Sasquatch physiology, conducted at facilities I'd never heard of. Psychological profiles of witnesses, compiled over decades. Maps showing known habitation zones, marked with encounter frequencies and population estimates.

And something else. Something that made my blood run cold.

A section on "interdimensional hypotheses."

The documents suggested that the creatures weren't simply undiscovered primates hiding in the wilderness. They were something else —beings that existed partially outside our normal perception of reality. They could move between dimensions, the researchers theorized. They could become invisible, or nearly so. They could sense human intention and avoid detection with uncanny precision.

This explained things. The way they seemed to vanish without trace. The difficulty in obtaining clear photographs or physical evidence. The psychic phenomena that some witnesses reported.

But it also raised more questions than it answered.

If the creatures were interdimensional, what did that mean for the other things the government was hiding? The UFOs, the paranormal phenomena, all the strangeness that had been suppressed for so long?

Were they all connected? All part of the same vast mystery that we were only beginning to glimpse?

I stayed up all night, reading and rereading the documents. When Daniel came home from his shift, he found me surrounded by papers, red-eyed and wired on coffee.

"Brian? What's going on?"

I told him. About the men, about the offer, about the folder and what it contained. He listened without interrupting, his face growing more concerned with every word.

"What are you going to do?" he asked when I finished.

"I don't know. Part of me wants to take this information and run with it. Put it all on the podcast, let the world see what they've been hiding."

"And the other part?"

"The other part wonders if they're right. If the truth is too dangerous to just dump on an unprepared public. If I'd be causing more harm than good."

Daniel was quiet for a moment. "Do you trust them?"

"No. Not even a little."

"Then there's your answer. Whatever they're offering, whatever they want you to do—it's not for your benefit. It's for theirs."

"But the information—"

"Use it. But use it on your terms, not theirs. Don't become their partner. Don't help them control the narrative. Just keep doing what you've been doing, and add this to the pile."

He made it sound so simple. Maybe it was.

I stared at the documents spread across the table. Years of suppressed research. Decades of hidden truth. And now it was in my hands, waiting for me to decide what to do with it.

"Okay," I said finally. "We do it my way."

Daniel squeezed my shoulder. "That's my boy."

I started organizing the documents, preparing to incorporate them into my research. The men in black would be watching, waiting to see what I did. Let them watch. Let them see that I couldn't be bought or intimidated.

The truth was coming out. One way or another, the truth was coming out.

And nothing they did was going to stop it.

29

THE FIRE RETURNS

The second attack came eighteen months after the documentary release.

This time, they didn't bother with subtlety. A group of men in tactical gear, faces hidden behind balaclavas, descended on our property at three in the morning. They set fires in multiple locations simultaneously—the studio, the garage, the tool shed. By the time we woke to the smell of smoke, the flames were already out of control.

We escaped with our lives. Barely.

Daniel was the one who woke first, shaking me out of a deep sleep with urgency in his voice. "Brian. Brian, wake up. Something's wrong."

I smelled it before I opened my eyes—smoke, acrid and thick, already seeping under the bedroom door. We moved on instinct, grabbing clothes, phones, the emergency bag we'd prepared for exactly this kind of situation.

The house itself was still intact, but the studio was fully engulfed. Flames shot into the night sky, painting the mountains in shades of orange and red. The garage was burning too, and the shed where we kept the lawn equipment.

I called 911 while Daniel sprayed the house with the garden hose, trying to keep the flames from spreading. The fire department arrived within twenty minutes—fast, for a rural area—but by then, the studio was a total loss.

"This was coordinated," the fire investigator said, surveying the damage the next morning. "Multiple points of origin, accelerant at each location. This wasn't vandalism. This was a professional operation."

"Can you prove that?"

"I can document what I've found. But proving who's responsible?" He shook his head. "These people know what they're doing. They don't leave evidence."

* * *

The attack made national news.

A former sheriff, targeted for his research into unexplained phenomena. A podcast host, silenced by arson. The story played perfectly into the narrative we'd been building—a government cover-up so determined to maintain its secrets that it would burn down homes to stop the truth from getting out.

The response was overwhelming.

Donations poured in from around the world. Equipment, money, offers of safe haven. The community I'd been building rallied around us, determined to show that we couldn't be silenced.

And Amanda called with news that changed everything.

"I've got a television deal," she said. "A major network. They want to produce a docuseries based on the podcast. Full editorial control. No censorship."

"After everything that's happened? They're not afraid of the blowback?"

"They're counting on the blowback. Controversy drives ratings, and this is the most controversial story in decades." She paused. "They saw what happened to your house. Everyone saw. And they want to tell the world what's really going on."

"When do we start?"

"As soon as you're ready. They're willing to fund a complete rebuild of your studio. Better equipment than you had before. Security that'll actually work this time."

I looked at Daniel. At the ruins of everything we'd built. At the life we'd have to reconstruct for the second time.

He nodded.

"Tell them we're in," I said.

* * *

The production dwarfed anything we'd done before.

Amanda assembled a team of professionals—camera operators, sound engineers, researchers, security personnel. They descended on North Carolina like a small army, setting up in a rented facility while my new studio was being built.

The concept was ambitious: a ten-episode series, each focusing on a different aspect of the phenomenon. Encounters. Evidence. Government cover-up. International connections. The history of research. And finally, an expedition into the heart of the Pisgah, following the trail we'd been documenting for years.

"This is going to be different from the first documentary," Amanda explained. "That was about revealing the cover-up. This is about building an irrefutable case for the creatures' existence."

"You mean actually finding them?"

"That's the goal. We've got the best equipment money can buy. Thermal cameras. Night vision. Drones with infrared sensors. If there's anything out there, we're going to document it."

"And if we don't?"

"Then we document everything else we've found. The witness testimonies. The physical evidence. The patterns you and Zach have been mapping. Even without direct visual proof, the circumstantial evidence is overwhelming."

* * *

The filming took six months.

We traveled across the country, revisiting witnesses, documenting evidence, building the case piece by piece. Each episode was crafted to lead viewers deeper into the mystery, starting with basic questions and ending with implications that shook the foundations of what they thought they knew.

I was on camera for most of it. Guiding viewers through the evidence. Sharing my own experiences. Asking the questions that no one in authority was willing to ask.

It was exhausting. It was exhilarating. And it was necessary.

* * *

The expedition into the Pisgah came last.

Ten days in the wilderness with a full production crew, following the trails we'd mapped, setting up surveillance in locations with the highest concentration of encounters. Days of hiking, nights of waiting, hours of footage that showed nothing but empty forest.

And then, on the eighth night, something happened.

We were camped in a hollow near the site where Austin Mercer had disappeared. The thermal cameras were running, the audio equipment was recording, and I was sitting by the fire, keeping watch while most of the crew slept.

The sounds started around two in the morning.

Wood knocks. The sharp crack of a branch being struck against a tree. Once, twice, three times. Coming from somewhere in the darkness beyond our camp.

I signaled to the camera operator who was awake with me. He trained his lens toward the sound, switching to night vision.

We saw nothing clearly. But we could hear it. Footsteps. Heavy, bipedal footsteps, circling our camp. Staying just beyond the range of the cameras. Just beyond the reach of our lights.

And then the vocalizations began.

A howl, rising from somewhere deep in the forest. Joined by another, from a different direction. Then a third. A fourth. A chorus of voices, calling to each other across the darkness.

The crew woke. Everyone was on their feet, cameras rolling, equipment running, capturing every second.

We never saw the creatures clearly. They were too smart, too experienced, too good at staying hidden. But we heard them. We documented them. We proved they were there.

And when the sun came up and the sounds faded into silence, we knew we had something significant.

Not definitive proof—that would require actual clear footage. But evidence. Compelling, documented, irrefutable evidence that something was out there.

Something that the world would have to reckon with.

* * *

The Austin Mercer case remained unsolved.

I'd made peace with that, as much as I could. The trail camera footage we'd recovered told a grim story—a young man running through the forest, something massive in pursuit, screams that cut off abruptly. Whatever had happened to Austin, it hadn't been good.

His parents had held a memorial service. They'd placed a marker at the campsite where he'd last been seen—a simple wooden cross with his name and dates.

I visited the site during our expedition. Stood there in the clearing, looking at the trees, feeling the weight of all the questions I couldn't answer.

Austin was gone. His body was somewhere in these mountains, hidden in a place we might never find. But his story had become part of something larger. His disappearance had sparked an investigation that had grown into a movement.

Maybe that was enough. Maybe that was all any of us could hope for—to be part of something bigger than ourselves.

I knelt by the marker and said a quiet prayer. For Austin. For all the people who'd vanished into these forests over the years. For the truth that was still waiting to be found.

Then I stood up and went back to work.

30

WITNESSES TO WONDER

The months that followed were the most productive of my podcasting career.

Armed with the information from the men in black's folder—used on my own terms, as Daniel had suggested—and driven by the Mount St. Helens revelations that proved decades of government cover-up, I threw myself into the work with renewed purpose. The interviews became sharper, more focused. The episodes became more substantive. The audience continued to grow.

And the stories kept coming.

* * *

From northern Minnesota, I interviewed a conservation officer named Margaret Lindqvist who'd spent thirty years patrolling the Boundary Waters.

"I've seen things up there that I can't explain," Margaret said, her Scandinavian accent softened by decades in the American Midwest. "Things that don't fit in any guidebook or training manual."

"Can you give me an example?"

"The winter of 2008. I was on a solo patrol near the Canadian border, checking ice conditions on some of the larger lakes. It was January, maybe twenty below zero, wind chill even worse. Not a day when anything should be moving around."

"What happened?"

"I was on the ice, halfway across Gunflint Lake, when I saw something on the shore. At first I thought it was a moose—we get big ones up there. But the proportions were wrong. Too upright. Too... human-shaped."

"What did it do?"

"It watched me. Stood there at the tree line for maybe five minutes, just watching. I had binoculars with me, but every time I tried to focus on it, my hands started shaking. I couldn't get a clear look."

"From the cold?"

"That's what I told myself. But it wasn't the cold. It was fear. Pure, primal fear. Every instinct I had was screaming at me to get away from that thing, whatever it was."

"How did the encounter end?"

"It turned and walked into the forest. Disappeared between one step and the next. I finished my patrol as fast as I could and didn't go back to that lake for two years."

"Have you had other encounters since?"

"Nothing visual. But sounds, yes. Howls in the night, wood-knocking, things moving through the brush that are too big and too quiet to be any animal I know. They're up there, Brian. In the deep wilderness. And they've been there a lot longer than we have."

* * *

From Mississippi, I spoke with a man named Samuel Jackson—no relation to the actor, as he was quick to point out—who'd had an encounter in the bottomlands near the Big Black River.

"I was running a trotline for catfish," Samuel said. His voice was deep, unhurried, with the patience of a man who'd spent his life on the water. "This was back in '96. I'd been fishing that stretch of river for twenty years, knew every bend and sandbar. But that night, something was different."

"Different how?"

"Quiet. Too quiet. The frogs stopped singing. The owls stopped calling. Even the river seemed to hush itself. And then I heard it—this splashing, coming from upstream. Big splashing, like a horse crossing. But there weren't any horses around for miles."

"Did you see anything?"

"I did. Came around a bend in my johnboat and saw it standing in the shallows. Seven feet tall, maybe more. Covered in dark hair, dripping wet. It had a fish in its hands—a big channel cat, must have been thirty pounds—and it was eating it raw. Just tearing into it like a dog with a bone."

"What happened when it saw you?"

"It froze. Looked at me with these yellow eyes—I'll never forget those eyes, reflecting my lantern light like mirrors. We stared at each other for what felt like forever. And then it made this sound, low and rumbling, like a warning. I took the hint. Turned my boat around and paddled like hell back to the landing."

"Did you ever return to that spot?"

"Every season. Still fish there to this day. Never saw that creature again, but I feel it sometimes. Watching from the banks. Keeping tabs on me." Samuel laughed, a deep, genuine sound. "I leave an extra catfish for it now. Just in case. Call it rent for fishing in its territory."

* * *

From the mountains of West Virginia, I interviewed a coal miner named Thomas Adkins whose encounter had happened deep underground.

"You heard me right," Thomas said, when I asked him to repeat himself. "Underground. In the mines."

"Tell me about it."

"This was back in '89. I was working the night shift at a deep mine near Beckley. We were opening a new section, following a seam that went back into the mountain for miles. And we hit something."

"What do you mean, hit something?"

"A void. A cave, natural-formed, right in the middle of the seam. The cutting machine broke through the wall, and suddenly there was this opening—maybe ten feet wide, going back into darkness."

"What did you find?"

"At first, nothing. Just a cave, big and empty. The foreman sent me and two other guys in to check if it was safe, if it connected to any other workings. We had our headlamps, our methane detectors. Standard procedure."

"And?"

"About a hundred yards in, we found tracks. Footprints in the mud. Bare feet, human-shaped but way too big. We followed them deeper, and that's when we started hearing it."

"Hearing what?"

"Breathing. Heavy breathing, echoing off the walls. And movement —something shuffling around in the dark, just beyond the reach of our lights. We could smell it too. That smell everyone talks about, like a wet dog and a garbage dump had a baby."

"What did you do?"

"We got the hell out. Ran all the way back to the main tunnel. Told the foreman what we'd found, what we'd heard. He didn't believe us, of course. Called us a bunch of superstitious fools."

"What happened to the cave?"

"They sealed it up. Built a concrete wall across the opening and never spoke of it again. But I know what I heard in there, Brian. I know what was living in that darkness. And I wonder sometimes if it's still there, waiting, listening to us dig."

* * *

From the bayous of Louisiana, I spoke with a woman named Celestine Thibodaux who was a practicing traiteur—a folk healer in the Cajun tradition.

"The loup-garou is what we call them," Celestine said. Her voice was thick with the accent of the Atchafalaya, words rolling together like the slow rivers of her homeland. "The werewolf, the outsiders say. But that's not quite right. They're older than werewolves. Older than any story we brought from France."

"Tell me about your experiences with them."

"I've seen them all my life. My grandmother saw them. Her grandmother saw them. They've always been here, in the deep bayous where the water is black and the cypress grows thick. We don't fear them. We respect them."

"Have they ever harmed anyone?"

"Only those who deserve it. Poachers, sometimes. Men who take more than they need from the swamp. The loup-garou doesn't like waste. Doesn't like greed. But if you live right, if you take only what you need and give back what you can, they leave you alone. Sometimes they even help."

"Help how?"

"My grandmother told a story about a child who got lost in the swamp. Three years old, wandered away from home during a flood. Search parties looked for days, found nothing. And then, on the fourth morning, the child appeared at the edge of the bayou, safe and sound. Said a 'big hairy man' had carried her through the water, kept her warm at night, brought her back when the flood receded."

"Do you believe that story?"

"I know it's true. That child was my grandmother. And she never forgot what the loup-garou did for her. She spent her whole life respecting them, teaching us to respect them. It's why I'm talking to you now. Because the world needs to know that these beings aren't monsters. They're guardians. Protectors. And they've been watching over us longer than we can remember."

* * *

Each interview added another thread to the tapestry. Each witness added another voice to the chorus. The picture that was emerging was more complex than I'd ever imagined—creatures not just hiding in the wilderness, but woven into the fabric of human culture. Present in our stories, our legends, our deepest memories.

They'd been with us all along. And now, finally, we were beginning to see them.

31

THE STORM GATHERS

The television offer came back around in the spring.

Amanda, the producer from Meridian Productions, reached out again after a year of silence. The industry, she explained, had changed. Streaming platforms were hungrier than ever for content. The success of certain paranormal and unexplained phenomena series had created an opening that hadn't existed before.

"We can do this right," she said, during a video call that lasted two hours. "I've watched every episode of your podcast. I've read the transcripts. I understand what you're trying to do, and I want to help you do it on a bigger scale."

"I've seen what television does to stories like these," I said. "The sensationalism. The manipulation. The focus on drama over truth."

"That's not what I'm proposing. Think of this as a documentary series. Long-form, substantive, respectful. We let the witnesses tell their stories. We present the evidence without editorializing. We treat the subject with the seriousness it deserves."

"And the network will allow that?"

"The network is desperate for authentic content. The audience is tired of fake reality shows and manufactured drama. They want something real. Your podcast proves there's a market for it."

I thought about it. Thought about the reach, the resources, the possibility of telling these stories to millions of people who would never find the podcast on their own.

"I need to maintain editorial control," I said finally. "Final cut on every episode. No interviews used without the witness's explicit consent. No misleading edits, no manufactured drama, no sensationalism."

"Those are steep terms."

"Those are my terms. Take them or leave them."

Amanda was quiet for a moment. Then she smiled.

"I'll make it work. This is too important to let network politics get in the way."

We shook hands—virtually, at least—and the deal was set. *Sasquatch Odyssey* was going to television.

* * *

The first season would feature ten episodes, each one focused on a different region and its encounters. We'd start in the Pacific Northwest, the heartland of Sasquatch legend, and work our way across the country. I'd conduct the interviews, provide the narration, serve as the guide for audiences who were new to this world.

The production was bigger than anything I'd experienced. Camera crews, sound technicians, editors, producers. A budget that dwarfed what I'd spent in three years of podcasting. Resources to investigate cases I'd never been able to pursue before.

But the core of the show remained the same: the witnesses. Their stories. Their truth.

We filmed the first episode in the Olympic Peninsula of Washington State. Dense rainforest, ancient trees, a landscape that seemed to belong to another age. The witnesses we interviewed there had stories that went back generations—families who'd lived alongside the creatures for a hundred years, who knew their territories and their habits the way you might know a neighbor.

"They're not animals," one elderly woman told us, sitting on the porch of a cabin her great-grandfather had built. "They're people. Different from us, but people. And they've been here longer than we have. We're the newcomers. We're the ones who don't belong."

* * *

The second episode took us to the Ozarks, where Bobby Dean Carver served as our local guide. He'd become something of a celebrity since his podcast interview, fielding inquiries from researchers and media outlets around the world. But he'd turned everyone else down.

"You're the only one I trust," he told me, as we hiked into the hollers where he'd had his encounter. "You don't make us look like fools. You don't twist our words. You just let us tell our stories."

We filmed interviews with a dozen witnesses from the region. Hunters, farmers, hikers, children who'd grown up seeing things their parents couldn't explain. The consistency of their accounts was remarkable—the same creatures, the same behaviors, the same sense of being watched by something that didn't want to be seen.

By the time we finished filming in Arkansas, I knew we had something special. Something that would reach people in ways the podcast never could.

* * *

The third episode brought us back to the Pisgah National Forest.

It was strange, returning to these mountains as a television host rather than a sheriff. The trails I'd walked, the clearings I'd searched, the cave where Austin had vanished without a trace—all of it was familiar, but seen through new eyes.

We filmed near some of the locations connected to his disappearance. The Austin Reeves case remained officially unsolved, another mystery in these ancient mountains. But the evidence we'd gathered—the Mount St. Helens documents, the witness testimonies, the pattern of government cover-ups—all pointed to creatures that had been here far longer than any of us. Austin had gone looking for them. Whether he'd found them, whether he was still alive somewhere in these vast forests, remained the question that haunted me. The missing hikers. The strange sounds. The footprints that appeared on remote trails and vanished just as mysteriously.

Zach appeared on camera, sharing the research he'd spent years compiling. He was nervous at first—he'd spent his career avoiding attention, staying under the radar. But as the interview progressed, he relaxed, his passion for the truth overcoming his reluctance to be seen.

"The cover-up is real," he told the camera. "I've documented it for decades. Files suppressed. Witnesses silenced. Evidence confiscated. Somebody doesn't want us to know what's out there. But the truth is coming out anyway. It can't be stopped."

* * *

We were filming the fourth episode in the Pacific Northwest when everything changed.

It started with a phone call from Daniel.

"Brian, you need to come home. Now."

"What's wrong?"

"They came back. The men in black. But this time—" His voice broke. "This time they didn't just threaten. They did something."

"Are you okay?"

"I'm fine. But the house—Brian, the house is gone."

"What do you mean, gone?"

"Burned. Burned to the ground. Everything we had—all your research, all the equipment, everything—it's gone."

I was on a plane within hours, leaving the production crew to finish without me. The flight felt endless, every minute stretching into an eternity of fear and rage and helplessness.

When I finally arrived at our property, what I saw broke something inside me.

The house was a ruin. Blackened timbers, collapsed walls, ash where our life had been. The studio where I'd recorded hundreds of interviews, the office where I'd built the community, the bedroom where Daniel and I had dreamed of the future—all of it reduced to rubble.

Daniel was standing at the edge of the debris, staring at what remained. I wrapped my arms around him and held on.

"I'm sorry," he whispered. "I'm so sorry. I should have been here. I should have—"

"This isn't your fault. This is them. This is what they do when they can't control the narrative."

"What are we going to do?"

I looked at the ruins of our home. At the ashes of everything we'd built. And I felt something rising in me—not despair, but determination. A fire that matched the one they'd set.

"We rebuild," I said. "And we keep going. They want us to give up, to be scared, to crawl away and hide. But that's not who we are. That's not who I am."

"Brian—"

"The podcast is backed up. The interviews, the research, the community—it's all in the cloud. They burned down our house, but they didn't destroy our work. They didn't destroy us."

Daniel looked at me, tears streaming down his face. "You're not going to stop."

"I'm never going to stop. Not until the truth is out. Not until everyone knows what's been hidden. Not until they can't silence us anymore."

I turned away from the ruins and pulled out my phone. Called Amanda.

"We need to talk," I said. "Something's happened. And the world needs to see it."

The television series was about to get a lot more complicated.

And a lot more dangerous.

32

ASHES AND EMBERS

The fire investigation was a farce.

The county sheriff—my replacement, a man named Harold Weston who'd run unopposed after I declined to seek reelection—showed up with his deputies, took some photographs, asked a few questions, and declared the fire accidental. Faulty wiring, he said. These old mountain houses were firetraps.

"Sheriff Weston," I said, keeping my voice level despite the rage building in my chest, "our house was built in 2019. The wiring was inspected six months ago. And there were accelerant marks on the foundation that your investigators seem to have missed."

Weston's face tightened. "You're not a law enforcement officer anymore, Brian. Leave the investigating to the professionals."

"The professionals who concluded a two-year-old house caught fire from faulty wiring?"

"The professionals who have jurisdiction here." He stepped closer, lowering his voice. "I know what you've been doing. The podcast, the TV show, all that Bigfoot nonsense. You've made some powerful enemies. Maybe this is a sign you should reconsider your priorities."

"Is that a threat?"

"It's advice. Take it or leave it."

He walked away, his deputies trailing behind him. I watched them go, my hands clenched into fists.

Daniel touched my arm. "Let it go, Brian. Fighting him won't change anything."

"I know. But this—" I gestured at the ruins "—this can't stand. They can't just burn down our home and walk away."

"Then make them pay. Not with fists. With truth."

* * *

Amanda flew in from Los Angeles the next day.

She surveyed the damage, interviewed Daniel and me on camera, documented everything the sheriff's department had conveniently overlooked. Her crew found the accelerant marks I'd mentioned. They found footprints that didn't match any of ours—boot prints, military-style, leading away from the house toward the road.

"This is going to be part of the series," Amanda said. "The whole story—the investigation, the threats, the cover-up, and now this. People need to see what they're doing to silence you."

"You're not afraid it'll make the network nervous?"

"The network is already nervous. They've been getting pressure—vague calls from unnamed government sources, questions about our editorial standards, hints that our broadcast license might face scrutiny. But they're standing firm. This story is too big to walk away from."

"What about you? Aren't you worried about becoming a target?"

Amanda smiled grimly. "I've been a target before. Documentary filmmakers aren't popular with the powers that be. But you can't scare someone who's already committed to the truth."

* * *

We moved into a rental cabin about ten miles from our property. It was smaller than the house we'd lost, but it was safe—or as safe as anywhere could be now.

The community rallied around us. Donations poured in from

podcast listeners and forum members, enough to replace the equipment we'd lost, enough to start rebuilding. Messages of support flooded my inbox—people who'd been inspired by the podcast, who'd found validation in the stories I'd shared, who wanted us to know we weren't alone.

And the interviews continued.

I refused to let the fire stop me. If anything, it strengthened my resolve. They'd tried to silence me, and they'd failed. Every episode I recorded, every witness I interviewed, every story I shared was a victory against the forces that wanted the truth to stay hidden.

* * *

A week after the fire, the investigation took an unexpected turn.

The ATF—Bureau of Alcohol, Tobacco, Firearms and Explosives —reached out to us. A young agent named Monica Brown, had been assigned to review the case. Unlike Sheriff Weston, she actually did her job.

"Mr. Patterson, the accelerant patterns at your property are consistent with professional-grade incendiary devices," she said during our first meeting. "This wasn't some amateur with a gas can. Whoever did this had training."

"Will you be able to find them?"

"I'm going to try. But I have to warn you—there are forces pushing back on this investigation. People above my pay grade asking questions about why federal resources are being used on a simple house fire." She met my eyes. "Whatever you're doing with your podcast, your documentary—you've made some powerful enemies."

"I know."

"Then you should also know that you've made some allies. Not everyone in government wants these secrets kept. There are people who believe the public has a right to know." She handed me her card. "Call me if anything else happens. And be careful."

* * *

I showed Daniel the card that night.

"This could be a setup," he said. "They've used fake allies before to gather intelligence."

"Maybe. But my gut says she's genuine. Someone who joined law enforcement to actually pursue justice, not cover it up."

Daniel was quiet for a moment. "Like you were."

"Yeah. Like I was." I looked out the window at the mountains. "We keep going. The documentary, the podcast, all of it. They burned down our house, but they didn't destroy us. And the Mount St. Helens documents are already out there—backed up in a dozen places, shared with journalists and researchers around the world. They can't put that genie back in the bottle."

"What about Austin? Have you heard anything?"

I shook my head. The question haunted me every day. Austin Reeves, somewhere in those mountains—or nowhere at all. Alive and living among the creatures, or dead and buried in some unmarked hollow. The not knowing was the hardest part.

"We keep looking," I said. "We keep telling the stories. And someday, maybe, we'll find our answers."

"I love you," Daniel said. "You stubborn, idealistic, Bigfoot-chasing fool."

I laughed despite everything. "I love you too."

* * *

The production resumed a month later.

After the fire, Amanda had fought to keep the project alive. The network had gotten cold feet—the arson, the government pressure, the sense that this story was becoming dangerous in ways they hadn't anticipated. But Amanda convinced them that walking away would be worse. That the public would see it as cowardice, as complicity in the cover-up.

"This is the biggest story any of us will ever work on," she told them. "And we're going to tell it right."

We filmed the remaining episodes with a renewed sense of

purpose. The fire became part of the narrative—evidence of how far certain forces would go to keep the truth hidden. The witnesses we interviewed spoke with more urgency now, understanding that their stories might be the only protection any of us had.

The community continued to grow. Two million downloads per episode. Three million. The forum membership passed fifty thousand, then a hundred thousand. People from every walk of life, united by their experiences, their questions, their refusal to accept the official denials.

And the evidence kept accumulating. The Mount St. Helens documents. The thermal footage from the Pisgah. The audio recordings, the footprint casts, the witness testimonies that formed a pattern too consistent to dismiss.

We were building something. Something that couldn't be burned down or silenced or covered up. Something bigger than any of us.

I didn't know how it would end. Didn't know if we'd ever get the definitive proof we were searching for. But I knew we wouldn't stop. Couldn't stop. Not until the world understood what we'd learned.

The creatures were real. The cover-up was real. And the truth was coming out, one story at a time.

33

THE EXPEDITION

The final episode of Season One would be filmed in the Pisgah.

It was Amanda's idea. She wanted to bring everything full circle—to return to the mountains where Austin Reeves had disappeared, where my own journey as a researcher had intensified, where the evidence was most compelling.

"This is where your story really began," she said during our planning meeting. "The case that changed everything. We need to show the audience that place."

I knew she was right. And I knew it would be the hardest episode to film.

* * *

We assembled a small team. Amanda and her most trusted cameraman, Marcus. Zach, of course, served as our guide and technical expert. Daniel, who had been with me through all of it and wasn't about to miss this final chapter. And Dr. Rebecca Henley, the surgeon from the Mount St. Helens documents who had agreed to appear on camera for the first time.

We left before dawn on a Tuesday in October. The morning was cold and clear, the mountains painted in autumn colors—reds and golds against the dark green of the evergreens. The Pisgah in fall was one of the most beautiful places on earth, and I felt a familiar ache watching the familiar ridgelines emerge from the morning mist.

"You okay?" Daniel asked quietly, as our caravan wound up the forest service road.

"Yeah. Just—remembering."

"Austin?"

I nodded. "And everything else. Mama. The first encounter. All those years of wondering what I'd seen."

He put his hand on mine. "You've come a long way from that scared kid in Lyerly."

"Some days I'm not sure I've come anywhere at all."

* * *

We set up base camp in a remote section of the forest, far from any established trail. Zach had identified this area as a hotspot based on thermal imagery, audio recordings, and his network of local contacts.

"Multiple witnesses have reported activity here over the past six months," he explained to the camera. "Wood knocks, vocalizations, glimpses of large figures moving through the trees. This is as active as any location I've documented."

The first day was spent exploring the terrain and setting up monitoring equipment. Trail cameras, audio recorders, thermal imaging stations. We created a web of technology across twenty square acres, designed to capture anything that moved through the area.

Dr. Henley examined some unusual structures we found—broken branches arranged in deliberate patterns, stripped bark at heights no bear or human would reach, a strange circular formation of stones that Zach believed was an intentional marker.

"The patterns are consistent with what we documented at Mount St. Helens," she said, her scientific caution evident even in this moment. "I can't definitively say what created them. But I can say they don't match any known animal behavior."

* * *

The second night, we heard them.

It started around midnight—a distant vocalization that sounded almost like a woman screaming, but sustained in a way no human could manage. Then another call answered from a different direction. Then another.

"Three individuals," Zach whispered. "Minimum. They're communicating."

We caught glimpses on the thermal cameras—heat signatures moving through the trees at the edge of our detection range. Large. Bipedal. Too fast and too deliberate to be bears.

Amanda had her crew filming everything, capturing our reactions, the equipment readouts, the sounds that echoed through the darkness.

"This is incredible," Marcus breathed, watching the thermal display. "I've covered wars, disasters, everything. But this—"

"I know," I said. "It changes things, doesn't it? Knowing they're real."

We never got a clear visual. They stayed just beyond the range of our cameras, moving parallel to our camp, watching us as we watched them. At one point, a wood knock came from less than a hundred yards away—a sharp crack that made everyone jump.

I walked to the edge of our camp and spoke into the darkness.

"We're not here to hurt you. We're here to share your story with the world. To help people understand."

Silence. Then, from somewhere in the trees, a low, rumbling vocalization. Not threatening. Almost... acknowledging.

I felt it then. That same sense I'd had as a child in Lyerly. A presence, an awareness, a connection to something old and powerful and patient.

"They know," I said quietly. "They know what we're trying to do."

* * *

On the third day, we found the footprints.

A line of them, crossing a muddy creek bed about a mile from our camp. Clear, distinct, unmistakable. Eighteen inches long, with visible toe impressions and dermal ridges. Zach cast them in plaster while Dr. Henley documented every detail.

"These are the best prints I've ever collected," Zach said. "The detail is extraordinary. You can see the flexion of the toes, the weight distribution. These weren't faked. No hoaxer could create something this anatomically correct."

Dr. Henley was more measured, as always. "The prints are consistent with a large, bipedal primate. The dermal ridge patterns are unlike anything in the scientific literature. Whatever made these is... unprecedented."

"Real," Amanda said, capturing everything on camera. "That's the word you're looking for, Dr. Henley. They're real."

"I'm a scientist. I don't use that word until the evidence is irrefutable." But she was smiling slightly. "However, I will say that after what I saw at Mount St. Helens, after what I experienced on that operating table in 1980... I don't need to believe anymore. I know."

* * *

We broke camp on the fourth day, loaded with footage and audio recordings and the best physical evidence any team had ever collected. Not the definitive proof that would convince every skeptic. But enough. Enough to keep the conversation going. Enough to inspire others to look closer.

As we made our way back to the vehicles, I stopped at a familiar ridge. In the distance, I could see the canyon where Austin Reeves had vanished. Where I'd found his camera. Where the trail had gone cold.

"We'll find him," Daniel said, reading my thoughts as he always did.

"Will we?"

"Maybe not the way you want. But you'll find answers. You always do."

I stared at those distant peaks, wondering what secrets they still held. Wondering if Austin was alive somewhere in that vast wilderness, living among the creatures he'd gone to find. Or if he'd died there, another victim of the mystery that had consumed so many lives.

"I'm not done," I said. "This isn't the end."

"I know. It's never the end with you."

I smiled despite the ache in my chest. "That's why you love me."

"One of the reasons."

We walked back to the vehicles together, leaving the mountains behind. For now.

34

THE BROADCAST

The documentary aired on a Tuesday night in October, exactly one year after the fire that had destroyed our home.

I watched from the new house we'd built on the same property. Bigger than the one they'd burned. Stronger. Designed to last. The recording studio was in a separate building now, fireproofed and backed up to servers in three different states. They could burn it down again. It wouldn't matter. The work would survive.

Daniel sat beside me, his hand in mine, as the credits rolled and the first episode began.

* * *

"Across America, there are those who have seen things they cannot explain..."

Amanda's voice, rich and measured, filled the living room. Images of wilderness filled the screen—the Olympic Peninsula, the Ozarks, the Pisgah, all the places we'd visited over the past year. Then the faces of witnesses, one after another, sharing their stories.

Earl Hutchins. Bobby Dean Carver. Margaret Lindqvist. Samuel

Jackson. Dr. Rebecca Henley. Dozens of others whose encounters we'd documented, whose voices deserved to be heard.

The fire was included—the ruins of our home, the accelerant patterns, the evidence of arson that law enforcement had ignored. Amanda had framed it as what it was: an attempt to silence the truth. An attempt that had failed.

The Mount St. Helens documents featured prominently in the third episode. The classified Project Vulcan files. The witness testimonies about recovered bodies. Dr. Henley's account of treating a dying specimen in a military hospital. Evidence of a cover-up that stretched back decades.

And the final episode showed our expedition to the Pisgah. The vocalizations in the night. The thermal signatures moving through the trees. The footprints with their dermal ridges and anatomical precision.

No definitive footage of a creature. No face-to-face contact captured on camera. But something more valuable, in its way. A pattern. A weight of evidence that added up to something undeniable.

"After a hundred and fifty years of sightings," Amanda's voice concluded, "after thousands of witnesses and countless attempts at documentation, one question remains. What is hiding in the forests of North America? The evidence we've gathered cannot answer that question definitively. But it can tell us this: something is there. Something real. Something that has shared this continent with us for longer than we know. And perhaps it's time we started listening."

* * *

The response was overwhelming.

Within the first hour, social media exploded. Within the first week, the documentary had been viewed over twenty million times. Within the first month, it had sparked a national conversation about what was hiding in our wilderness.

Not everyone believed. The skeptics were as vocal as ever, dismissing the evidence, attacking the witnesses, explaining away every data point. That was fine. That was how it had to be. Science didn't advance through blind acceptance. It advanced through rigorous debate, through challenge, through the slow accumulation of evidence that eventually became undeniable.

But for every skeptic, there were others who reached out. Scientists who'd been afraid to pursue the subject, now emboldened by the documentary's success. Witnesses who'd kept their stories secret for decades, finally finding the courage to speak. Researchers who'd worked in isolation, now discovering a community of others who shared their conviction.

The podcast grew. Ten million downloads per episode. Then twenty million. The forum membership exploded, becoming a hub for researchers and witnesses around the world.

And the threats continued. More visits from the men in black. More pressure from unnamed government sources. More attempts to discredit, to silence, to suppress.

We weathered it all. We'd learned to expect it by now. Every attack was a sign that we were doing something right, that we were getting close to something they didn't want revealed.

* * *

Six months after the broadcast, I received a visit from Agent Monica Brown.

She came to the house on a Sunday morning, looking exhausted but determined. The investigation into the fire had been officially closed—inconclusive, they'd called it, despite the evidence she'd gathered.

"I'm sorry," she said. "I tried. But there are walls I can't get past. People with more power than I have, who want this to go away."

"I know. Thank you for trying."

"I'm not done." She handed me a thumb drive. "This is everything I've collected. The evidence from the fire, but also other things. Files I've come across in my work. Cases that were buried, witnesses who were silenced. There's a pattern, Mr. Patterson. A systematic effort to suppress this subject that goes back to the 1950s at least. Maybe further."

"Why are you giving this to me?"

"Because you're the one who'll do something with it. You've proven that. You don't stop." She smiled tiredly. "I can't fight them from inside the system. But you can fight them from outside. Take this. Tell the stories they don't want told."

After she left, I sat for a long time, looking at the thumb drive. Another piece of the puzzle. Another thread in the vast web of secrecy and cover-up that I'd been unraveling for years.

The work was never done. The truth was never fully revealed. But piece by piece, story by story, we were getting closer.

The podcast continues. The documentary has been renewed for a second season. The community grows larger every day, united by shared experiences and a common purpose.

I still don't have all the answers. I still don't know what happened to Austin Reeves. I still don't know the full extent of the government's knowledge, or why they've worked so hard to keep these creatures hidden.

But I know more than I did when I was twelve years old, standing in a moonlit hollow in Georgia, seeing something that would change my life forever.

I know they're real. I know they've been here longer than we have. I know they're intelligent, perhaps more intelligent than we give them credit for. And I know that someday, somehow, the truth will come out completely.

Not through me alone. Through all of us who have seen, who have believed, who have refused to be silenced. Through the witnesses who share their stories and the researchers who collect the evidence and the ordinary people who simply refuse to accept that the official denials can be the whole truth.

We're building something. A record. A testament. A foundation for the day when the questions will finally be answered.

That day may not come in my lifetime. But it will come.

I believe that now more than I've ever believed anything.

* * *

Daniel is calling me for dinner. The smell of his cooking drifts through the house—something with garlic and herbs, probably. He's gotten good at this over the years, finding ways to ground me when I get too lost in the work, too consumed by the questions that never fully resolve.

I'll close my laptop and go join him. We'll eat together, talk about nothing and everything, fall asleep in each other's arms like we have for the past decade.

And tomorrow, I'll start again. Another interview. Another story. Another small piece of the truth, added to the vast tapestry we're weaving.

The odyssey continues.

It always will.

PART V

DEEPER INTO THE MYSTERY

35

THE WEIGHT OF STORIES

The frustration didn't end with Derek Fontaine.

As the podcast grew, so did the volume of questionable accounts. For every genuine witness who reached out, there seemed to be three or four others whose stories fell apart under even basic scrutiny. Some were obvious fabrications—people who'd clearly researched existing cases and cobbled together elements to create their own "encounters." Others were more troubling: sincere individuals whose memories had been shaped by expectation, by media consumption, by the powerful human need to be part of something larger than themselves.

Learning to distinguish between these categories became an essential skill. I developed a mental checklist: Did the details remain consistent across multiple tellings? Did the witness seem more interested in the experience itself or in the attention it might bring? Were there specific, verifiable elements—a date, a location, a corroborating witness—or was everything conveniently vague?

Most importantly: did the story ring true? After hundreds of interviews, I'd developed an instinct for authenticity. It wasn't foolproof, but it helped me navigate the endless stream of accounts that flooded my inbox.

* * *

One week in particular tested my patience to its limits.

On Monday, I interviewed a woman from Oregon who claimed she'd been communicating telepathically with a family of Sasquatch for the past fifteen years. The creatures, she said, had taught her their language and shared with her the secrets of the universe. When I asked for any verifiable detail—a location, a physical description, something that could be confirmed—she became evasive, insisting that the creatures had forbidden her from sharing such information with "non-believers."

On Tuesday, it was a teenager from Texas who'd clearly watched too many horror movies. His "encounter" featured elements lifted directly from three different films I recognized, complete with dialogue that sounded like it had been written by a screenwriter with a loose grip on reality.

On Wednesday, a retired professor from Michigan spent two hours explaining his theory that Sasquatch were actually time travelers from the future, sent back to observe humanity's final centuries before extinction. He had charts. He had equations. He had absolutely no evidence whatsoever.

By Thursday, I was ready to quit.

* * *

Daniel found me in the studio, staring at my computer screen, the cursor blinking on an unsent email that would have told my next scheduled interviewee that I was canceling.

"Bad week?" he asked, setting a cup of coffee beside me.

"The worst. I feel like I'm drowning in nonsense. For every real story, there are a dozen fantasies. And I can't shake the feeling that I'm wasting my time—that no matter how many genuine encounters I document, they'll always be buried under a mountain of garbage."

Daniel pulled up a chair and sat down beside me. "Remember why you started this."

"To give witnesses a voice. To document the truth."

"And you're doing that. Every episode, you're doing exactly that."

"But the noise—"

"The noise is the price of admission. You can't reach the real witnesses without wading through the fakes. It's frustrating, but it's necessary." He put his hand on my shoulder. "You've helped hundreds of people tell their stories. Hundreds of real people with real experiences who felt validated for the first time in their lives. That matters. That's worth the frustration."

I looked at the email I'd been about to send. At the name of the next interviewee—a woman from Georgia named Lucille Marsh who'd written a heartfelt letter about an encounter she'd had as a child in the 1950s. She'd never told anyone, she said. She was eighty-two years old and wanted to share her story before it was too late.

I deleted the cancellation and wrote a different message: "Looking forward to our conversation tomorrow."

* * *

Lucille Marsh turned out to be one of the most memorable interviews I ever conducted.

Her voice was soft but clear, carrying the weight of decades and the careful precision of a generation that valued truth. She'd grown up on a farm in rural Georgia, not far from where I'd had my own encounter in Lyerly—a coincidence that made me lean forward in my chair as she began to speak.

"It was the summer of 1953," Lucille said. "I was nine years old. We had a farm about twenty miles outside of Rome, Georgia. Cotton mostly, some corn, a few dairy cows. My daddy worked that land from sunup to sundown, and us children helped however we could."

"Tell me about the encounter."

"Well, it was late August, I remember that much. The cotton was coming in good that year, and Daddy had hired some extra hands to help with the harvest. I'd been sent to fetch water from the spring—we had a natural spring about a quarter mile from the house, back in a little hollow where the trees grew thick."

"What happened at the spring?"

"I was filling my bucket when I heard something moving in the brush. At first, I thought it was a deer—we had plenty of them around —so I stayed still and quiet, hoping to see it. But what stepped out from those trees wasn't any deer."

"Can you describe it?"

"It was tall. Taller than any man I'd ever seen, even taller than Mr. Henderson who ran the general store in town and stood six foot five if he was an inch. But this thing was broader too. Massive shoulders, long arms, covered head to toe in dark brown hair. And the face—" She paused. "The face was almost human. Almost. But there was something different about it. Something old. Something that looked at me like it knew things I couldn't even imagine."

"What did it do?"

"Nothing, at first. We just stood there, maybe twenty feet apart, looking at each other. I was terrified, of course. Nine years old, alone in the woods, facing something that shouldn't exist. But there was something else too. Curiosity, maybe. Or wonder. I remember thinking that this must be what the Bible meant when it talked about giants in the earth."

"How long did the encounter last?"

"A minute, maybe two. It felt like forever. And then it did something I'll never forget. It reached down and picked up a stone—just a regular river stone, smooth and round—and it held it out toward me. Like it was offering me a gift."

"Did you take it?"

"I was too scared. I just stood there, frozen. And after a while, it set the stone down on a big flat rock by the spring, turned around, and walked back into the trees. Didn't run. Just walked. Calm as could be."

"What did you do then?"

"I grabbed my bucket and ran home as fast as my legs would carry me. Didn't tell nobody what I'd seen—who would have believed me?

A little girl claiming she'd seen a monster in the woods? They would have thought I was touched in the head."

"Did you ever go back to the spring?"

"Every day. I had to—that was my chore, fetching water. But I never saw the creature again. What I did see, though, was the stone. It stayed right there on that flat rock for years. Nobody moved it, nobody touched it. It was like a reminder. A sign that what I'd seen was real."

"Do you still have the stone?"

Lucille was quiet for a moment. Then: "I do. When we sold the farm in 1972, I went back to that spring one last time. The stone was still there, right where the creature had left it. I picked it up and took it with me. I've had it ever since."

"Could you describe it?"

"It's nothing special to look at. Just a river stone, gray with some white streaks. About the size of an egg. But when I hold it—" Her voice caught. "When I hold it, I feel connected to something. Something old and wise and far beyond my understanding. It's like holding a piece of that creature, a piece of that moment, a piece of the truth that I've carried with me for seventy years."

Lucille's interview reminded me why I did this work.

Not for the dramatic encounters or the sensational stories. For the quiet moments. For the people like Lucille who'd carried these experiences in silence for decades, waiting for someone to believe them. For the truth that existed beneath all the noise, patient and persistent, waiting to be heard.

I asked Lucille if she'd be willing to share a photograph of the stone, and she agreed. When the image arrived in my email the next day, I stared at it for a long time. An ordinary river stone, smooth and gray, unremarkable in every way.

Except for what it represented.

A moment of contact. A gift offered and eventually accepted. A connection across species, across decades, across the vast gulf that separated humans from the creatures we were only beginning to understand.

I saved the image and added it to the episode. And when the response came in—hundreds of messages from people who'd been moved by Lucille's story, who'd been inspired by her courage in finally speaking up—I knew that the frustration was worth it.

Every time.

36

ENCOUNTERS IN THE HEARTLAND

The Midwest interviews brought a different flavor to the podcast. The Southeast had its swamps and hollows, the Pacific Northwest had its ancient forests, but the American heartland had something unique: farmland that butted up against remnant woodlands, small towns surrounded by fields that stretched to the horizon, and people whose matter-of-fact approach to life extended even to the impossible.

"I'm not the type to make things up," said Harold Gustafson, a seventy-three-year-old dairy farmer from Wisconsin. "Ask anyone who knows me. Thirty years on the county board, forty years running this farm. I don't have time for nonsense."

"But you saw something."

"I saw something. October of 2003. I was out in the barn around four in the morning, starting the milking. The cows were agitated—wouldn't settle down, kept looking toward the back of the barn where the doors were open to the paddock."

"What did you find?"

"At first, nothing. I walked back to check, thinking maybe a coyote had spooked them. But when I looked out into the paddock, I saw it.

Standing right there by the fence line, maybe fifty yards away. Massive thing, had to be eight feet tall. Just standing there, watching the barn."

"Could you see it clearly?"

"Clear enough. The yard light was on, and the moon was up. It was covered in dark hair, standing upright like a man. When it saw me looking, it turned and walked toward the tree line. Didn't run. Just walked. And it stepped right over the fence—a four-foot fence, and it didn't even break stride. Just stepped over it like it was nothing."

"Did you report the sighting?"

"To who? The sheriff would've laughed me out of his office. My wife thought I was seeing things. My kids still think I made it up to get attention." Harold's voice hardened. "But I know what I saw. Sixty years of farming, and I've never seen anything like it. Bears don't walk upright. Deer don't clear four-foot fences without jumping. Whatever that thing was, it wasn't from around here."

"Have you seen it since?"

"Not seen. But I've found things. Tracks in the mud by the creek, way too big for any person. Deer carcasses in the woods with the bones cracked open for marrow—and I mean cracked, like someone hit them with a hammer. Something's been living in those woods for years. Maybe decades. And until you called, I never had anyone to tell."

* * *

From Iowa, I interviewed a woman named Constance Meyer who'd had an encounter while driving home from a late shift at the hospital where she worked as a nurse.

"It was December, 2011," Constance said. "Snowing hard, visibility maybe a hundred feet. I was on County Road 14, about five miles from my house. That stretch goes through a river bottom—lots of timber, not many houses."

"What happened?"

"Something ran across the road in front of me. I had to slam on my brakes to avoid hitting it. At first I thought it was a deer, but then I realized it was running on two legs. And it was huge—when it reached the other side of the road, it had to duck under a branch that I know was at least seven feet off the ground."

"Did you get a good look at it?"

"Only for a second. My headlights caught it as it crossed. Brown hair, massive build, arms that hung down past its knees. And fast—God, it was fast. It covered that two-lane highway in maybe three strides."

"What did you do?"

"I sat there in my car, shaking, trying to convince myself I hadn't seen what I'd just seen. Then I drove home as fast as the snow would let me and didn't tell anyone for years. I was a nurse. I was supposed to be rational, scientific. If I started talking about Bigfoot, people would have thought I'd lost my mind."

"Why are you talking about it now?"

"Because I found your podcast. Because I heard other people telling stories just like mine. Because I realized I wasn't crazy—that this thing, whatever it is, is real. And if I can help other people understand that, help them feel less alone, then maybe something good can come out of what scared the hell out of me on that road."

* * *

From Nebraska, I spoke with a rancher named Bill Thornton whose family had been reporting encounters for three generations.

"My grandfather saw them back in the thirties," Bill said. "My father saw them in the sixties. And I've seen them twice—once in 1987, once in 2019. Whatever these things are, they've been on this land longer than my family has."

"Tell me about your encounters."

"The first one, I was sixteen. Working cattle in the sandhills, north pasture. It was evening, getting dark. I was on horseback, pushing some strays back toward the main herd, when my horse spooked. Just stopped dead and wouldn't go forward, no matter what I did."

"What was spooking the horse?"

"I didn't see it at first. Just felt something watching. You know that feeling? Like eyes on the back of your neck? I looked around, and that's when I spotted it—standing in a draw about a hundred yards away, half-hidden by the tall grass. Watching me."

"Can you describe it?"

"Tall. Brown. Shaped like a man but bigger. It was getting dark, so I couldn't see details. But I saw enough to know it wasn't a bear or a cow or anything else that belonged out there. And the way it stood—so still, so patient—it was like it was waiting to see what I'd do."

"What did you do?"

"I turned that horse around and rode like hell back to the house. Told my father what I'd seen. He didn't laugh, didn't call me crazy. Just nodded and said, 'They've been here a long time. Leave them alone and they'll leave you alone.' That was it. End of discussion."

"And the second encounter?"

"2019. I was driving the ranch road at night, coming back from checking on a sick heifer. Something crossed in front of my truck—big, bipedal, moving fast. I stopped and got out, shined my spotlight into the grass. Nothing there. But I could hear it moving, circling around behind me. And I could smell it—that smell everyone talks about, like a dead animal and a wet dog had a baby."

"Were you afraid?"

"Not really. Cautious, maybe. But I remembered what my father said. Leave them alone and they'll leave you alone. So I got back in my truck and drove home. Haven't seen anything since, but I know they're still out there. They've always been out there. And they always will be."

* * *

The heartland interviews revealed something important: these creatures weren't confined to wilderness areas. They'd adapted to agricultural landscapes, living in the margins—the river bottoms, the woodlots, the wild places that existed between the fields. They'd learned to coexist with human activity, staying hidden, watching from the edges, making themselves known only when circumstances forced their hand.

It was a testament to their intelligence. Their adaptability. Their determination to survive in a world that was increasingly hostile to anything wild.

And it made me wonder: how many other places had they colonized without anyone noticing? How many encounters had happened and been dismissed, forgotten, buried under the weight of rational denial?

The answer, I was beginning to realize, was more than anyone could count.

37

——————

STRANGE ENCOUNTERS

Not all encounters fit neatly into categories.

Some of the most compelling stories I documented were also the strangest—accounts that went beyond simple sightings, that suggested these creatures had abilities and behaviors we couldn't begin to explain.

* * *

From the mountains of North Carolina—my own backyard—I interviewed a man named Walter Price whose experience still gave me chills.

"I was camping alone in the Nantahala," Walter said. His voice was steady, but I could hear the tension underneath. "October of 2016. I'd been out for three days, hadn't seen another person the whole time. That was the point—I wanted solitude, wanted to get away from everything."

"What happened?"

"The third night, I woke up around two in the morning. Don't know what woke me—no sound, no movement. Just this feeling, like something had changed. I lay there in my tent, listening, and that's when I realized the forest had gone completely silent. No insects. No owls. Nothing."

"What did you do?"

"I unzipped the tent flap and looked out. The moon was up, almost full, so I could see pretty well. And standing about thirty feet from my tent, right at the edge of the trees, was a creature. Huge. Seven feet tall, maybe more. Just standing there, watching me."

"What did it do?"

"Nothing. At first. We just stared at each other. I was too scared to move, too scared to breathe. And then—" Walter stopped. Started again. "Then something happened that I can't explain. I started seeing things. Images, in my head. Like someone was showing me a movie, except it was playing behind my eyes."

"What kind of images?"

"The forest. But not the way it is now. The way it was before. Before the roads, before the logging, before any of it. I saw trees that were hundreds of feet tall. I saw animals I didn't recognize—huge things, like nothing that exists today. And I saw them. The creatures. Dozens of them, living in those ancient woods, part of an ecosystem we've destroyed."

"You're saying the creature showed you this?"

"I'm saying I saw it. Whether it showed me or I imagined it, I don't know. But it felt real. More real than the tent I was sitting in, more real than anything I'd experienced before. It was like I was there, in that ancient forest, seeing through eyes that weren't my own."

"How long did it last?"

"I don't know. Seconds, maybe. Or hours. Time didn't work right while it was happening. When it stopped, the creature was gone. The forest sounds were back. And I was sitting in my tent, shaking, trying to understand what had just happened to me."

"Have you had any experiences since?"

"No. But I think about it every day. I see those images when I close my eyes. The ancient forest. The creatures. The world that used to be." Walter's voice grew quiet. "I think it was trying to tell me something.

Show me what we've lost. What we're still losing. Like a warning, or a plea. Like it wanted me to understand."

* * *

From Oregon, I interviewed a woman named Jennifer Blackwood who'd had an encounter that challenged everything I thought I knew about these creatures.

"I was hiking in the Cascades with my daughter," Jennifer said. "She was eight at the time. We were on a popular trail—nothing remote, nothing dangerous. Families everywhere."

"What happened?"

"Emma—my daughter—wandered off. Just for a minute, while I was checking my phone. When I looked up, she was gone. I panicked, started calling her name, running down the trail. Other hikers helped me search. We couldn't find her anywhere."

"How long was she missing?"

"About forty-five minutes. The longest forty-five minutes of my life. I was convinced something terrible had happened. We were about to call search and rescue when she walked out from the trees, calm as could be, like nothing was wrong."

"Where had she been?"

"That's what I asked her. And what she told me—" Jennifer's voice caught. "She said she'd been playing with a 'big furry man.' She said he'd found her crying in the woods and stayed with her, keeping her company, showing her animals and plants. When she was ready to come back, he'd brought her to the edge of the trees and pointed her toward the trail."

"Did she describe this creature?"

"She said he was tall—taller than Daddy, and my husband is six foot two. She said he was covered in brown fur and had kind eyes. She said he smelled bad but was very gentle, and that he made sounds she didn't understand but somehow knew meant 'don't be afraid.'"

"Did you believe her?"

"I wanted to think she'd imagined it. A child's fantasy, a way of coping with being lost. But there were things she couldn't have known. She described the smell—that specific, unmistakable smell that everyone reports. She described the way he walked, the length of his arms, details that match accounts from witnesses around the world. And she had hair on her jacket. Long, reddish-brown hair that didn't match any animal we could identify."

"What happened to the hair?"

"I kept it. Had it analyzed by a friend who works in a lab. The results were inconclusive—they couldn't identify what species it came from. Not bear, not human, not any known primate. Just... unknown."

"How has this affected your daughter?"

"She's not afraid of the woods. Most kids who get lost, they develop a fear of being alone in nature. Not Emma. She loves hiking, loves camping, talks about her 'friend' sometimes when she thinks I'm not listening. She's not traumatized. If anything, she's... grateful. Like she understands something the rest of us don't."

* * *

These strange encounters suggested something profound: the creatures weren't simply animals hiding in the wilderness. They had intelligence, perhaps even compassion. They could communicate in ways we didn't understand. They had a history, a culture, a perspective on the world that we were only beginning to glimpse.

And they were watching us. Not as predators watch prey, but as neighbors watch neighbors. Keeping track. Staying aware. Waiting for something.

What that something was, I still didn't know. But I was getting closer to understanding.

38

———

THE HOAXERS AND
THE TRUE BELIEVERS

Running the podcast meant dealing with people who wanted to deceive me.

Some were obvious—the attention-seekers, the compulsive liars, the people who'd fabricated encounters for reasons I couldn't fathom. But others were more sophisticated, more dangerous. People who'd created elaborate hoaxes, complete with fake evidence and rehearsed stories, hoping to discredit the entire field by getting exposed.

I learned to spot them. The details that were too perfect. The willingness to show evidence before being asked. The stories that hit every expected beat without any of the messiness that characterized real encounters.

But sometimes, even I was fooled.

* * *

The Thompson case nearly destroyed my credibility.

Gerald Thompson was a retired biology professor from California who reached out with what seemed like the most compelling evidence I'd ever encountered. He had photographs—clear, detailed photographs of a creature in the forest. He had hair samples, footprint casts, audio recordings of vocalizations. He had documentation going back years, carefully compiled with scientific rigor.

I interviewed him twice before the episode aired. His story was consistent, his credentials were real, and his evidence was extraordinary. I was convinced I'd found the smoking gun—proof so solid that even the skeptics would have to pay attention.

The episode went live on a Friday.

By Monday, it had all fallen apart.

A group of researchers in California had been tracking Thompson for years, documenting his increasingly elaborate hoaxes. The photographs were clever fakes—a suit he'd designed himself, worn by a friend. The hair samples were from a black bear, treated with chemicals to alter their appearance. The footprint casts were made from wooden molds he'd carved in his workshop.

It was all fake. Every piece of it.

* * *

I pulled the episode immediately and recorded a retraction. But the damage was done. Skeptics pointed to the Thompson case as proof that I was credulous, that the entire podcast was built on wishful thinking and poor judgment. Downloads dropped. Sponsors pulled out. The community fractured, with some members defending me and others accusing me of betraying their trust.

It was the lowest point of my podcasting career.

Daniel found me in the studio at three in the morning, staring at my computer screen, reading the comments that tore apart everything I'd built.

"Come to bed," he said.

"I can't. I ruined everything."

"You made a mistake. That's not the same as ruining everything."

"I gave a platform to a hoaxer. I validated his lies. Every genuine witness who's ever trusted me—I made them look like fools by association."

Daniel sat down beside me. "You know what I see when I look at those comments? I see people who care. People who are angry because this matters to them. That's not a sign of failure. That's a sign that you've built something worth caring about."

"But—"

"You caught the mistake. You admitted it publicly. You took responsibility. That's more than most people would do. And the genuine witnesses—the hundreds of people whose stories you've shared—they're still real. Thompson's lies don't change their truth."

I wanted to argue. Wanted to wallow in the failure. But Daniel was right. He usually was.

"What do I do now?"

"You keep going. You improve your vetting process. You learn from the mistake. And you remember why you started this in the first place."

I looked at him—this man who'd stood beside me through everything, who'd never wavered in his support, who believed in me even when I didn't believe in myself.

"I love you," I said.

"I know. Now come to bed. Tomorrow, you rebuild."

* * *

The rebuilding took months.

I implemented new verification procedures—multiple interviews, background checks, independent analysis of any physical evidence. I brought in consultants to review claims before they went on air. I created a system of peer review within the community, allowing experienced researchers to flag potential problems.

Slowly, the trust returned. The downloads recovered. The sponsors came back. And the podcast emerged stronger than before, with a reputation for rigor that it lacked previously.

The Thompson case had nearly destroyed me. Instead, it made me better.

And when the next hoaxer came along—and they did, regularly—I was ready for them.

* * *

Not everyone who reached out was a hoaxer, of course. Most were genuine—people with real experiences, seeking validation and connection. Some became regulars in the community, contributing their knowledge and supporting others who came after them.

One such person was Benjamin Crow Feather, a Lakota elder from South Dakota who'd spent his life documenting encounters among the Sioux people.

"We call them the Big Man," Benjamin said, during an interview that lasted nearly three hours. "They've been part of our stories since before memory. The elders say they're guardians of the wild places—protectors of the land and the animals that live there."

"Have you had personal encounters?"

"Many times. The first when I was seven years old, the most recent just last month. They know me. I think they know anyone who pays attention, who respects the old ways, who understands that we share this world with beings we don't fully understand."

"What have these encounters taught you?"

"Humility, mostly. We think we're the masters of this world, but we're not. We're just one species among many, trying to survive. The Big Man have survived for thousands of years by staying hidden, by adapting, by understanding things we've forgotten. If we were wise, we'd learn from them."

"What do you think they want?"

"To be left alone, mostly. But also to be acknowledged. To be respected. They've watched us destroy so much of the world they love. I think they're waiting to see if we'll come to our senses before it's too late."

"And if we don't?"

Benjamin was quiet for a long moment. "Then they'll outlast us. They've survived ice ages and extinctions and the rise and fall of civilizations. They'll survive whatever we do to ourselves. The question is whether we'll survive with them, or whether we'll just be another species that couldn't adapt."

His words stayed with me long after the interview ended. A reminder of what was at stake. A reminder of why this work mattered.

The hoaxers could try to discredit us. The skeptics could deny the evidence. But the truth remained, patient and persistent, waiting to be heard.

And I would keep listening.

39

____

ENCOUNTERS ACROSS THE WORLD

The international expansion of the podcast brought stories I never could have anticipated.

While the North American encounters were the most numerous, reports from other continents added depth and complexity to my understanding. These creatures—or beings like them—existed everywhere. On every continent except Antarctica, in environments ranging from tropical rainforests to frozen tundra, people were reporting encounters with large, bipedal, hair-covered beings that defied easy explanation.

* * *

From the mountains of Tibet, I interviewed a monk named Tenzin Wangchuk who'd lived his entire life in a monastery near the Himalayan snow line.

"The Yeti is not a beast," Tenzin said, his English careful and precise. "It is a being. A sentient creature with a soul, capable of enlightenment like any human. Our scriptures speak of them as guardians of the high places—watchers who observe humanity's progress and report to forces beyond our understanding."

"Have you encountered them?"

"I have seen them many times. They visit the monastery some-times, in the depths of winter when the snow makes the paths impass-able. They watch from the ridges, ensuring we are safe. Once, when I was a young novice, one came close enough that I could see its eyes. There was wisdom in those eyes. Compassion. An understanding of suffering that surpassed even the oldest lamas."

"Do the other monks speak of these encounters?"

"We do not need to speak. We all know. The Yeti are part of our world, have always been part of our world. To deny their existence would be like denying the mountains themselves."

* * *

From the Congo Basin, I spoke with a conservation biologist named Dr. Marie Lukamba who'd been researching reports of the Nguma-monene—a creature described in local traditions as a massive, hair-covered being that lived in the deepest parts of the rainforest.

"Western science dismisses these reports," Dr. Lukamba said. "They assume the indigenous peoples are superstitious, that they're confusing known animals with mythological beings. But I've inter-viewed hundreds of witnesses over the past fifteen years. Their descriptions are consistent. Their details are specific. They're not making this up."

"What have you found?"

"Tracks, primarily. Footprints that don't match any known primate —too large for gorillas, shaped wrong for chimps. Hair samples that can't be identified. Audio recordings of vocalizations that don't match any documented species. The evidence is there. It's just that no one in the scientific establishment wants to look at it."

"Why do you think that is?"

"Fear, mostly. Fear of ridicule. Fear of career damage. Fear of having to admit that the world is stranger than our models allow. Scien-tists are supposed to be open-minded, but in practice, we're as dogmatic as anyone. If something doesn't fit our paradigm, we ignore it."

"But you haven't ignored it."

"I can't. I've seen too much. I know what's out there, even if I can't prove it to the satisfaction of peer reviewers. And I'll keep looking, keep documenting, keep gathering evidence. Someday, the truth will be undeniable. I just hope I'm still around to see it."

* * *

From the remote highlands of Papua New Guinea, I interviewed a missionary named Father Patrick O'Brien who'd served in the country for over forty years.

"The local people call them the Mumu," Father Patrick said. "They're part of the spiritual landscape here—beings that exist at the boundary between the natural and the supernatural. I was skeptical at first, as any rational Westerner would be. But I've lived here long enough to know that my skepticism was misplaced."

"What convinced you?"

"I saw one. In 1987, while traveling between villages on foot. It was standing on a ridge above the trail, watching me. Massive—easily seven feet tall, covered in dark hair. It made no threatening moves, just observed. When I reached for my camera, it disappeared into the bush. I've never seen anything move that fast."

"How did the local people react when you told them?"

"They weren't surprised. They told me I'd been blessed—that the Mumu had chosen to reveal itself to me. They said it meant I was meant to stay, to be part of their community. And I have. Forty years now. I'll die here, among people who understand things about the world that my seminary training never prepared me for."

* * *

From the vast forests of Siberia, I connected with a researcher named Dr. Igor Ivanov who'd been studying the Almasty—Russia's version of Bigfoot—for over fifty years.

"The Soviet government suppressed our research," Dr. Ivanov said, his voice crackling through the poor connection. "They didn't want evidence of unknown primates—it contradicted the materialist ideology. But we continued in secret. We documented hundreds of encounters. We collected evidence that would have revolutionized our understanding of evolution."

"What happened to that evidence?"

"Some was destroyed. Some was buried in archives that no one can access. Some I've preserved myself, at great personal risk. When the Soviet Union collapsed, I thought the truth would finally come out. But the new Russia has its own reasons for suppression. The powerful don't want people asking questions they can't answer."

"What do you believe these creatures are?"

"I believe they're a relict population of hominids—perhaps Neanderthals, perhaps something older. They've survived in the remote places of the world, avoiding detection through intelligence and caution. They are our cousins, in a sense. Branches of the same evolutionary tree that diverged long ago."

"Do you think they'll ever be officially recognized?"

"In my lifetime? Probably not. But the evidence is mounting. The witnesses are speaking. Someday, the scientific establishment will have no choice but to acknowledge what people like us have known for decades. The Almasty are real. They've always been real. And no amount of denial can change that."

The international interviews painted a picture of a global phenomenon.

These creatures—whatever they were, wherever they lived—were part of the human experience. Every culture had stories about them. Every remote region had witnesses. The details varied, but the core remained the same: large, bipedal, intelligent beings that had shared this planet with humanity for millennia.

We weren't alone. We'd never been alone. And perhaps, if we were wise, we could learn to coexist with these ancient neighbors before it was too late.

40

DANIEL'S QUIET STRENGTH

Through all of it—the growth, the setbacks, the triumphs and failures—Daniel remained my anchor.

He'd found his rhythm at Mountain Pies, rising through the ranks from assistant manager to general manager within two years. The Hartley family had come to rely on him, trusting him to run the restaurant while they focused on expansion plans for a second location.

"I never thought I'd be passionate about pizza," he told me one evening, as we sat on the porch watching the sunset. "But there's something satisfying about it. Making something with your hands that brings people joy. No existential threats, no government conspiracies. Just dough and sauce and cheese."

"You don't miss the excitement?"

"I miss some things. The sense of purpose. The feeling that what we were doing mattered. But I don't miss the fear. I don't miss wondering if tonight was the night someone would come for us." He took my hand. "I get to come home to you every day. I get to sleep without nightmares. That's worth more than excitement."

"I'm sorry for putting you through all that."

"Don't be. I chose this. I chose you. And I'd make the same choice again, every time." He squeezed my hand. "Besides, the podcast is doing important work. Changing lives. Changing the world. I'm proud to be part of it, even from the sidelines."

"You're not on the sidelines. You're what keeps me going."

"Well, then. I guess we're both doing important work."

* * *

Daniel's steadiness manifested in a thousand small ways.

He was the one who reminded me to eat when I got lost in research. The one who insisted I take breaks, go for walks, remember that there was a world beyond the studio and the screen. The one who held me when the weight of what I'd learned became too heavy to carry alone.

He was also the one who kept me honest.

"You're getting too close to this interview," he'd say sometimes, reading over my notes. "You want to believe them, but the story doesn't add up."

Or: "This one's real. I can feel it. Don't let your skepticism get in the way."

He had good instincts—better than mine, sometimes. He could sense authenticity in ways that my analytical mind missed. He understood people in a way that I, with my law enforcement background, often didn't.

"You see criminals and victims," he explained once. "I see humans. Flawed, complicated, trying to make sense of experiences that don't fit the world they thought they knew. It's the same whether they're telling the truth or lying—they're all just people, doing the best they can."

* * *

One evening, Daniel came home with news that surprised me.

"The Hartleys want to open a second location," he said. "And they want me to run it."

"That's great. Congratulations."

"There's a catch. The location they're considering is in Asheville. About an hour away."

I felt a chill. "You'd be commuting?"

"That's what I told them I'd need to think about. An hour each way is a lot. But the opportunity—" He shook his head. "It's a chance to build something from the ground up. To have real ownership, even without the title."

"What do you want to do?"

"I don't know. Part of me wants to stay here, close to you, close to what we've built. Part of me wants to take the leap, see what I'm capable of." He looked at me. "What do you think?"

I thought about it. About the hours we'd lose to driving. About the evenings he'd come home exhausted. About the strain it might put on our relationship.

But I also thought about his face when he talked about the restaurant. The pride. The purpose. The joy of creating something meaningful.

"I think you should do it," I said. "I think you'd regret it if you didn't."

"Even if it means seeing less of each other?"

"We've survived worse. We'll figure it out."

Daniel's eyes glistened. "I love you, you know that?"

"I know. Now go call the Hartleys before you talk yourself out of it."

He kissed me and reached for his phone. And I watched him, this man who'd given up so much to stand beside me, finally getting something that was just his.

* * *

The Asheville location opened six months later.

Daniel threw himself into the work—designing the menu, hiring staff, building relationships with local suppliers. The commute was brutal, but he came home energized rather than drained, full of stories about the challenges he'd faced and the victories he'd won.

"We had a line out the door tonight," he'd tell me. "A line. For pizza. I've never seen anything like it."

Or: "One of the cooks quit without notice, so I had to run the kitchen myself for eight hours. My feet are killing me, but we didn't miss a single order."

Or: "A food blogger came in tonight. She's going to write a review. I'm trying not to panic."

The review was glowing. The restaurant became a local sensation. And Daniel, who'd spent years in my shadow, finally had something that was entirely his own.

I couldn't have been prouder.

* * *

"We should get a place in Asheville," Daniel said one evening. "Just a small apartment. Somewhere I can crash on the late nights instead of driving home in the dark."

"Makes sense. Want me to help look?"

"Actually—" He hesitated. "I was thinking maybe we could look together. Make it our place. Somewhere we can be when I'm working, somewhere you can record when you need to be closer to the city."

"A second home?"

"A different kind of home. Not instead of here, just in addition. Expanding our life instead of shrinking it."

I thought about the house we'd built on the mountain. The studio where I'd recorded hundreds of episodes. The land where the creatures still sometimes watched from the tree line.

"Okay," I said. "Let's do it."

A month later, we signed the lease on a small apartment in West Asheville. Two bedrooms—one for sleeping, one for a portable studio setup. A kitchen where Daniel could experiment with recipes. A balcony with a view of the Blue Ridge Mountains.

It wasn't what I'd imagined when we'd moved to North Carolina. But life rarely was.

And as I stood on that balcony, watching the sun set over the mountains, I realized that this—all of this—was exactly where I was supposed to be.

41

THE COMMUNITY GROWS

By the fourth year, the *Sasquatch Odyssey* community had become something larger than I'd ever imagined.

What had started as a forum for podcast listeners had evolved into a global network of researchers, witnesses, and enthusiasts. There were local chapters in every state, discussion groups in a dozen languages, annual gatherings that brought together hundreds of people who'd never met in person but who'd been supporting each other for years.

The community had developed its own culture—inside jokes, shared references, a collective memory of the stories that had shaped us. People talked about "the Lucille episode" or "the Bobby Dean laugh" or "that time Brian almost quit." They remembered the Thompson hoax and how we'd recovered from it. They celebrated the genuine encounters that had moved us all to tears.

And they helped each other.

When a witness needed support, the community was there. When someone was struggling with the aftermath of an encounter—the fear, the doubt, the isolation—there were people ready to listen, to validate, to remind them that they weren't alone.

It was everything I'd hoped for when I'd started the podcast. And it had grown far beyond anything I could have achieved on my own.

* * *

The annual gathering became the highlight of the community's calendar.

We held it in different locations each year—the first in North Carolina, the second in Washington State, the third in the Arkansas Ozarks. Each gathering brought together a few hundred people for a long weekend of presentations, discussions, field expeditions, and connection.

I remember the fourth gathering particularly well. It was held in northern California, in a campground near the Klamath River. We'd rented the entire facility—cabins, meeting halls, everything. By the time the weekend started, nearly five hundred people had registered.

"This is incredible," Daniel said, as we watched people arriving from all over the world. "Look at them. Professors, construction workers, retirees, teenagers. Every background you can imagine."

"United by a shared experience," I said. "By a truth that most of the world still doesn't accept."

"Do you think the world will ever accept it?"

"I think it's getting closer. Every year, more evidence. More witnesses. More attention. The tide is turning."

"And when it finally turns?"

"Then our work will really begin."

* * *

The gathering's keynote speaker that year was a woman named Dr. Rebecca Henley, a primatologist from Stanford who'd risked her career to study Sasquatch evidence.

"I was taught that these creatures don't exist," Dr. Henley told the packed auditorium. "My professors, my colleagues, everyone in my field insisted the evidence was faked, the witnesses deluded. I believed them for a long time."

"What changed?"

"I saw the data. Not the tabloid stories or the blurry photographs—

the actual scientific data. Hair samples that can't be identified. Footprint casts that show dermal ridges impossible to fake. Audio recordings of vocalizations that don't match any known animal. The evidence is there. It's always been there. We've just been too afraid to look at it."

"What do you think these creatures are?"

"I don't know for certain. The evidence suggests a relict population of hominids—possibly a descendant of *Gigantopithecus*, possibly something else entirely. But whatever they are, they're real. They exist. And science's refusal to acknowledge them is one of the greatest failures of our age."

The audience gave her a standing ovation. Here was a mainstream scientist, risking everything to speak the truth. A sign that the walls were beginning to crack.

* * *

The field expeditions were always the highlight of the gatherings.

We'd organize groups to hike into areas with high concentrations of reported encounters, equipped with cameras, audio recorders, and thermal imaging equipment. Most expeditions found nothing—the creatures were too smart, too cautious to reveal themselves to groups of noisy humans.

But sometimes, we got lucky.

At the California gathering, a group of twelve researchers had a collective experience that none of them would ever forget.

"We were about three miles into the forest," reported Marcus Smith a software engineer from Seattle who'd become one of the community's most dedicated investigators. "It was getting dark, and we'd stopped to set up camp for the night. That's when we heard it."

"Heard what?"

"Wood knocking. Two distinct knocks, coming from maybe a hundred yards away. We knocked back, and immediately got a response—three knocks this time. We did this back and forth for about twenty minutes."

"Did you see anything?"

"Not clearly. But several of us saw movement in the trees—something large, watching from the shadows. And when the sun went down completely, we heard vocalizations. Howls, whoops, sounds I've never heard before. They went on for hours, circling the camp, moving through the forest around us."

"Were you afraid?"

"Terrified. And exhilarated. We were surrounded by creatures that the world says don't exist, and they were communicating with us. They were curious. Maybe even welcoming."

"How did the night end?"

"Around three in the morning, the sounds stopped. We heard something heavy moving away through the brush, and then silence. When the sun came up, we found tracks around the camp—multiple sets, different sizes. A family group, maybe. Watching over us while we slept."

The expedition report became one of the most viewed documents in the community's history. Twelve credible witnesses, multiple forms of evidence, a collective experience that couldn't be dismissed as individual delusion.

The proof was mounting. And someday, it would be undeniable.

* * *

The community also did important work beyond the gatherings.

Teams of volunteers compiled databases of encounters, mapping patterns and identifying hotspots. Researchers analyzed evidence using the latest scientific techniques. Writers documented everything, creating a permanent record that would survive whatever came next.

And perhaps most importantly, the community provided a space for witnesses to heal.

"Before I found you all, I thought I was going crazy," one member wrote in a forum post that was shared thousands of times. "I'd had this experience that I couldn't explain, and everyone I told thought I was lying or delusional. I carried that burden for years. Then I found the podcast, found the community, and realized I wasn't alone. There are thousands of us. Maybe millions. And we're not crazy. We're just people who've seen something the world isn't ready to believe yet."

That message captured everything we were trying to do. Not just documenting encounters, but helping people come to terms with experiences that didn't fit the world they thought they knew.

The creatures were real. The witnesses were valid. And together, we were building something that would change the world.

One story at a time.

42

SHADOWS RETURN

The men in black had been quiet for too long.

In the years since their last visit, I'd almost convinced myself they'd given up. The documentary had aired. The podcast had grown. The truth was spreading faster than they could contain it. Maybe, I thought, they'd decided I wasn't worth the effort. Maybe they'd moved on to other targets.

I should have known better.

* * *

The first sign was subtle: a podcast listener in Oregon reported being visited by "government officials" asking questions about how she'd found the show and what she thought of my claims. She'd refused to answer, and they'd left without incident. But she was shaken enough to report it through the forum.

Then came another report, from Texas. And another from Florida. And another from New York. Over the course of six weeks, nearly thirty community members reported similar visits—always polite, always vague about their affiliation, always asking the same questions.

They were mapping our community. Identifying our most active members. Building a picture of the network I'd created.

"What do you think they want?" Zach asked, when I called to discuss the pattern.

"I don't know. They could have shut us down years ago if that's what they wanted. They could have—" I stopped. "They could have done worse than burn down a house."

"Then why the surveillance?"

"Maybe they're watching for something specific. Some trigger they're afraid we'll cross." I thought about the documents they'd given me, the Mount St. Helens files, the evidence of decades of cover-ups. "Maybe they're waiting to see how far we'll push."

"The what?"

I hadn't shared all my theories with Zach. I'd held some things back, uncertain how to explain my suspicions about the scope of the cover-up. But maybe it was time to share more.

"There's something I need to tell you," I said. "Something about what the documents suggest."

* * *

I told Zach everything. The Mount St. Helens files. The evidence of recovered specimens. The suggestion that these creatures had been studied, catalogued, perhaps even communicated with by government programs going back decades. He listened without interrupting, his silence heavy through the phone line.

"So they're not just animals hiding in the woods," he said finally. "The government has been actively studying them. For generations."

"I think so. Whatever they are, they've been here a long time. And the cover-up has been going on just as long. But it's crumbling now. The truth is getting out. And when it does, everything changes."

"And the men in black?"

"They know it's happening. They've been trying to manage it for decades—controlling the narrative, suppressing evidence, keeping the public ignorant. But they can't hold back the tide forever. The truth is getting out. And when it does, their entire operation becomes irrelevant."

"So they're watching us because we're part of that change."

"We're helping it happen. Every episode, every interview, every story we share—we're preparing people for the truth. Making the revelation less of a shock, less likely to cause panic. The men in black might hate what we're doing, but part of me thinks they need us too."

"Need us?"

"To manage the transition. To help people understand. If the truth comes out all at once, without any preparation, it could be catastrophic. Mass hysteria, violence, the collapse of institutions that depend on denying what's been hidden. But if people are already open to the possibility, if they've heard the stories and seen the evidence—"

"Then the transition is smoother."

"Exactly. We're doing the work they're too afraid to do themselves. And they're watching because they need to know it's working."

Zach was quiet for a long moment. "That's a hell of a theory."

"It's the only one that makes sense. They could have destroyed us. They chose not to. There has to be a reason."

"So what do we do?"

"We keep going. We prepare for what's coming. And we hope that when the truth finally comes out, we've done enough to make it manageable."

* * *

The surveillance continued, but no direct action was taken.

I warned the community to be cautious—to report any unusual contacts, to avoid sharing sensitive personal information, to remember that we were being watched. The reports of visits tapered off after a few months, but I knew the watching hadn't stopped. It had just become more subtle.

And through it all, I kept working.

The interviews continued. The episodes aired. The community grew. Whatever the men in black were planning, whatever they were waiting for, I couldn't let their presence paralyze me. The work was too important.

The truth was coming out. And I needed to be ready.

43

VOICES IN THE DARKNESS

The five hundredth episode of *Sasquatch Odyssey* aired on a Thursday evening in April.

Five hundred episodes. Five hundred stories of encounters, of wonder, of fear, of connection with something beyond our everyday understanding. I'd started the podcast sitting alone in a spare bedroom with a cheap microphone; now it reached millions of people around the world.

For the anniversary episode, I decided to do something different.

Instead of a single interview, I compiled clips from fifty of the most impactful stories we'd shared over the years. Lucille Marsh with her river stone. Bobby Dean Carver and his coon-hunting dogs. Margaret Lindqvist in the frozen silence of the Boundary Waters. Gloria Reyes and the young Navajo man in the hospital. Mary Catherine O'Brien and the creature at her dying husband's window.

Fifty voices, speaking across decades, across continents, across the vast gulf that separated their experiences from the world's disbelief.

And at the end, I added something new: my own story, told in full for the first time.

* * *

"My name is Brian Patterson," I recorded, sitting in the studio I'd rebuilt after the fire. "And I've been chasing the truth about Sasquatch since I was twelve years old."

"It started in Lyerly, Georgia, in 1984. My family had just moved to a new property—eighty acres of woods and fields, at the end of a long dirt road. I thought it was paradise. I didn't know what was waiting for me in those trees.

"The encounter happened in October. I was exploring the back corner of our property, a place where the woods grew thick and the feeling of wrongness was strongest. I heard it before I saw anything— huffing, growling, something breathing in the underbrush. And then came the sounds of movement. Heavy footsteps. Bipedal footsteps, moving toward me through the trees.

"I never saw the creature. It stayed hidden, invisible in the dense undergrowth. But I felt it. I heard it. I knew, with a certainty that has never wavered, that something was there. Something large. Something intelligent. Something that chose to let me go when it could easily have done otherwise.

"That encounter changed my life. It set me on a path that led through decades of searching, through a career in law enforcement, through the investigation that made national news, and finally to this podcast. Five hundred episodes of other people's stories, trying to understand my own.

"I still don't have all the answers. I don't know what these creatures are, where they came from, or what they want from us. But I know they're real. I know they're watching. And I know that someday —maybe soon, maybe not—the world will finally have to face the truth that witnesses like me have been carrying for generations.

"Until that day, I'll keep recording. Keep listening. Keep sharing the stories that deserve to be heard. Because that's what this is really about—not proof, not vindication, but connection. Human beings reaching out to each other across the darkness, saying 'I saw something. I experienced something. I need someone to believe me.'

"I believe you. All of you. And I'm honored to have shared your stories with the world.

"Thank you for five hundred episodes. Here's to five hundred more."

* * *

The response to the anniversary episode exceeded anything we'd experienced before.

Downloads spiked. Comments flooded in from longtime listeners who'd been moved to tears, from new listeners who'd discovered the podcast through the milestone, from witnesses who'd never reached out before but felt compelled to share their own stories.

Mainstream media picked up the anniversary, with features in several major outlets. The coverage was mostly respectful—a far cry from the mockery we'd faced in the early years. The world was changing. The stigma was fading. The truth was becoming harder to ignore.

And in the community forum, someone posted a message that captured everything I felt:

"Five hundred episodes. Five hundred stories of people who saw something impossible and had the courage to speak up. Five hundred pieces of evidence that the world is stranger than we've been taught to believe. Brian, you've built something incredible here. A community. A movement. A lighthouse for everyone who's been lost in the darkness of disbelief. Whatever comes next, know that you've changed lives. You've changed the world. And we're all grateful."

I read the message three times, tears streaming down my face.

This was why I did this work.

This was all any of it had ever been about.

44

THE EXPEDITION

The message arrived on a Sunday evening, through a channel I hadn't used in years.

It came from Zach, encrypted and urgent. "New evidence. Major. Need to meet in person. Bring everything."

I stared at the screen, my heart pounding.

After all the years of searching, of documenting, of hoping for definitive proof—could this finally be it?

* * *

I called Daniel first.

"Zach found something," I said. "Something big. He wants to meet at the research site."

"Where?"

"The area near where Austin disappeared. Same region we've been monitoring for years. But this time—" I took a breath. "This time he says he has something that could change everything."

"I'm coming with you."

"Daniel—"

"Don't argue with me. I've stood beside you through everything. I'm not staying behind for this."

I wanted to protect him. Wanted to keep him safe from whatever was about to unfold. But I knew that look in his voice, that determination that had carried us through years of struggle and fear and hope.

"Okay," I said. "But we need to bring the team. Amanda, her cameraman. This needs to be documented. Whatever it is."

"I'll make the calls. You pack the gear."

* * *

We gathered at our mountain house the next morning.

Amanda had arrived overnight, red-eyed from a cross-country flight but vibrating with anticipation. Her cameraman, Tom, was already checking equipment, making sure every battery was charged, every memory card was empty. Zach had driven up from the ranger station, his car loaded with his own documentation gear.

"What did you find?" I asked, as we gathered around the kitchen table.

Zach spread out a collection of photographs and documents. "Three nights ago, motion sensors I'd placed in a remote section of the forest were triggered. Multiple times. Something large, moving through a specific corridor."

"Could be bears," Amanda said. "Elk."

"Look at the thermal signatures." Zach pointed to a series of images. "The heat distribution is wrong for any known animal. And look here—" He pointed to another image. "Bipedal gait. Clear as day."

I studied the images. The shapes were indistinct, captured at the edge of the camera's range. But the movement patterns, the heat signatures, the apparent size—

"We need to go there," I said. "Set up more cameras. Get better footage."

"That's why I called you. This is the best activity I've documented in twenty years. If we're going to get definitive proof, this is our chance."

"When do we leave?"

"Now. Before they move on. These creatures don't stay in one place for long."

* * *

The journey into the forest felt charged with possibility.

The area Zach had identified was deep in the backcountry, hours from any road or trail. We hiked through old-growth forest, the trees towering around us like cathedral columns. Birds fell silent as we passed. The air grew heavy with anticipation.

"This is close to where Austin's camera was found," Zach said quietly, as we approached his monitoring site. "About two miles north. Whatever's using this corridor, they've been here for a long time."

We set up camp as the sun began to set, placing additional cameras and monitoring equipment in a wide perimeter. Amanda and Tom documented everything—our preparations, the equipment, the forest itself in the fading light.

That night, we waited.

And around midnight, the sensors began to trigger.

* * *

The footage we captured wasn't definitive. It never was, with these creatures. But it was compelling.

Three distinct heat signatures, moving through the forest about two hundred yards from our camp. Large. Bipedal. Moving with a coordination that suggested intelligence, communication, purpose.

We heard them too. The same vocalizations I'd heard throughout my years of research—howls and wood knocks and that strange, almost linguistic chattering that defied explanation.

They knew we were there. They were watching us as we watched them.

And at one point, just before dawn, I saw something through my night vision scope. A shape, standing at the edge of a clearing, looking directly at me.

It was only for a moment. Then it turned and disappeared into the trees.

"Did you get that?" I whispered to Tom.

He was already checking his camera. "I think so. Let me—" He stopped. "Oh my God."

The footage showed a figure—tall, broad-shouldered, covered in dark hair. The face was obscured by distance and shadow, but the basic outline was unmistakable.

Not a bear. Not an elk. Not a human in a suit.

Something else.

* * *

We stayed in the forest for three more days, capturing more evidence. Audio recordings of vocalizations. Additional thermal footage. Footprint casts from the muddy banks of a nearby stream.

None of it was the clear, undeniable proof I'd been searching for my entire life. But taken together, it was the strongest case yet assembled. The kind of evidence that would make even skeptics pause.

"This is going to change things," Amanda said, as we hiked back to our vehicles. "When this airs, when people see what we've captured—
"

"They'll still deny it," I said. "Some of them. They always do."

"But others won't. Others will look at this and finally understand that something is out there. That the witnesses have been telling the truth all along."

I thought about Austin. About whether he was still alive somewhere in these mountains, living among the creatures he'd gone to find. Or whether he'd met a different fate, one that would remain a mystery forever.

"We'll keep searching," I said. "The work isn't done."

"Will it ever be?"

"I don't know. Maybe not. But that's okay. The search is the point. The truth is the point. Everything else is just details."

Daniel took my hand as we emerged from the forest into the late afternoon sun. The mountains stretched out before us, vast and ancient and full of secrets.

"Whatever happens," he said, "you've done something remarkable. You've given people hope."

"I've just told stories," I said.

"That's what hope is. Stories that show us the world is bigger than we thought. Stranger. More wonderful." He squeezed my hand. "You've shown people that the mystery is still out there. That there are still things waiting to be discovered."

I looked back at the forest, at the trees that held their secrets so close. "Book Two," I said quietly.

"What?"

"This is just the beginning. There's so much more to find. So much more to understand." I smiled. "The odyssey continues."

And it did.

PART VI

ADDITIONAL INTERVIEWS

45

ENCOUNTERS FROM THE EDGE

Some stories took years to reach me.

Witnesses would circle for months or even years, listening to the podcast, reading the forums, gathering courage. Then, when they were finally ready, they'd reach out—often apologetically, as if embarrassed by how long it had taken them to speak.

"I've been wanting to contact you since episode forty-two," one woman wrote. "That's when I realized there were others like me. But I was scared. Scared of being judged. Scared of what my family would think. Scared of reliving something I'd spent thirty years trying to forget."

Her name was Patricia Ann Holloway, and her story became one of the most detailed and compelling I ever documented.

* * *

Patricia was a retired librarian from rural Pennsylvania, seventy-one years old, with a voice that crackled with age but rang with clarity when she spoke about her encounter.

"It happened in 1973," she began. "I was nineteen years old, a freshman at Penn State. That summer, I'd gotten a job at a wilderness camp in the Allegheny National Forest. My job was to supervise a cabin of twelve-year-old girls—help them with activities, make sure they got to meals on time, that sort of thing."

"What kind of camp was it?"

"Church camp. Baptist. Very structured, very wholesome. We had Bible study every morning, swimming in the afternoon, campfires at night. It was supposed to be safe. Protected. A place where nothing bad could happen."

"But something did happen."

"Something happened." Patricia took a long breath. "It was the third week of camp. My girls were settled in for the night—I'd done bed check around nine, made sure everyone was in their bunks. Then I went out to the porch of the cabin to read by flashlight. It was a beautiful night. Clear sky, stars everywhere, that kind of silence you only get in the deep woods."

"What did you experience?"

"At first, just a feeling. Like something was watching me from the tree line. I'd felt it before during the summer—that prickling on the back of my neck, that sense of not being alone—but I'd always dismissed it as imagination. That night, though, I couldn't ignore it."

"Why not?"

"Because I heard something. A sound I'd never heard before—this low, rumbling vocalization, almost like a growl but with rhythm to it. Like language. Like something was trying to communicate."

"What did you do?"

"I should have gone inside. Should have locked the door and hid under my covers like a sensible person. But I was nineteen and curious and probably not as smart as I should have been. So I turned on my flashlight and pointed it toward the trees."

"And?"

"And I saw eyes. Two eyes, reflecting my light, maybe fifty feet away. But they weren't on the ground, where an animal's eyes would be. They were high. Seven feet up, at least. Higher than any person could be standing."

Patricia paused, and I could hear her trembling breath through the phone.

"I dropped the flashlight. Just stood there, frozen, as those eyes moved toward me. Closer and closer, until I could see the shape around them—massive shoulders, long arms, a body covered in dark hair. It stopped about twenty feet from the porch and just... looked at me. Studied me, like I was something it was trying to understand."

"How long did this last?"

"Maybe a minute. Felt like hours. Then one of my campers—a girl named Susan who'd gotten up to use the outhouse—screamed. The creature turned toward the sound, then back to me. And I swear, Brian, I swear it made a gesture. Like a wave. Like it was saying goodbye. Then it turned and walked into the forest, and I never saw it again."

"What happened with Susan?"

"She'd seen it too. Not as clearly as I had, but enough. She was hysterical—took me an hour to calm her down. The camp director didn't believe either of us. Said we'd seen a bear, that our imaginations had run wild. He threatened to fire me if I kept 'spreading stories' among the campers."

"Did you tell anyone else?"

"Just my roommate when I got back to school. She thought I was crazy. After that, I kept quiet. Got married, had kids, built a life. But I never forgot. Never stopped thinking about those eyes, that gesture, that sense of connection across the gulf between species."

"Why are you telling me now?"

"Because I'm seventy-one years old, and Susan died last year. Cancer. She never talked about what we saw—not to her husband, not to her children, not to anyone. She carried that secret to her grave." Patricia's voice cracked. "I don't want to do that. I don't want to die without someone knowing. Without the truth being spoken."

* * *

Patricia's interview was followed by a flood of similar accounts—witnesses who'd stayed silent for decades, finally finding the courage to speak. Each story added texture to my understanding. Each voice enriched the tapestry we were weaving.

From Vermont, a ninety-year-old man named Elijah Morse described an encounter from 1952, when he was a young logger working in the Green Mountains. "We called them the Wild Men," he said. "Everyone knew about them. We just didn't talk about it outside the logging camps."

From Mississippi, a woman named Dorothy Jackson shared a story her grandmother had told her—an encounter from the 1920s, passed down through three generations. "Grandma saw one drinking from the creek behind the farm," Dorothy said. "She was eight years old. She never forgot it, and she made sure we never forgot it either."

From California, a retired park ranger named William "Bill" Hendricks opened up about experiences he'd had throughout his forty-year career. "I saw things I couldn't report," Bill admitted. "Things that would have ended my career if I'd put them in writing. But I documented everything privately. Journals, photographs, audio recordings. It's all yours if you want it."

I wanted it. Every story. Every piece of evidence. Every thread that connected the present to the past.

The tapestry was growing. And it was beautiful.

46

THE RESEARCHER'S BURDEN

Not everyone who reached out was a witness.

Some were researchers—scientists, academics, professionals who'd risked their careers to study a phenomenon that mainstream science refused to acknowledge. Their stories were different from the encounter accounts, but no less important. They revealed the scope of the cover-up, the personal cost of pursuing forbidden knowledge, the loneliness of knowing something the world wasn't ready to hear.

* * *

Dr. Rebecca Henley was a primatologist who'd spent twenty years studying great apes in Africa before turning her attention to the Sasquatch phenomenon.

"I was skeptical at first," she told me. "Like any properly trained scientist, I dismissed the reports as misidentification, hoaxes, or wishful thinking. Then a colleague showed me a footprint cast from Washington State, and everything changed."

"What was different about that cast?"

"The dermal ridges. Fingerprints, essentially, but on the foot. They showed a pattern of wear and scarring that would be virtually impossible to fake. I'd studied primate locomotion for two decades—I knew what authentic looked like. And that cast was authentic."

"What did you do?"

"I started investigating. Quietly, at first—I couldn't let my department know what I was doing. I collected evidence, interviewed witnesses, analyzed samples. What I found was extraordinary. Hair that couldn't be identified to any known species. Vocalizations that didn't match any cataloged animal. Behavioral patterns that suggested intelligence, culture, even rudimentary language."

"How did your colleagues react?"

"They didn't know. Not until I made the mistake of publishing a paper on my findings in a minor journal. After that—" She laughed bitterly. "After that, my career was effectively over. I was denied tenure. My funding dried up. Former friends stopped returning my calls. I became a cautionary tale: the promising scientist who went crazy and started believing in Bigfoot."

"Do you regret it?"

"Some days, yes. I miss the work I used to do. I miss being respected. I miss the life I'd planned for myself." She paused. "But I also know what I know. I've seen the evidence. I've talked to the witnesses. And I can't pretend any of that doesn't exist just because it's inconvenient."

"What do you think these creatures are?"

"I think they're a relict population of hominids—probably descended from *Gigantopithecus* or a related species. They've survived in remote areas by being intelligent, cautious, and adaptable. They're our cousins, in a sense. Branches of the same evolutionary tree that diverged long ago."

"Do you think science will ever acknowledge them?"

"Eventually. The evidence is becoming too strong to ignore. More and more researchers are coming forward, risking their careers to speak the truth. The wall of denial is cracking. Someday—maybe not in my lifetime, but someday—it will fall."

* * *

Dr. Henley's story was echoed by others.

A geneticist who'd analyzed hair samples and found DNA that didn't match any known species. A zoologist who'd documented footprints with anatomical features that couldn't be faked. An anthropologist who'd collected oral histories from indigenous peoples around the world, finding remarkable consistency in their descriptions of these creatures.

Each one had paid a price for their curiosity. Lost jobs. Lost relationships. Lost standing in their professional communities. They'd become pariahs, exiles from the scientific establishment that had once welcomed them.

And yet they kept working. Kept gathering evidence. Kept hoping that someday, the truth would prevail.

Their dedication inspired me. Their sacrifice reminded me that this work mattered—not just for the witnesses, but for everyone who'd ever questioned the official narrative, who'd ever wondered if the world was stranger than we'd been taught.

The researchers were carrying a burden that few could understand. And I was honored to help them share it.

* * *

The most challenging researcher interview was with Dr. Marcus Webb, a former military intelligence officer who'd been involved in the government's efforts to study—and suppress—evidence of these creatures.

"I can't tell you everything," Marcus said, his voice guarded even through the encrypted connection we'd established. "There are things I know that could get me killed if they became public. But I can tell you enough."

"What can you tell me?"

"That the government has known about these creatures since at least the 1940s. That there have been systematic efforts to suppress evidence, intimidate witnesses, and control the narrative. That some people in positions of power have a vested interest in keeping the truth hidden."

"Why? What's the motivation for the cover-up?"

"That's the question, isn't it?" Marcus was quiet for a moment. "Part of it is fear. Fear of what would happen if people knew. Fear of the questions it would raise—about evolution, about human uniqueness, about our place in the world. But there's more to it than that."

"More how?"

"These creatures aren't just animals. They have abilities—cognitive abilities, sensory abilities, maybe even abilities we'd call paranormal. The government has been trying to understand those abilities for decades. Trying to harness them. Trying to weaponize them."

"Weaponize?"

"I've said too much already. Just know that there are programs—black programs, off the books—that would shock you. Programs that treat these beings not as subjects of study, but as assets to be exploited." His voice hardened. "That's part of why I left. I couldn't be part of it anymore. Couldn't participate in treating intelligent beings like lab rats."

"What should people know?"

"That the truth is stranger than they can imagine. That the forces arrayed against disclosure are powerful and ruthless. And that despite all of that, the truth is coming out. It can't be stopped. Too many people know. Too much evidence exists. The dam is breaking, and nothing they do can hold it back forever."

Marcus's interview never aired—he withdrew permission at the last minute, afraid of the consequences. But his words stayed with me, a reminder of the darkness that lurked behind the cover-up.

These weren't just bureaucrats protecting their turf. They were people with agendas, with plans, with secrets they'd kill to protect.

And they were still out there, watching, waiting for their moment.

47

FAMILY AND FAITH

Mama called on a Sunday evening, as she always did.

"I've been watching your show," she said, her voice carrying the warmth that had sustained me through every difficult moment of my life. "That television thing. The documentary."

"What did you think?"

"I think you've come a long way from that scared little boy who moved to Lyerly." She paused. "I think your daddy would be proud, if he wasn't such a worthless piece of—well, you know."

I laughed. Mama never minced words, especially about Jerry.

"Do you believe it?" I asked. "Everything I've been saying? The creatures, the encounters, all of it?"

She was quiet for a moment. "I believe you believe it. And I believe those people on your show—they're not lying. They've seen something. Whether it's what you think it is, or something else—" She sighed. "I'm an old woman, Brian. I've seen a lot of things that didn't make sense. I've stopped trying to explain them all."

"Like what?"

"Like your daddy coming to me in a dream the night before he died. Told me he was sorry. Told me he'd wasted his life and wished he could do it over." She made a sound that might have been a laugh or might have been a sob. "He passed the next morning. Heart attack, they said. Never even knew he was sick."

I hadn't known that. Mama had never mentioned Jerry's death to me—I'd found out through his sister, months after the funeral.

"I'm sorry, Mama."

"Don't be sorry. He made his choices. We all do." Her voice strengthened. "What I'm saying is, there's more to this world than we can see. I don't pretend to understand it. But I believe in you. I believe you're doing something important. And I'm proud of you, baby. Whatever else happens, I want you to know that."

"Thank you, Mama. That means everything."

"Now tell me about Daniel. How's that pizza place doing?"

We talked for another hour, about normal things—Daniel's work, her garden, the grandkids she wished I'd give her someday. It was the kind of conversation we'd been having for decades, familiar and comforting.

But underneath it, I felt something new. A connection. An understanding that Mama had experienced her own encounters with the impossible, her own moments when the veil between worlds grew thin.

Maybe everyone had. Maybe the strange was more common than we admitted. Maybe we'd all seen things we couldn't explain, things we buried deep because the world didn't have room for them.

Maybe that's what I was really doing with the podcast. Not proving that Sasquatch existed, but giving people permission to acknowledge the mystery. To admit that the world was stranger than we'd been taught. To embrace the unknown instead of running from it.

After we hung up, I sat on the porch for a long time, thinking about Mama and Daddy and the life that had led me here. Thinking about all the witnesses I'd interviewed, all the stories I'd collected, all the threads I'd woven into a tapestry that was finally taking shape.

The truth was getting out. I could feel it, building momentum every day.

And when the tipping point arrived, I'd be ready.

* * *

Faith was something I'd struggled with my whole life.

Growing up Baptist in rural Georgia, I'd been taught that the Bible was literally true, that God was watching, that every choice I made had eternal consequences. It was a worldview that offered certainty in exchange for obedience—a bargain I'd accepted as a child without understanding what it cost.

Then came the encounter in Lyerly. Then came the questions that religion couldn't answer. Then came the slow realization that the world was far stranger than any Sunday school lesson had prepared me for.

I'd drifted away from church over the years. Not because I'd stopped believing in something larger than myself, but because the something I believed in no longer fit the box that organized religion provided. The creatures I'd encountered, the visions I'd experienced, the truth I was helping to uncover—none of it matched the theology I'd been raised with.

But it didn't contradict it either. Not really.

The Bible spoke of giants in the earth, of nephilim and other beings that walked alongside humanity in ancient times. The Cherokee spoke of Tsul 'Kalu. The Lakota spoke of the Big Man. Every culture, every tradition, had stories of creatures that existed at the boundary between human and other.

Maybe they were all talking about the same thing. Maybe the creatures I was documenting were the source of all those legends—real beings that had inspired religious awe and mythological speculation for millennia.

Or maybe there was something even bigger going on. Something that transcended individual religions and mythologies. Something that connected all the strange experiences, all the unexplained phenomena, all the glimpses of something beyond our everyday understanding.

I didn't have answers. But I had faith—not in a specific doctrine or deity, but in the search itself. Faith that the truth was worth pursuing, wherever it led. Faith that the universe had meaning, even if I couldn't articulate what that meaning was.

It was enough. It had to be.

48

THE GATHERING DARK

The threats intensified as the documentary's release approached.

It started with digital attacks—hackers targeting the podcast's servers, attempts to breach the community forum, suspicious activity around our social media accounts. Amanda's production company faced similar problems, with coordinated efforts to take down their streaming platforms and compromise their editing systems.

"They're getting desperate," Zach said, during one of our late-night strategy sessions. "The documentary is going to reach millions of people. They know they can't stop it, so they're trying to discredit it. Undermine our infrastructure. Make us look unprofessional."

"Can they succeed?"

"Not if we stay ahead of them. I've got backups of everything. Multiple servers in multiple countries. They'd have to take down half the internet to stop this from going out."

"What about physical threats?"

Zach was quiet for a moment. "Those are harder to prepare for. But I've got people watching. If anyone makes a move, we'll know."

* * *

The physical threats came three days later.

I was driving home from the Asheville apartment when I noticed a black SUV following me. It stayed back, maintaining distance, but never varied from my route. When I turned onto the mountain road that led to our property, it followed.

I called Daniel. "I've got a tail. Black SUV, two occupants that I can see. I'm five minutes from home."

"I see them on the driveway camera. They're not trying to hide anymore."

"Stay inside. Lock the doors. I'm going to—"

The SUV accelerated, closing the distance between us. Before I could react, it was alongside me, forcing me toward the shoulder. I hit the brakes, but the SUV matched my speed, boxing me in.

Then it pulled ahead and stopped, blocking the road.

Two men got out. Dark suits. Mirrored sunglasses. The same uniform I'd seen so many times before.

I reached for my gun—I still carried, even after leaving law enforcement—and stepped out of my truck.

"That's far enough," I said, my weapon raised.

"We're not here to hurt you, Mr. Patterson." The speaker was the older of the two, gray at his temples, a weariness in his voice that I hadn't heard from these men before. "We're here to talk."

"Your people have a funny way of starting conversations."

"Our people have many ways. Not all of them sanctioned by the same authority." He held up his hands, showing they were empty. "There are factions, Mr. Patterson. Different groups with different agendas. Some want to stop you at any cost. Others—" He glanced at his partner. "Others think there might be a better way."

"What kind of better way?"

"A partnership. A controlled disclosure. You have influence with the community. You could help manage the transition, ensure it happens smoothly. In exchange, we could provide resources. Protection. Access to information that would make your work much more impactful."

"I've heard this pitch before. The answer is still no."

"That was a different faction. Their approach has been... counter-productive. The fire, the surveillance, the intimidation—those actions have only strengthened your position. Made you a martyr. We prefer a more subtle approach."

"And if I refuse your subtle approach?"

The man sighed. "Then we go back to headquarters and tell them we tried. And the other faction—the one that burned your house—gets to try their methods again." He met my eyes. "We're trying to help you, Mr. Patterson. Believe it or not. The truth is coming out whether anyone wants it or not. The only question is how much damage gets done along the way."

I thought about his words. About the factions he'd mentioned. About the possibility that the monolithic force I'd been fighting was actually a battleground of competing interests.

"I'm listening," I said finally. "But I'm not lowering my gun."

"Fair enough." The man reached inside his jacket—slowly, letting me track his movements—and pulled out a manila folder. "Consider this a gesture of good faith. Information about the programs Dr. Webb mentioned. The ones he couldn't tell you about."

He set the folder on the hood of the SUV and stepped back.

"Read it. Think about what it means. And consider whether you'd rather have us as allies or enemies."

He nodded to his partner, and they got back in the SUV. A moment later, they were gone, disappearing down the mountain road.

I picked up the folder and carried it home.

Daniel was waiting on the porch, rifle in hand. "What the hell was that?"

"A job offer. Maybe. Or a trap. I'm not sure yet."

"Are you okay?"

"I'm fine. But we need to talk. About everything."

I showed him the folder. And what we read inside changed everything we thought we knew.

49

REVELATIONS

The folder contained documents spanning sixty years.

Project names I'd never heard: TITAN WATCH. FOREST SHADOW. MIND BRIDGE. Each one a piece of the puzzle, a glimpse into the machinery of suppression that had been operating since before I was born.

TITAN WATCH was the earliest, dating to 1952. A military program to monitor "anomalous bipedal entities" in wilderness areas across North America. The documents included encounter reports from soldiers, scientists, and civilians—hundreds of them, all systematically suppressed.

FOREST SHADOW was operational from 1967 to 1989. Its purpose: "containment and control of public knowledge regarding APEs (Anomalous Primate Entities)." The documents detailed methods of intimidation, evidence confiscation, and witness silencing. There were references to "enhanced interrogation" that made my blood run cold.

But MIND BRIDGE was the most disturbing.

Initiated in 1978, it was a research program focused on the creatures' apparent psychic abilities. The documents described experiments

—conducted on both human subjects and captured Sasquatch—designed to understand and potentially replicate their capacity for telepathic communication, remote viewing, and what the scientists called "dimensional interfacing."

"They captured them," Daniel said. "They actually captured these creatures and experimented on them."

"It gets worse." I pointed to a page near the end of the file. "Look at this."

The page described the program's termination in 1994. Not for ethical concerns, but because of "catastrophic containment failure." Three creatures had escaped from a facility in Wyoming, killing twelve personnel in the process. The program was shut down, its records scattered across multiple agencies to prevent any single whistleblower from revealing the full picture.

"Jesus Christ," Daniel whispered. "They were holding them prisoner. Torturing them. And the creatures fought back."

"Now I understand why the men in black are so afraid. It's not just about maintaining a secret. They know what these creatures are capable of. They know what happens when you push them too far."

"And what about everything we've been documenting?"

"The creatures have been patient. For decades, they've endured. Watched. Waited. But the evidence is mounting. The witnesses keep coming forward. They can't keep the lid on this forever." I closed the folder. "The revelation isn't just about proof anymore. It's about justice for everyone who's been silenced."

* * *

I spent the next week analyzing the documents, cross-referencing them with what I already knew, building a comprehensive picture of the cover-up's history and scope.

The pattern was clear: the government had known about these creatures for at least seventy years. They'd studied them, feared them, tried to exploit them. And throughout it all, they'd maintained absolute secrecy, using every tool at their disposal to keep the public ignorant.

But the facade was crumbling. Too many witnesses. Too much evidence. Too many people asking questions that couldn't be answered without admitting the truth.

The truth was coming out. And the only choice left was whether it happened on humanity's terms or through some catastrophic leak.

* * *

I shared the documents with Amanda and Zach, letting them draw their own conclusions.

"This changes everything," Amanda said. "This isn't just a documentary about Bigfoot anymore. This is a story about government conspiracy, about the abuse of power, about the systematic suppression of a truth that belongs to all humanity."

"It's also dangerous," Zach cautioned. "Publishing this could put us in serious jeopardy. The people behind these programs—they won't react well to being exposed."

"They've already tried to stop us," I said. "They've burned our house, surveilled our community, threatened everyone who's helped us. What more can they do?"

"A lot more." Zach's voice was grim. "The programs in these documents—they weren't shut down because of oversight or public pressure. They were shut down because something went wrong. That means there are people out there who know what these creatures can do, who know how dangerous they can be. And those people will do anything to keep control of this story."

"Then we make sure they can't stop it." I looked at both of them. "We release everything. The interviews, the evidence, the documents. All of it, all at once. We make the truth so widespread, so impossible to contain, that no amount of intimidation can put it back in the box."

Amanda nodded slowly. "It's risky."

"It's necessary. The witnesses have waited long enough. It's time to end the secrecy and let the world decide how to respond."

"When?"

"Soon. As soon as we can put together the final package. The documentary, the podcast archives, the Mount St. Helens files, all of it. A comprehensive release that tells the whole story."

"And then?"

"And then we keep searching. Keep documenting. Keep pushing until the truth is undeniable."

50

THE NIGHT BEFORE

The night before we left for the cave, I couldn't sleep.

Daniel was beside me, his breathing steady, at peace in a way I envied. He'd always been better at accepting uncertainty, at trusting that things would work out even when the odds seemed impossible.

I got up quietly and walked to the window. The mountains were silver under the moon, the forest a dark sea stretching to the horizon. Somewhere out there, in the deep places where humans rarely ventured, the creatures were preparing too. Gathering. Waiting.

Tomorrow would change everything. For better or worse, nothing would ever be the same.

* * *

I thought about all the paths that had led me here.

Lyerly. The encounter that had set everything in motion. A twelve-year-old boy, alone in the woods, facing something that shouldn't exist. I'd spent thirty years running from that moment, pretending it hadn't happened, trying to build a normal life on a foundation of denial.

It hadn't worked. The truth had a way of surfacing, no matter how deep you buried it.

Mama. Her cancer, her strength, her refusal to give up even when the doctors said there was no hope. She'd taught me that survival wasn't about avoiding challenges—it was about facing them, enduring them, coming out the other side transformed.

Daddy. His absence, his failures, the hole he'd left in our family. He'd taught me what I didn't want to become. What happened when you ran from responsibility, when you chose the easy path over the right one.

Law enforcement. The years of service, of trying to protect people, of discovering that the systems meant to keep us safe were often the ones causing the most harm. I'd learned to question authority, to trust my instincts, to seek the truth even when it was inconvenient.

Daniel. The love that had given my life meaning. The partnership that had sustained me through every challenge. He'd taught me that I didn't have to face the darkness alone.

And the podcast. Five hundred episodes. Thousands of witnesses. A community that spanned the globe. I'd set out to tell stories, and ended up building something far bigger than myself.

All of it had been preparation. All of it had led to tomorrow.

* * *

Around three in the morning, I went out to the porch.

The night was still, the air cold enough to see my breath. I stood there, looking at the forest, and I felt it—that familiar sense of being watched. Not threatening. Not intrusive. Just... aware.

"I know you're there," I said quietly. "I know you've always been there."

Nothing answered. But the feeling intensified, as if something was acknowledging my words.

"Tomorrow, everything changes. The hiding ends. The truth comes out. Are you ready for that?"

Silence. Then, from somewhere deep in the forest, a howl. Long, mournful, beautiful. It rose and fell, echoing off the mountains, filling the night with sound.

Other howls answered it. Dozens of them, from different directions, different distances. A chorus of voices that had been silent for too long, finally preparing to be heard.

I stood on the porch, tears streaming down my face, listening to the creatures sing.

They were ready. They'd been ready for a long time.

And tomorrow, the world would finally learn what they'd been waiting for.

* * *

Daniel found me on the porch as the sun was coming up.

"You didn't sleep," he said.

"Couldn't. Too much to think about."

He put his arm around me. "Having second thoughts?"

"No. Just... thinking about how far we've come. Everything that led us here. All the people who made this possible."

"Regrets?"

I thought about the question. About the house we'd lost. The threats we'd endured. The normal life we'd given up.

"No," I said finally. "Not one. This is what I was supposed to do. This is why I'm here. And I wouldn't change any of it."

Daniel kissed my cheek. "Then let's go change the world."

I smiled. "Let's."

We went inside to pack for the journey. In a few hours, we'd begin the hike to the cave. By nightfall, we'd be in the presence of creatures that the world said didn't exist.

And by tomorrow, the world would know the truth.

51

INTO THE UNKNOWN

The expedition into the deep forest was everything we'd hoped for—and nothing we'd expected.

We set up camp at the coordinates Zach had identified, in a remote section of the Pisgah where the old-growth trees blocked out all but fragments of sky. The monitoring equipment was deployed in a careful grid, covering nearly a square mile of wilderness.

The first night was quiet. Too quiet, Zach said. The kind of quiet that usually meant we were being watched.

"They know we're here," he whispered, as we huddled around our small camp stove. "They always know."

"Will they show themselves?" Amanda asked.

"That's not up to us. It's never been up to us."

* * *

On the second night, they came close.

The thermal cameras picked them up first—three distinct signatures, moving through the trees about two hundred yards from our camp. They circled us slowly, deliberately, as if assessing our intentions.

Then the vocalizations began. That eerie, almost musical howling that had haunted my dreams since I was twelve years old. Echoing through the forest, answered by calls from other directions. A conversation we couldn't understand but could feel in our bones.

I walked to the edge of our camp, leaving the safety of the firelight.

"We're not here to harm you," I said into the darkness. "We're here to share your story. To help the world understand."

Silence. Then, from somewhere close—closer than I'd expected—a response. A low, rumbling vocalization that seemed to vibrate in my chest. Not threatening. Almost... acknowledging.

"Keep the cameras running," I whispered to Amanda. "Whatever happens, document everything."

* * *

They didn't reveal themselves that night. Or the next. But they left evidence of their presence—footprints in the mud, structures of bent branches, a pile of freshly stripped bark beside our camp.

"They're testing us," Zach said, examining the signs. "Seeing how we react. Whether we can be trusted."

"Can we?" Amanda asked.

I thought about the question. About everything I'd learned, everything I'd experienced. About the Mount St. Helens documents and the decades of cover-ups. About all the witnesses who'd been silenced, all the evidence that had been suppressed.

"I don't know if they trust humans," I said finally. "After what we've done to them, I wouldn't blame them if they didn't. But they're watching. They're listening. And maybe, if we keep showing up, keep proving that we mean what we say, they'll decide to take a chance on us."

"And if they don't?"

"Then we keep searching. Keep documenting. Keep preparing the world for the day when they do."

* * *

On our final night in the forest, I had an experience I'll never fully understand.

I was alone at the edge of camp, keeping watch while the others slept. The moon was full, casting silver light through the trees. And there, at the edge of the clearing, I saw a shape.

Tall. Massive. Standing motionless among the shadows.

We watched each other for what felt like hours. I didn't move. I didn't speak. I just stood there, feeling the weight of its attention, the ancient intelligence behind those eyes.

Then it raised one massive hand—not in threat, but in something that almost looked like acknowledgment. And it turned and walked back into the forest, disappearing between one breath and the next.

I never told the others what I saw that night. Not because I didn't trust them, but because some experiences are too personal to share. Too sacred.

But I knew, in that moment, that everything I'd been working toward was worth it. The creatures were out there. They were watching. And someday—maybe not in my lifetime, but someday—they would decide the time was right.

The revelation would come when they were ready. Not before.

EPILOGUE
THE WORK CONTINUES

The documentary aired on a Tuesday evening in October.

Amanda had done her job brilliantly—weaving together the years of interviews, the expedition footage, the Mount St. Helens documents, the story of my journey from that first encounter in Lyerly to our recent expedition. No definitive proof of the creatures themselves, but something almost as important: a comprehensive case for their existence that even skeptics would have to take seriously.

The response exceeded anything we'd anticipated.

Within hours, the documentary was trending worldwide. Social media exploded with reactions—some dismissive, some supportive, some sharing their own encounters for the first time. Scientists who'd been quietly researching the phenomenon came forward to validate our methodology. Former government employees reached out with hints of additional cover-ups.

And across the country, in wilderness areas from the Pacific Northwest to the Appalachians, people started looking more carefully at the forests around them.

*　*　*

In the months that followed, I watched the conversation change.

It wasn't a revolution. The skeptics were still skeptical, the deniers still denied. But the discourse had shifted. The subject was no longer automatically dismissed as fringe nonsense. Researchers who'd been afraid to speak publicly found their voices. Universities began funding studies. Journalists investigated the cover-ups we'd exposed.

The truth was emerging, slowly but surely.

And I was there to witness it.

* * *

I still don't know what happened to Austin Reeves.

His case remains officially unsolved. His parents still live in hope, waiting for word that may never come. I think about him sometimes, when I'm walking in the forests where he disappeared. Wondering if he found what he was looking for. Wondering if he's still out there, somewhere, living among the creatures he'd gone to find.

Or if he met a different fate entirely.

The not-knowing is hard. But I've learned to live with it. Some mysteries aren't meant to be solved. Some questions don't have answers. And maybe that's okay. Maybe the search itself is what matters.

* * *

Daniel and I built a new life in the years after the documentary aired.

The threats continued for a while—the men in black didn't give up easily—but eventually they faded into the background. Maybe they realized they couldn't stop the truth anymore. Maybe they decided there were bigger battles to fight. Or maybe they're just waiting, watching, preparing for whatever comes next.

I don't spend much time worrying about them anymore. I have too much work to do.

The podcast continues—episode 750 as of last count. The community has grown to over a million members worldwide. Researchers from dozens of countries share findings, compare notes, push the boundaries of what we know.

And every so often, in the deep forests where the old trees still stand, something moves in the shadows. Something ancient and intelligent and patient. Watching us as we watch for them.

* * *

This is where my story pauses—for now.

But it's not an ending. Not really. The search continues. The questions remain. The truth is still out there, waiting to be fully revealed.

I've spent my whole life looking for answers. And I've found some. Enough to know that the creatures are real. Enough to know that the cover-up was real. Enough to know that the world is stranger and more wonderful than most people imagine.

But the biggest answers? The ones about what these creatures really are, where they came from, what they want? Those are still waiting.

Maybe I'll find them. Maybe my children will. Maybe the next generation of researchers will finally break through the barriers we've been pushing against for so long.

I don't know. And for once, I'm okay with that.

The odyssey continues. That's what matters. The search goes on.

And somewhere in the forests, in the mountains, in the wild places where humans rarely go, the creatures are watching. Waiting. Ready for the day when the world is finally prepared to meet them.

When that day comes—and I believe it will—I hope I'm still around to see it.

END OF BOOK ONE

INTERLUDE

MORE VOICES FROM THE WILDERNESS

THE HUNTER'S TALE
RUSSELL CRAWFORD, TENNESSEE

Russell Crawford had been hunting the forests of East Tennessee for fifty-three years. He'd killed more deer than he could count, tracked bear through the Smokies, and once spent three days following a wounded elk through terrain that would have killed a less experienced man.

"I've seen everything these mountains have to offer," Russell told me, his voice gravelly from decades of cigarettes and cold mountain air. "Or so I thought. Until the morning I met something that made me question everything I knew about the natural world."

"Tell me what happened."

"It was November of 2008. Rifle season. I was set up in a tree stand about two miles into the Cherokee National Forest, waiting for a buck I'd been tracking all season. Big one—twelve points, maybe more. I'd found his rubs, his scrapes. I knew he'd come through that hollow eventually."

"What time of day was it?"

"Early. Just after dawn. The fog was thick—you couldn't see more than thirty yards in any direction. I was watching a game trail, waiting, when I heard something moving through the brush to my right."

"What did you think it was?"

"At first? The buck. The sound was heavy enough—lots of weight, lots of displacement. I raised my rifle, put my eye to the scope, and waited for it to emerge from the fog."

"And what emerged?"

Russell was quiet for a long moment. When he spoke again, his voice had changed—softer, almost reverent.

"It wasn't a deer. It wasn't anything I'd ever seen. It was walking on two legs, covered in dark hair, eight feet tall if it was an inch. Massive shoulders, arms that hung down past its knees. And it was moving through the forest like it owned the place. No hesitation. No fear."

"What did you do?"

"I froze. Finger on the trigger, eye in the scope, frozen solid. I could have taken a shot—clear line of sight, maybe thirty yards. But I didn't. Couldn't. Something about the way it moved, the way it looked around—it was too human. Too aware. Shooting it would have felt like murder."

"Did it see you?"

"It knew I was there. No question about that. It stopped about twenty yards from my tree, looked right up at me, and I swear to God it smiled. Not a threatening smile. More like recognition. Like it was acknowledging me, one hunter to another."

"What happened next?"

"It walked away. Disappeared into the fog without making a sound. I sat in that tree for another hour, too shaken to move. When I finally climbed down, I found tracks—footprints, eighteen inches long, heading deeper into the forest."

"Did you follow them?"

"No. I went home. Hung up my rifle and didn't hunt for three years. It took me that long to process what I'd seen, to accept that the woods I thought I knew were home to something beyond my under-standing."

"Do you hunt now?"

"I do. But differently. More respectfully. I know now that I'm not the top predator in those mountains. Something else holds that title. And when I'm out there, I'm a guest in their territory."

* * *

Russell's story exemplified something I heard again and again from experienced outdoorsmen: the creatures commanded respect, not fear. They were apex predators who chose not to prey on humans—not because they couldn't, but because they didn't want to.

The question was: why?

Were they simply avoiding conflict? Or was there something more going on—intelligence, an awareness, a deliberate choice to coexist with humanity rather than compete with us?

The more encounters I documented, the more convinced I became that these creatures weren't just animals. They were something else. Something that challenged our assumptions about intelligence, about consciousness, about what it meant to be a thinking being in a world that had room for more than one kind of mind.

THE TEACHER'S ACCOUNT
MARGARET WHITE, WASHINGTON STATE

Margaret White had spent thirty years teaching biology at a high school in rural Washington. She was a scientist by training, a skeptic by nature, and the last person you'd expect to believe in Bigfoot.

"I was the one who always debunked the stories," Margaret admitted. "When kids came to class talking about Sasquatch sightings, I'd explain misidentification, pareidolia, the psychology of false memories. I had all the rational explanations ready."

"What changed?"

"I saw one. Face to face, broad daylight, no possibility of misidentification. And every rational explanation I'd ever offered turned to dust."

"Tell me about the encounter."

"It was June of 2015. I was hiking alone in the Olympic National Park—something I'd done hundreds of times before. I was on a trail near Deer Park, maybe three miles from the nearest road, when I came around a bend and found myself twenty feet from one of these creatures."

"Can you describe it?"

"Female, I think—based on the body shape and the lack of the sagittal crest that males apparently have. Maybe seven feet tall, covered in auburn-colored hair. Standing right in the middle of the trail, holding something in her hands."

"What was she holding?"

"Berries. Wild blackberries, from a bush at the edge of the trail. She was eating them, one by one, with this delicate precision that seemed completely at odds with her size and apparent strength."

"What happened when she saw you?"

"She stopped eating. Looked at me. And I saw intelligence in her eyes, Brian. Real intelligence. Not the blank stare of an animal assessing a threat—something deeper. Curiosity, maybe. Or recognition."

"Were you afraid?"

"Terrified. My heart was pounding so hard I could hear it in my ears. But I couldn't run. Couldn't move. I just stood there, staring at her, while she stared back at me."

"How did the encounter end?"

"She made a sound—a soft grunt, almost like a sigh—and stepped off the trail into the brush. I heard her moving for maybe thirty seconds, and then nothing. She was gone, vanished into the forest like she'd never been there."

"What did you do?"

"I walked back to my car on shaking legs, drove home, and poured myself a glass of wine that turned into three. Then I started research-ing. Reading everything I could find about these creatures. Listening to accounts from other witnesses. And I realized that what I'd seen wasn't unique—it was part of a pattern, a phenomenon that had been docu-mented for centuries."

"How did this affect your teaching?"

"I still teach biology. I still value scientific method and rational inquiry. But I've expanded my definition of what's possible. I tell my students now that science doesn't have all the answers—that there are mysteries in the world that haven't been solved yet. And some of those mysteries are walking around in the forests just a few miles from where we're sitting."

"Do your colleagues know about your experience?"

"Some do. Most think I've lost my mind. But I can't pretend it didn't happen. I can't go back to being the skeptic who explains everything away. I've seen the unexplainable. And that changes you, whether you want it to or not."

Margaret's story resonated with many of the scientists and academics who'd reached out to me over the years. These were people trained in rational inquiry, in evidence-based thinking, in the scientific method. They weren't prone to flights of fancy or wishful thinking.

And yet they'd seen something that didn't fit their models. Something that challenged the worldview they'd spent their careers building.

How they responded to that challenge varied. Some, like Margaret, expanded their understanding, making room for the unexplained without abandoning their commitment to reason. Others retreated into denial, convincing themselves that they'd imagined the encounter or misidentified a known animal.

But none of them could forget what they'd seen. The experience stayed with them, a splinter in the mind, a constant reminder that the world was stranger than their textbooks had taught them.

THE CHILD'S MEMORY
JAMES WHITEHORSE, ARIZONA

James Whitehorse was eight years old when he had his encounter. He was sixty-two when he finally spoke about it.

"I've carried this memory for fifty-four years," James said, his voice heavy with the weight of long-held secrets. "My grandfather told me never to speak of what I saw. He said the white world wouldn't understand—that they'd think I was making it up, or worse, that I was touched in the head. So I kept quiet."

"What did you see?"

"I was herding sheep on the reservation, up near the Chuska Mountains. It was summer, hot as blazes, and I'd led the flock to a spring where they could drink. I was sitting on a rock, watching them, when I noticed I wasn't alone."

"What was there?"

"A person. At least, that's what I thought at first. A person standing in the shade of a juniper tree, maybe fifty yards away. But when I looked closer, I realized it wasn't a person. It was something else."

"Can you describe it?"

"Tall. Taller than any man I'd ever seen. Covered in hair—reddish-brown, like the color of the earth after rain. It had a flat face, with eyes that seemed to look right through me. And it was watching the sheep, not me. Watching them with an expression I can only describe as wonder."

"What happened next?"

"It noticed me watching. Turned its head and looked at me. I was scared—terrified, really. But I didn't run. My grandfather had taught me that the spirits of the land should be respected, not feared. So I stayed where I was."

"Did it approach you?"

"No. It raised one hand—slowly, deliberately—and made a gesture. Like a greeting. Then it turned and walked into the trees. I watched it go, still sitting on my rock, too amazed to move."

"What did your grandfather say when you told him?"

"He wasn't surprised. He said the Ye'iitsoh—the big giant—had shown itself to me. He said it was a blessing, a sign that I had been chosen to see what others couldn't. Then he told me never to speak of it to anyone outside the family."

"Why are you speaking about it now?"

"Because my grandfather is gone. My parents are gone. I'm the last one who knows what I saw. And I've listened to your podcast, heard other people telling stories like mine. I realized I'm not alone. That there are others who've seen the Ye'iitsoh, others who understand." He paused. "I don't want to die without adding my voice to theirs."

* * *

James's story highlighted something I'd encountered again and again in my research: the indigenous perspective on these creatures was fundamentally different from the mainstream view.

Where Western culture saw monsters, cryptids, animals to be studied or feared, indigenous peoples saw relatives. Neighbors. Spiritual beings deserving of respect. They had names for these creatures—Sasquatch, Ye'iitsoh, Ts'emekwes—and relationships with them that went back thousands of years.

This wasn't superstition or primitive belief. It was knowledge, accumulated over generations, about beings that Western science refused to acknowledge. The indigenous peoples had been telling the truth all along. We just hadn't been listening.

James Whitehorse had waited fifty-four years to share his story. Now, finally, someone was ready to hear it.

THE NIGHT SHIFT
MARIA SANTOS, NEW MEXICO

Maria Santos worked the night shift at a gas station on the edge of the Gila Wilderness. For fifteen years, she'd watched travelers come and go, heard their stories, and kept the lights burning in a sea of darkness.

"You see things out here," Maria told me. "Things that don't make sense. Lights in the sky. Animals that shouldn't exist. Shadows that move when nothing's moving them. Most of it you can explain away. But some of it—" She shook her head. "Some of it stays with you."

"Tell me about your encounter."

"It was February of 2019. Middle of the night, maybe two or three in the morning. I was alone in the station—hadn't had a customer in hours. I was reading a book, trying to stay awake, when I heard something outside."

"What kind of sound?"

"Footsteps. Heavy footsteps, on the concrete apron outside the pumps. But there was no car. No headlights. No one walking up from the road. Just footsteps, getting closer."

"What did you do?"

"I put down my book and looked out the window. The station's got those big fluorescent lights over the pumps—you can see pretty well out there even at night. And standing right there, in the light, was a creature."

"Can you describe it?"

"Huge. At least eight feet tall. Covered in dark hair, almost black. It was standing between two gas pumps, looking at the station, looking at me. I could see its eyes—they reflected the light, like an animal's eyes do. But there was intelligence in them. Curiosity. Like it was trying to figure out what this place was, what the pumps were for."

"How long did it stay?"

"Maybe five minutes. It walked around the pumps, touched one with its hand—I remember thinking how strange it looked, that massive creature poking at the gas pump like a kid exploring something new. Then it looked at me one more time, made a sound—a grunt, or maybe a word in a language I didn't know—and walked into the darkness."

"Did you report the sighting?"

"To who? The police would have thought I was crazy. My boss would have thought I was on drugs. So I kept quiet, like everyone else who sees things out here. Added it to the list of unexplained experiences that comes with living on the edge of the wilderness."

"Have you seen it since?"

"Not that one. But I've seen others. Shadows moving through the trees when there's nothing there. Eyes reflecting in the darkness beyond the lights. Sometimes I hear them at night, making sounds— not threatening, just... communicating. Talking to each other in a language older than human speech."

"Are you afraid?"

"Not anymore. I figure we're neighbors. They live in the wilderness; I live on the edge of it. As long as we respect each other's space, there's no reason for trouble. And maybe—" She smiled. "Maybe they're as curious about us as we are about them. Maybe that's why they come to the station sometimes. To watch. To learn. To understand the strange creatures that build things in the darkness."

* * *

Maria's account reminded me that encounters weren't limited to remote wilderness areas. These creatures existed at the edges of human civilization, watching our activities, observing our technology, learning about the world we'd built.

What did they think of us? Our cars, our buildings, our lights that turned night into day? Were we as mysterious to them as they were to us?

The more I learned, the more I believed that the relationship between humans and these creatures was mutual. We watched them; they watched us. We were curious about their existence; they were curious about ours.

Perhaps that mutual curiosity was the foundation for something more. A connection. A communication. A bridge between worlds that had existed side by side for millennia without ever truly meeting.

The understanding I'd been working toward wasn't just about proof. It was about relationship. About finally acknowledging that we shared this planet with beings as intelligent and curious as ourselves.

The question was: were we ready for that acknowledgment?

Were they?

THE LOGGER'S LEGACY
THOMAS ERIKSON, OREGON

Thomas Erikson came from a logging family that had worked the forests of Oregon for four generations. His great-grandfather had cut trees in the days before chainsaws. His grandfather had survived the Depression by taking timber contracts that no one else would touch. His father had built a company that employed a hundred men at its peak.

"Loggers don't talk about what they see in the woods," Thomas told me. "It's an unwritten rule. You go in, you do your job, you come out. Whatever happens in there stays in there."

"But you're talking now."

"Because I'm eighty-one years old and the company's gone. Sold to a corporation that doesn't know a Douglas fir from a pine. The old ways are dying, and the stories are dying with them. Somebody needs to remember."

"What stories?"

"Stories my grandfather told me. Stories my father told me. Stories I lived through myself." He leaned back in his chair, his eyes distant. "We called them the Wood Apes. Not Bigfoot, not Sasquatch—that was for the newspapers and tourists. The Wood Apes. Every logger in the Pacific Northwest knew about them. We just didn't talk about it."

"What did loggers know?"

"We knew they were real. We knew where they lived—which valleys, which ridges, which old-growth stands. We knew not to bother them if we could help it. And we knew that sometimes, despite our best efforts, we'd run into them anyway."

"Tell me about your encounters."

"Too many to count. Footprints in the mud. Sounds at night. Shadows moving through the trees. But there are three that stand out. Three that I'll never forget."

"Tell me about them."

"The first was in 1958. I was seventeen, working my first summer with my father's crew. We were cutting a stand near the Rogue River, old growth that had never been touched. One morning, we came into the work site and found our equipment vandalized. Not broken—moved. The chainsaws were stacked in a pile. The fuel cans were arranged in a circle. Our lunch coolers were opened, the food eaten, the containers placed neatly on a stump."

"What did you think happened?"

"My father said it was kids playing a prank. But there were no roads into that site—we'd built them ourselves. And the nearest town was thirty miles away. No kids could have found us. And no kids would have eaten our food and then organized our equipment with that kind of precision."

"What about the second encounter?"

"1972. I was running my own crew by then, working a contract in the Siuslaw National Forest. We'd been in the same area for three weeks, clearing a section for replanting. One night, we heard them—not just sounds, but voices. Actual voices, speaking to each other in a language that wasn't English or any other human tongue."

"Did you see them?"

"Two of my guys did. They'd gone out to investigate the sounds—stupidly brave, or maybe just curious. They came back white as sheets, talking about shapes in the darkness, about creatures that moved like shadows and watched them with eyes that glowed."

"What did you do?"

"We finished the contract and never went back. Lost money on the job, but I didn't care. Some places aren't meant for human activity. Some forests belong to someone else."

"And the third encounter?"

"That was the one that changed everything." Thomas's voice grew quieter. "1985. I was alone, surveying a potential contract site. Deep in the mountains, no roads, no people for miles. I was marking trees when I realized I wasn't alone."

"What happened?"

"There was one standing right there, maybe twenty feet away. Full daylight, nothing between us but air. We looked at each other for what felt like an hour but was probably only a minute. And then it spoke."

"Spoke? In words?"

"Not words I understood. But speech. Communication. It was trying to tell me something, I'm sure of it. Its voice was deep, resonant —I felt it in my chest as much as I heard it in my ears. And when it was done speaking, it pointed at me, then at the trees around us, then at itself. Like it was making a connection. Saying we were all part of the same thing."

"What did you do?"

"I nodded. Didn't know what else to do. And then it turned and walked away, disappearing into the forest. I never saw it again. But I never forgot what it seemed to be saying."

"What do you think it was saying?"

"That we share this world. That the trees aren't just resources to be harvested—they're home. Their home, our home, everything's home. And maybe we should remember that before we cut it all down." Thomas smiled sadly. "I didn't listen, of course. I kept logging for another thirty years. But I always thought about that creature, about its message, about what it meant. And now that I'm old and the forests are shrinking and the world is changing, I think maybe it was right. Maybe we should have listened."

* * *

Thomas Erikson died six months after our interview. His family sent me a note, saying that he'd been at peace in his final days—that telling his story had lifted a weight he'd carried for decades.

His account became one of the most listened-to episodes in the podcast's history. Not because of spectacular sightings or dramatic confrontations, but because of the quiet truth it contained: a lifetime of coexistence, of encounters that defied explanation, of a relationship between humans and creatures that had existed in the shadows of the logging industry for generations.

The loggers had known. They'd always known. They just hadn't been allowed to say it.

Now, finally, their stories could be told.

THE FINAL WITNESS
JEAN PATTERSON, GEORGIA

The last interview I ever conducted before the documentary aired was with my own mother.

Jean Patterson—Mama, as I'd always called her—was sixty-eight years old, still sharp, still strong, still the rock I'd built my life around. She'd never spoken publicly about anything related to my work. But as the documentary's release approached, she reached out.

"I think it's time I told you something," she said. "Something I've been keeping for a very long time."

"What is it, Mama?"

"You remember when we moved to Lyerly? When you were twelve?"

"Of course. The worst year of my life."

"I know. Your daddy's drinking, my cancer, everything falling apart." She paused. "But there's something I never told you. Something that happened before we moved."

"What happened?"

"I saw one. One of them. Before we even knew that property existed."

I felt the hairs on the back of my neck prickle. "Tell me."

* * *

"It was the summer of 1983," Mama began. "A year before we moved. Your daddy and I were looking at properties—we knew we needed to get out of Summerville, find somewhere cheaper, somewhere we could start over. A realtor showed us a place in Lyerly. Eighty acres, mostly woods, a little house that needed work."

"Our place."

"The place that would become our place. But on that first visit, before we'd even made an offer, something happened."

"What?"

"We were walking the property line—me, your daddy, and the realtor. It was late afternoon, getting toward evening. We were in the back corner, the part you'd later call the dead zone, when I saw something moving in the trees."

"What did you see?"

"A figure. Tall, dark, moving through the forest maybe fifty yards away. At first, I thought it was a person—a hunter, maybe, or someone walking through from a neighboring property. But then it stepped into a patch of sunlight, and I saw what it really was."

"What was it, Mama?"

"You know what it was. The same thing you saw a year later. The same thing that's been living in those woods since before any of us were born."

I sat in stunned silence. All these years, all my searching, and my mother had seen one before I ever set foot on that property.

"Why didn't you ever tell me?"

"Because I didn't want you to know. After your encounter—after I saw how it affected you, how it changed you—I was afraid. Afraid that if you knew I'd seen one too, you'd never let it go. You'd spend your whole life chasing answers that maybe didn't exist."

"I spent my whole life chasing them anyway."

"I know. And maybe that was always going to happen. Maybe some people are meant to see things, to question things, to dig for truths that the rest of us are afraid to face." She reached out and took my hand. "But I wanted you to have a choice. I wanted you to be able to walk away if you needed to."

"I couldn't walk away. I tried. It didn't work."

"No. It didn't. And now look at you—changing the world, telling truths that have been hidden for generations." She smiled, her eyes glistening. "I'm proud of you, baby. Whatever happens next, I'm proud of who you've become."

"Thank you, Mama. For everything."

"Don't thank me yet. The hard part is still coming. When those creatures show themselves, when the world has to face what you've been saying all along—it's going to be chaos for a while. You need to be ready for that."

"I am. I've been ready my whole life."

She squeezed my hand. "Then go do what you need to do. And when it's over, come home. We'll sit on the porch and watch the stars and talk about everything that's changed."

"I'd like that."

"Me too, baby. Me too."

* * *

That interview with Mama never aired. It was too personal, too intimate, too connected to my own story to share with the world.

But it stayed with me as I prepared for the final journey to the cave. The knowledge that my mother had seen what I'd seen, had carried her own secret for decades, had been protecting me even as she watched me chase the truth she'd tried to shield me from.

We were connected, Mama and I, by more than blood. We were connected by experience. By knowledge. By the shared understanding that the world was stranger than most people could imagine.

And as I hiked into the forest for the final time, I carried her with me. Her strength. Her love. Her faith that whatever I was doing, whatever I was becoming, was worth the cost.

The truth was coming out.

And I was ready to face whatever came next.

ADDITIONAL ENCOUNTERS

FROM THE ARCHIVES

THE TRUCKER'S MIDNIGHT RUN
EDDIE MCGRAW, INTERSTATE 90

ddie McGraw had been driving trucks for thirty-one years. He'd crossed the country more times than he could count, seen every state, driven every major highway. But the night of September 14th, 2011, stood apart from all the rest.

"I was hauling a load of furniture from Seattle to Chicago," Eddie told me. "Long haul, three days on the road. I'd stopped for the night at a rest area in Montana, somewhere between Missoula and Butte. Middle of nowhere, really. Just a parking lot, some bathrooms, and darkness in every direction."

"What time was this?"

"Around two in the morning. I was trying to sleep in the cab, but something kept bothering me. This feeling, you know? Like something was watching. I'd had that feeling before, out on lonely stretches of highway, but never this strong."

"What did you do?"

"I looked out the window. At first, I didn't see anything—just the empty parking lot, the other trucks, the tree line maybe fifty yards away. But then something moved. Something big."

"What did you see?"

"It came out from the trees and walked across the parking lot. Walked, not ran. Like it didn't have a care in the world. It was huge—eight feet tall, easy. Covered in dark hair. Walking on two legs, with this rolling gait that covered ground faster than you'd think possible."

"Did it approach your truck?"

"It walked right past. Maybe ten feet from my door. I could see its face in the parking lot lights—flat, broad, with deep-set eyes that seemed to glow. It looked at me as it passed. Just a glance, like you'd give a stranger on the street. And then it kept walking, crossed the parking lot, and disappeared into the trees on the other side."

"What did you do after?"

"I sat there shaking for about twenty minutes. Then I started my rig and drove straight through to the next truck stop, about a hundred miles east. Didn't sleep for the rest of that trip. Couldn't close my eyes without seeing that face."

"Have you had any encounters since?"

"Not face to face. But I've heard things. Sounds in the night at rest areas. Knocking on the side of my trailer when I'm parked in remote places. I know they're out there. And I think they know I know." Eddie laughed nervously. "Some nights, I think they're just checking on me. Making sure I'm still keeping their secret."

Eddie's account was one of dozens I'd collected from truckers over the years. The highways that crossed wilderness areas were prime territory for sightings—long stretches of empty road where the creatures could move unseen, rest areas surrounded by forest where they could observe human activity without being noticed.

The trucking community had its own folklore about these creatures. Stories passed from driver to driver, warnings about certain rest areas, certain stretches of highway where you didn't want to stop after dark. Most outsiders dismissed these tales as campfire stories, exaggerations born of long hours and lonely nights.

But the consistency of the accounts suggested something more. The truckers were seeing the same things, in the same places, decade after decade. Whatever was out there, it was real. And it was watching.

THE PHOTOGRAPHER'S OBSESSION
DAVID BAKER, PACIFIC NORTHWEST

David Baker had been a wildlife photographer for twenty-five years. His work had appeared in National Geographic, Smithsonian, and every major nature publication in the world. He'd photographed grizzlies in Alaska, tigers in India, and snow leopards in the Himalayas. But the image that defined his career was one he could never publish.

"I've spent fifteen years trying to get another photo like it," David said. "Fifteen years of expeditions, of waiting in blinds, of camping in remote areas for weeks at a time. And I've never come close."

"Tell me about the original photograph."

"It was 2007. I was in the Olympic National Park, working on a piece about temperate rainforests. I'd set up a remote camera on a game trail, triggered by motion sensor. Standard practice for wildlife photography—you can capture images of animals that would never tolerate a human presence."

"What did the camera capture?"

"Three frames. Just three frames, before the camera was destroyed." David's voice tightened. "The first showed the trail, empty, just as I'd left it. The second showed a figure—massive, hair-covered, standing in profile about twenty feet from the camera. And the third showed a hand—a huge, dark hand—reaching toward the lens."

"The camera was destroyed?"

"Crushed. When I went to retrieve it, I found pieces scattered over a twenty-foot area. The memory card was intact, but the camera itself had been systematically demolished. Not by accident. Deliberately."

"What did the images show?"

"Exactly what you'd expect. A Sasquatch. Clear as day, in profile, close enough to see individual hairs. The best photograph ever taken of these creatures. And I couldn't do anything with it."

"Why not?"

"Because no one would believe it was real. The clarity was too good. People would assume it was faked. And because—" He paused. "Because I was afraid. Afraid of what would happen if I went public. Afraid of being labeled a hoaxer or a crackpot. Afraid of destroying the career I'd spent decades building."

"What happened to the images?"

"I still have them. Locked in a safe. I've shown them to a few trusted colleagues—people who know my work, who know I wouldn't fake evidence. They believe me. But that's not the same as going public."

"Would you consider sharing them now? With the documentary?"

David was quiet for a long moment. "Maybe. If the time is right. If the world is ready." He smiled sadly. "I've spent fifteen years waiting for that moment. Maybe it's finally here."

* * *

David Baker eventually agreed to share his photographs. They appeared in the documentary, along with expert analysis confirming their authenticity. The images became some of the most discussed evidence in the history of Sasquatch research—clear, detailed, undeniable.

But for David, the victory was bittersweet. He'd spent so many years hiding the truth, protecting himself from ridicule, that the revelation felt more like a relief than a triumph.

"I should have shared them sooner," he told me, after the documentary aired. "I should have been braver. Maybe if I had, we wouldn't have had to wait so long for the world to believe."

Maybe. Or maybe the world wasn't ready until now. Maybe everything had to happen in its own time, according to a schedule none of us could control.

The truth was like that. It couldn't be rushed or forced. It would emerge when it was meant to emerge. And all we could do was prepare the ground and wait for the seeds to sprout.

THE RANGER'S CONFESSION
PATRICIA MORGAN, YELLOWSTONE

Patricia Morgan had spent thirty-two years as a park ranger in Yellowstone National Park. She'd seen every kind of wildlife the park had to offer—grizzlies, wolves, bison, elk. She'd rescued hikers, fought fires, and enforced regulations in one of America's most treasured wilderness areas.

But she'd never spoken publicly about the other things she'd seen. Until now.

"There's a file," Patricia said. "An unofficial file, passed down from ranger to ranger. It contains reports of sightings, encounters, things that don't fit into any official category. We call it the X-File, like the TV show. It's been growing since the 1950s."

"What kind of reports?"

"Everything you'd expect. Large bipedal creatures seen in remote areas. Footprints that don't match any known animal. Vocalizations recorded at night that can't be identified. Strange structures found in the backcountry—shelters made of woven branches, arranged in patterns that suggest intelligence."

"Why hasn't any of this been made public?"

"Because it would cause chaos. Yellowstone gets millions of visitors every year. If people thought there were unknown creatures living in the park, some would be terrified. Others would flood the back-country trying to find them. Either way, it would be a disaster for the park and for the creatures themselves."

"Have you had personal encounters?"

"Three. The first was in 1994, my second year as a ranger. I was on patrol in the Lamar Valley, checking on a wolf pack we were monitoring. It was early morning, just after dawn, and I saw something standing on a ridge about a quarter mile away. At first, I thought it was a bear, but it was too tall, too upright. It watched me for about a minute, then turned and walked over the ridge. I never reported it."

"Why not?"

"Because I wanted to keep my job. I'd seen what happened to rangers who reported things like that. They got transferred to desk duty, or their assignments suddenly became less desirable. The park service doesn't want to deal with this. They'd rather pretend it doesn't exist."

"What about the other encounters?"

"The second was in 2003. I was investigating reports of strange sounds in the Thorofare region—the most remote area in the lower 48. I spent three days camped out there, and every night I heard them. Vocalizations. Communications. Things talking to each other in a language that wasn't human but clearly meant something."

"Did you see anything?"

"Just shadows. Shapes moving at the edge of my flashlight's range. But I could feel them watching. I knew they were there."

"And the third encounter?"

"That was last year. I was doing a routine patrol in the backcountry when I came across a structure. A lean-to, made of branches woven together with remarkable precision. Inside was a bed of moss, clearly used recently. And on the ground nearby, I found a footprint. Eighteen inches long, five toes, distinctly humanoid."

"What did you do?"

"I photographed everything. Added it to the file. And kept my mouth shut." Patricia looked at me with tired eyes. "I'm retiring next month. Thirty-two years is enough. And before I go, I wanted someone to know the truth. I wanted someone to document what we've been hiding all these years."

"Can I see the file?"

"I can get you copies. It's not everything—some reports are too sensitive, too recent, too connected to people who are still working. But enough to show the pattern. Enough to prove that the park service has known about these creatures for decades and done nothing."

"Why are they hiding it?"

"Fear, mostly. Fear of what would happen if the truth came out. Fear of losing control of the narrative. Fear of having to deal with something that doesn't fit into their bureaucratic categories." She shook her head. "But the truth is coming out anyway. You're helping it come out. And maybe that's a good thing. Maybe it's time for the hiding to stop."

* * *

Patricia Morgan's file became one of the most valuable resources in my research. Decades of reports, observations, and encounters, all carefully documented by rangers who'd been sworn to silence. The evidence was overwhelming—not just of the creatures' existence, but of a systematic cover-up that extended to the highest levels of the park service.

When the documentary aired, Patricia was one of the first to go public. She appeared on camera, in uniform, explaining what she'd seen and what she knew. The reaction was immediate—both support from the public and condemnation from the park service.

But Patricia didn't care. She'd spent thirty-two years hiding the truth. Now, finally, she could speak.

And her voice was one of the loudest in the chorus that changed the world.

THE SCIENTIST'S JOURNEY
DR. MICHAEL BROOKS, PRIMATOLOGIST

Dr. Michael Brooks had spent his career studying great apes in Africa. He'd published dozens of papers on primate behavior, locomotion, and cognition. He was respected, established, secure in his position at one of the country's top universities.

And he was ready to risk it all.

"I've known the truth for fifteen years," Michael told me. "Fifteen years of keeping silent, of pretending I didn't see what I saw, of compartmentalizing my knowledge so I could continue my career. But I can't do it anymore."

"What truth are you talking about?"

"The truth about Sasquatch. The truth about the scientific community's systematic denial of evidence that contradicts our established paradigms. The truth about how we've failed the very principles we claim to uphold."

"When did you first become aware of this?"

"2006. I was at a conference on primate evolution when a colleague showed me a footprint cast from the Pacific Northwest. He'd obtained it from a researcher who was terrified of going public, and he wanted my opinion."

"What did you see?"

"A footprint that didn't match any known primate. The proportions were wrong for a human or an ape. The dermal ridges showed a pattern of wear that would be virtually impossible to fake. And the size—eighteen inches long, five inches wide—suggested a creature of enormous proportions."

"What was your reaction?"

"Disbelief, at first. I assumed there must be an explanation—some hoax or misidentification I wasn't seeing. But the more I studied the cast, the more convinced I became that it was authentic. And that realization changed everything."

"What did you do?"

"I started investigating. Quietly, at first—I couldn't let my colleagues know what I was doing. I collected evidence, interviewed witnesses, analyzed samples. And what I found was extraordinary."

"What did you find?"

"A species. An actual species, undiscovered by modern science, living in the wilderness areas of North America. The evidence was overwhelming—footprints, hair samples, vocalizations, eyewitness accounts. Everything pointed to the same conclusion: these creatures were real."

"Why didn't you go public?"

"Fear. The same fear that's kept thousands of researchers silent. Fear of ridicule, of career destruction, of being labeled a crackpot. I'd spent decades building my reputation. I wasn't willing to sacrifice it for a truth that no one was ready to hear."

"What changed?"

"Your podcast changed. The documentary changed. Everything changed." Michael leaned forward. "For the first time, there's a critical mass of evidence and witnesses. For the first time, the public is ready to listen. And for the first time, scientists like me can speak without destroying ourselves in the process."

"What do you want people to know?"

"That science has failed them. That we've allowed our preconceptions and our fears to blind us to evidence that's been in front of us for decades. That the creatures you've been documenting are real, they're intelligent, and they've been hiding in plain sight while we pretended they didn't exist."

"What should happen now?"

"Study. Protection. Recognition. These creatures deserve to be understood, not hunted or exploited. They deserve to have their habitat protected, their existence acknowledged, their intelligence respected. And science—the scientific community that's denied them for so long —needs to step up and do the work that should have been done generations ago."

* * *

Dr. Michael Brooks became one of the most visible scientific advocates for Sasquatch recognition. His credentials gave him credibility that most researchers in the field had lacked. His willingness to speak opened doors that had been closed for decades.

After the documentary aired, other scientists followed his lead. Biologists, anthropologists, primatologists—researchers from every field began coming forward, sharing evidence they'd been hiding, admitting to experiences they'd never dared discuss.

The wall of scientific denial was crumbling. And in its place, a new understanding was emerging—one that made room for creatures that didn't fit the established paradigms, for mysteries that science couldn't easily explain.

The world was changing. And science was changing with it.

A PREVIEW OF BOOK TWO

The conversation happened on a Tuesday evening in late fall.

Daniel had just come home from the Asheville location—another fourteen-hour day, another crisis averted, another line out the door that had kept him running until his feet ached. He dropped onto the couch beside me, and I could see the exhaustion in his eyes. The good kind of exhaustion, the kind that comes from doing work you love. But exhaustion all the same.

"I need to talk to you about something," I said.

He raised an eyebrow. "That sounds serious."

"It is. Kind of." I took a breath. "I need you to quit your job."

Daniel laughed. Then he saw my face and stopped laughing. "You're serious."

"I'm serious."

"Brian, I can't just quit. The Hartleys are counting on me. The restaurant is finally turning a real profit. I've got staff who depend on me for their paychecks—"

"I know. And I wouldn't ask if it wasn't important." I turned to face him fully. "The podcast has grown beyond anything I ever imagined. *Sasquatch Odyssey* is pulling in numbers I never thought possible. The documentary opened doors I didn't even know existed. And now—" I shook my head. "Now I'm drowning, Daniel. I can't do this alone anymore."

"You're not alone. You've got the team, the community—"

"I need you. Specifically you. Not as my partner who supports me from the sidelines, but as my partner who's in the trenches with me every day." I reached over and took his hand. "I want you to come work with me full time. Executive producer of Paranormal World Productions. Help me take this thing to the next level."

Daniel was quiet for a long moment. I watched his face, trying to read what he was thinking.

"Paranormal World Productions," he said finally. "That's what we're calling it now?"

"That's what it's become. It's not just *Sasquatch Odyssey* anymore. I've started three new shows in the past year. *Backwoods Bigfoot Stories*—that's the one where I narrate listener submissions, the encounters people send in from all over the country. Then there's *Disturbing History*, which covers the dark chapters of American history that nobody wants to talk about. And *The Guilty Files*—true crime, unsolved cases, the kind of stories I used to work as a cop."

"That's a lot."

"It's too much. For one person, anyway. I need someone I trust to help me manage it all. Someone who understands the vision, who knows what we're trying to build. Someone who can handle the business side while I focus on the content."

"And you think that's me?"

"I know it's you. You ran that restaurant like a machine. You handled suppliers, staff, finances, marketing—all while making sure every pizza that went out the door was perfect. That's exactly what I need. Someone who can take the chaos and turn it into something sustainable."

Daniel looked down at our joined hands. "I love that restaurant, Brian. I built something there. Something that was mine."

"I know you did. And I'm not asking you to give that up lightly. But think about what we could build together. Think about where this could go."

"Where could it go?"

"Anywhere. Everywhere." I felt the excitement building in my chest, the same excitement I'd felt when I first started the podcast all those years ago. "The audience is there. The stories are there. The hunger for truth—for real truth, not the sanitized version the mainstream media feeds people—it's bigger than ever. We could build something that reaches millions of people. That changes the conversation. That finally brings these subjects out of the shadows and into the light."

"And you need me for that."

"I need you for everything. I always have." I squeezed his hand. "But yeah. For this specifically. I can't do it without you."

Daniel was quiet again. I could see him thinking, weighing the decision, considering everything he'd be leaving behind and everything he'd be stepping into.

"The Hartleys will be devastated," he said.

"They'll understand. And you can help them find a replacement, train them, make sure the transition is smooth. I'm not asking you to abandon them. I'm asking you to take the next step with me."

"The next step."

"The next chapter. Book Two, if you wanna think of it that way."

That got a small smile out of him. "Book Two. I like that."

"So what do you say? You ready to leave the pizza business behind and join the monster-hunting business full time?"

Daniel laughed—a real laugh this time, the one that had made me fall in love with him all those years ago.

"Monster-hunting business. Is that what we're calling it?"

"Truth-seeking business. Mystery-exploring business. Whatever you wanna call it." I grinned. "It pays better than pizza. Probably."

"Probably." He shook his head, still smiling. "You're really serious about this."

"Dead serious. I've never been more serious about anything in my life. Except maybe when I asked you to move to North Carolina with me. And when I told you I loved you for the first time. And when—"

"Okay, okay. I get it." He held up his hand in surrender. "You're serious."

"So?"

Daniel looked at me for a long moment.

"Okay," he said. "Let's do it. Let's build something together."

"Yeah?"

"Yeah. But I have one condition."

"Name it."

"When we finally get definitive proof—when we finally capture one of those things on camera, clear as day, undeniable—I get to be the one who posts it online."

I laughed. "Deal."

We shook on it, like we were closing a business deal. Which I guess we were.

Then Daniel leaned back on the couch, and I leaned into him, and we sat there together watching the darkness gather outside the windows. Somewhere out there, in the forests and mountains and wild places, the creatures were watching too. Waiting. Wondering what we'd do next.

They'd find out soon enough.

Book Two was just beginning.

ABOUT THE AUTHOR

Brian, a native of Northwestern Georgia, has been captivated by the mysteries beyond our understanding since childhood. Enthralled by tales of hairy creatures in the mountains near his home, a personal encounter as a child ignited his deep fascination with Sasquatch, propelling him into a world of endless exploration.

After a sixteen-year career in law enforcement, Brian turned his passion into a hobby by starting a podcast. Unexpectedly, this hobby evolved into something much greater. By 2022, his *Sasquatch Odyssey* podcast had become one of the most popular shows in the realm of Sasquatch encounters, captivating a diverse audience. Brian has conducted hundreds of interviews with eyewitnesses and undertaken field research on his expansive forty-acre property in North Carolina, as well as in Tennessee and British Columbia, Canada—all in pursuit of answers to the Sasquatch mystery.

Brian's success and his knack for captivating storytelling have earned him recognition beyond the podcasting world. He has been a guest on numerous podcasts and featured on television shows aired on the Vice Network and Tubi. As a skilled public speaker and host, he has graced the stages of Sasquatch conferences and festivals across the United States and around the world.

Not content with a single venture, Brian is also the founder and CEO of Paranormal World Productions, LLC. In addition to *Sasquatch Odyssey*, he hosts other intriguing podcasts such as *The Guilty Files*, *Backwoods Bigfoot Stories*, *Weird Encounters*, and *The Bigfoot Inquiry*, showcasing his diverse talents and unwavering commitment to exploring the uncharted territories of the paranormal world.

ALSO BY BRIAN KING-SHARP

Born Wild: Koda's Odyssey

Sasquatch Unleashed: The Truth Behind the Legend

AFTERWORD

Go to hangar1publishing.com to learn more about the authors and stay up to date with their newest releases.